Backbench Opinion

IN THE HOUSE OF COMMONS

Backbench Opinion

IN THE HOUSE OF COMMONS 1955–59

S. E. FINER, M.A.
Professor of Political Institutions

H. B. BERRINGTON, B.Sc.(Econ.)
Lecturer in Political Institutions

D. J. BARTHOLOMEW, B.Sc., Ph.D.
Lecturer in Social Statistics

UNIVERSITY COLLEGE OF NORTH STAFFORDSHIRE

PERGAMON PRESS
NEW YORK · OXFORD · LONDON · PARIS
1961

PERGAMON PRESS INC.
122 East 55th Street, New York 22, N.Y.
1404 New York Avenue N.W., Washington 5 D.C.

PERGAMON PRESS LTD.
Headington Hill Hall, Oxford
4 & 5 Fitzroy Square, London, W.1

PERGAMON PRESS S.A.R.L.
24 Rue des Écoles, Paris Ve

PERGAMON PRESS G.m.b.H.
Kaiserstrasse 75, Frankfurt am Main

Library of Congress Card Number: 61-17031

Set in Intertype Times 10 on 12pt. and printed in Great Britain by
ODHAMS (WATFORD) LTD.

Contents

Preface and Acknowledgments

MOST political sociology—and this study is a piece of political sociology—considers the base of our political life, establishing connexions between the attitudes and the characteristics of sections of the electorate. In contrast, this book takes a look at the apex: at the two great Parliamentary parties. In it we show the relationship between the social make-up of these two parties and the shades (or divisions) of political opinion to be found inside each of them. This has meant, in the first instance, establishing the political views of individual M.P.s on the one hand, and their political and social histories on the other.

This is a pioneer study, in two senses of the term. In the first place, the task has not previously been attempted in any shape or manner, nor has the basic source material (the Order Paper of the House of Commons) been explored systematically. In the second place, however, this study forms part of a wider one. It is concerned with the Parliament of 1955–59. A further inquiry, on the period 1945–55, is almost completed thanks to the generosity of the Nuffield Foundation who made us a research grant for that purpose. The preliminary conclusions for the Parliament of 1951–55, now available, have provided us with a valuable cross-check upon the conclusions of the present study.

To establish our conclusions we have had to apply statistical techniques. Consequently this book rests on a large mass of computational as well as parliamentary data. Had we incorporated this in our text, the result would have been largely unreadable and of interest only to specialists. Consequently we have, to begin with, used diagrams and graphs instead of columns of figures wherever this was possible. Next, we have segregated the data on which our conclusions rest from the book itself, by relegating it to a series of appendices. Even in this form, however, it threatened to become overwhelming; and, therefore, we have only presented a selection from it, chosen with an eye to intrinsic interest but (we trust) in sufficient quantity and variety to allow the specialists to examine both our methods and our assumptions. The remainder, we feel, is best presented in the form of contributions to academic journals.

The book is the product of co-operation between the three co-authors, but each has had special responsibilities. Professor Finer is primarily responsible for the sections on the Labour party, and Mr. Berrington for those on the Conservative party; while Dr. Bartholomew is primarily responsible for the statistical techniques and tests used throughout the study.

The manuscript has gone through several versions since we began, and our debt to friends and colleagues is very large. Among those who discussed the project with us, by correspondence or in person, we particularly wish to thank the Lord Privy Seal, The Rt. Hon. E. R. G. Heath, M.B.E., M.P., and the Minister of Health, The Rt. Hon. J. Enoch Powell, M.B.E., M.P.; together with Mr. Anthony Wedgwood Benn, Mr. Gresham Cooke, M.P., Mr. Geoffrey de Freitas, M.P., The Rt. Hon. D. P. T. Jay, M.P., Mr. Carol Johnson, M.P., Mr. H. N. Lever, M.P. and Mr. Nigel Nicolson. Sir Edward Fellowes, the Clerk of the House of Commons, gave us valuable technical information about the Order Paper, and Mr. Michael Fraser, Head of the Research Department of the Conservative Central Office, significantly added to our understanding of the Conservative Parliamentary Party.

We have benefited from the advice of our professional colleagues Professor Wilfrid Harrison, Mr. D. E. Butler, Mr. F. W. Bealey and Mr. Jean Blondel all read the work in an earlier version; and it is as a result of the views of the two first-mentioned that we decided to re-write the whole work in the interests of a more popular presentation. We wish to thank each of the four for their care and labour, which have much improved the book.

We wish to acknowledge a particular debt to three colleagues who have now left the University. Mr. John Thompson, B.A., M.Ed., and Miss Betty Thirsk, B.A., were the Senior and Junior Research Assistants respectively under the Nuffield Foundation project for the 1945–55 period, as mentioned above; but they gave us unsparingly of their leisure to check this manuscript for inaccuracies, while the work on which they were engaged provided many valuable checks on the present study's classifications and findings. Their help has been quite invaluable. The same is true of the help given us by Miss Pat Heneage, B.A., who has acted as computer. To her fell the laborious task of working out the statistical tests, and she has been good enough, too, to check the present manuscript for arithmetical and statistical inaccuracies.

Mr. Aubrey Noakes performed an indispensable task by copying the Early Day Motions for us from the file in the British Museum. His industry and accuracy enabled us to get on much faster than would have otherwise been possible.

Mrs. Marguerite Armstrong, and then Mrs. Josephine Herbert "typed, re-typed and typed again" the numerous versions through which the work has passed and we are much indebted to their unflagging cheerfulness and patience, as well as to the speed and accuracy with which they worked. Mr. Fred Rowerth, Chief Technician of the Physics Department, substantially helped us by his admirable drawings.

Mr. S. O. Stewart, the Librarian of the University College, and his staff were particularly helpful in providing us with the necessary parliamentary and reference sources and we wish to thank them for their courtesy and patience.

Finally—and placed here because of a more than ordinary importance—we owe a singular debt to Captain Robert Maxwell, our publisher. The speedy publication of this book owes everything to him.

S. E. FINER

H. B. BERRINGTON

Keele D. J. BARTHOLOMEW

Chapter 1 · Behind the Division Lists

THE PARLIAMENTARY ENIGMA

The practice of publishing division lists showing how M.P.s have voted on the questions of the day is little more than a century old. It was a further step in the democratization of British government, for it was hoped thereby that the electorate would take into account the voting record of their members when these presented themselves for re-election. "The people," wrote Burke, in his "Thoughts on the Cause of the Present Discontents", "ought to be excited to a more strict and detailed attention to the conduct of their representatives . . . Frequent and correct lists of the voters in all important questions ought to be procured . . ." "Members voting in the majority," said Lord John Russell later, "are unlimited kings . . . making laws, voting money, imposing taxes, sanctioning wars with all the plenitude of power and all the protection of obscurity—".* The publication of the lists was finally agreed to in 1836, and contemporaries thought it a very democratical device indeed. "So stringent a test," wrote the celebrated Erskine May, "had never been applied to the conduct of members; and if free constituencies have since failed in their duty of sending able and conscientious representatives, the fault has been entirely their own."†

Tempora mutantur. "Those who elect M.P.s to represent them," wrote Michael Foot in 1959, "can judge their conduct if they know how their representatives vote on the issues of real importance . . ." "*But,*" he added, "if the outside public chooses to study the division lists—now openly published after a long, historic struggle in the name of freedom—they will not discover the answer. It will be

---

* In 1819. Quoted from *May's Constitutional History of England* (1912 edition), I. p. 346.

† Ibid p. 346. The sentence was first published in the first edition in 1861.

discovered that an M.P. voted loyally with his party. But how did he speak and vote in the critical binding debate in the private meeting upstairs? Nobody can discover that except by rumour or leakage or on those infrequent occasions when an individual M.P. kicks over the traces."*

In the following pages it will be shown that Michael Foot is correct in his view that the division list today is useful only as an index of party loyalty but incorrect in saying that there is no means of detecting an M.P.'s personal sympathies. There is such a means. It can provide an X-ray of the two major parliamentary parties. The picture that emerges is a blurred one, for sure; but it is a picture nevertheless. This book presents the picture of the two parties as they were in the Parliament of 1955–59.

PARLIAMENTARY PARTIES AND PARLIAMENTARY VOTING

What has happened since 1861 when May regarded the division lists as "a stringent test of the conduct of members", to make them as useless or even misleading as Michael Foot protests? Simply, the continuous decline in cross voting and the corresponding rise of party discipline enforced by the Whips. The critical period of the changeover occurred as far back as the 1890's but party discipline has been on the increase ever since then; and with the decline of the independent Member, the abolition of the university seats, and the virtual elimination of the Liberals as a third parliamentary party, it is not surprising that it has appeared to observers as though "two great monolithic structures now face each other and conduct furious arguments about the comparatively minor issues that separate them."† As Christopher Hollis has put it, the M.P. is now so much a servant of his party machine that it would be simpler and much cheaper if a flock of tame sheep were kept to be driven through the division lobbies in the appropriate numbers, at the proper times.‡

But of course, this solidarity of party voting is illusory. Nothing is more certain or more obvious than the existence of wings,

---

* M. Foot, "Parliament in Danger!" *Pall Mall Pamphlet No. 4,* 1959.

† R. McKenzie, *British Political Parties,* p. 586.

‡ C. Hollis, *Can Parliament Survive?* pp. 64-5.

"factions" and cleavages in each of the two parties. The speeches which Members deliver often indicate such differences of opinion, and even more dramatically so, do floor revolts. One need only recall the Bevanite revolts in the Labour party between 1951 and and 1955, or the Suez rebels, and latterly Mr. Nabarro's "fuel furies" in the Conservative party to establish this point; but no more dramatic or conclusive illustration is required than the virtual civil war over the two issues—nationalization and unilateral nuclear disarmament—that had in 1960 brought the Labour party almost to the point of disintegration.

Yet surprisingly little attention has been paid, until very recently, to the organization of the parliamentary parties and particularly to the mechanisms they have evolved for reconciling their differences. For, as party discipline has increased since 1945, so have methods for sounding out and giving effect to the opinions within the parties. Before the war both parties established backbench committees to discuss special topics, but they were *ad hoc* and advisory only: the present elaborate system of specialist committees and sub-committees covering the whole field of policy, tied in with the full party-meeting and geared to the Whips' office, dates from 1944 in the Labour party and 1946 in the Conservative party. The evolution of the system has gone almost entirely unremarked, and even its operation, though now receiving more attention, has still not been described very thoroughly.*

It is here, in the party committees and no longer on the floor of the House, that views are uninhibited and the clashes of opinion take place. As Foot describes it: † "The Labour M.P. who seeks to change or affect great decisions must persuade his colleagues in the secret conclave of the party meeting. True, he will have had the chance of pressing his view at an earlier meeting of a specialized official group. But if his powers of advocacy fail there or if the political crisis in which he is concerned breaks suddenly, as most important crises do, it is in the party meeting—not on the floor of the House of Commons—that he will have the only opportunity to determine action." Hollis makes the same diagnosis, saying that:

---

* Cf. I. Bulmer-Thomas. *The Party System of Great Britain,* P. G. Richards. *Honourable Members.*

† *Op. cit.* p. 15.

"It is a disgraceful thing that Members of Parliament should express and vote for their real opinions in private behind closed doors and then come and give a merely automatic support to the party line in public."*

Hollis does admit, however, that these privately expressed opinions may compel a government to change its policy; and in June 1960, when the internal dissensions of the Labour party had almost annihilated its effectiveness as a parliamentary opposition, it was even possible to argue, seriously, that the Conservative party committees were, alone, "supplying the need for some sort of parliamentary opposition or challenge to the government". In one week, the Education Committee let the Minister of Education know that it was time to reappraise his policy over the Kidbrooke multilateral school; the Fuel and Power Committee protested to the Minister at the appointment of Mr. Robens to the Chairmanship of the National Coal Board; and the Foreign Affairs Committee demanded that the Government negotiate with the European Economic Community. "This," wrote the Political Correspondent of *The Times* (meaning by "This" the backbench committees)—"This is where things are being said and done that are more politically meaningful than a greal deal that passes in the Chamber itself." It would be fascinating, he goes on, to prove the influence of, say, the Finance Committee—fascinating, but, he adds with regret, "humanly impossible. Privacy is the essence of the backbench committee system".†

The division lists, then, no longer reveal a Member's private views; on the contrary, they conceal them. Outspoken comment is only to be heard "upstairs", or on the rare occasions of a floor revolt or the infrequent and usually unimportant free votes. Is there no way then of ascertaining the shades or divisions of party opinion other than the gossip of lobby correspondents, and the free votes and floor revolts which are too sporadic, and too infrequent, to allow us to generalize? There is indeed a way, as will be seen; but first, what is the utility of acquiring such information? Assuming that the personal views of Members on a range of topics could be made known, to what uses could this information be put?

---

* Hugh Thomas (ed.), *The Establishment*. p. 174.

† *The Times*, 27/6/60.

A PHYSIOLOGY OF THE PARTIES?

The two major political parties each consist of three parts: the Parliamentary Party, the voluntary mass organization, and the professional party bureaucracy. The parliamentary parties do not regard themselves as responsible to, or spokesmen for their mass organization in the country. If the party is in power, the government regards itself as responsible to the country as a whole: and if it is to make concessions to its followers, it is much more likely to make them to its parliamentary supporters (on whom its life depends) than to the party branches. In opposition it is, indeed, more likely to listen to those party branches than when it is bearing the responsibility of office; but even so, it will not regard itself as the mere agent of its mass organization. In both the parties the Parliamentary Party tends to be the energizing and creative body, albeit subject to the checks and balances imposed on it by its need for continued electoral assistance from its militants. Indeed, in the Conservative party, the primacy of the Parliamentary Party is not in doubt. "The Conservative Party in Parliament deliberately created [its] organization outside Parliament to recruit support among the mass electorate provided by the Reform Acts—."* Substantially it has retained that characteristic ever since. The Parliamentary Labour party's relationship to the party conference and national executive committee is indeed more ambiguous; but however the exact constitutional relationship be interpreted, it is demonstrable—and indeed McKenzie has demonstrated it—that the Parliamentary Party exerts an enormous *influence* in decision making.†

Given this powerful, even preponderant role of the parliamentary parties in the shaping of party policy, one might have expected that they would be subjected to a microscopic examination. If they, rather than their mass organizations, be the fountainhead of party

---

* McKenzie, *op. cit.* p. 12.

† McKenzie, *op cit. passim. cf.* S. Rose *Policy Decision in Opposition* (*Political Studies* Vol. IV No. 2 pp. 128-138) and R. McKenzie "Policy Decision in Opposition: A Rejoinder" (*Political Studies* Vol V No. 2 pp. 176-182).

cf. also the controversy, since the Scarborough Conference, 1960, on the degree of autonomy possessed by the Parliamentary Party.

policy, an understanding of their nature would seem to promise the most fruitful insights into British political behaviour. Yet the great bulk of inquiry and research has been devoted to the mass parties. For the nature of the parliamentary parties we have to rely on memoirs and the comments of political journalists. The supreme justification for information about the parliamentary parties is that it would illuminate a key sector of British political life.

If the individual views of M.P.s could be ascertained, the most obvious use to which this information could be put is the practical-political one: to inform constituents of the particular shade of conservatism or socialism which their Member represents. In this way the people could once more, in Burke's words "be excited to a more strict and detailed attention to the conduct of their representatives—". A less immediately obvious, more complicated, but certainly more fruitful use of the information would be to establish, however hazily, what may be styled the *physiology* of these parties. First of all, it would uncover causes and viewpoints to which minority sections of the parties are attached but which, over-ridden as they are by party loyalty, are not brought to public debate. It would establish the numbers of such dissidents and thus indicate the weight attaching to such a view. Finally, it might establish the *type* of the dissident. For the parties are not composed of identical persons. On the contrary, the members of each party differ from one another by virtue of occupation, or education, or age; some fought their first successful election long ago, others are recent entrants to the House; some sit for marginal and others for safe seats. It may be that some of these factors bear a firm relationship to a member's political attitudes. Is there a public school "style" in Parliament; or a Trades Unionist "style"; or a pre-war as against a post-war "style"? If this proved so, one could begin to analyse and interpret the parliamentary parties in terms of their various political, social and economic components: and, since these components alter from election to election, it might even prove possible, to some extent, to project forward the altering character of the parties.

The division lists, index or testimony to party discipline and loyalty, have so far thwarted any such analysis. There is, however, a source which offers in large measure the kind of information to make the enterprise possible. This source has never been explored systematically and indeed unless its exploration *is* both systematic and exhaustive, would prove seriously misleading.

BEHIND THE DIVISION LISTS

The division lists are contained in the Commons' Order Paper. They display the names of Members who voted for or against the Motions (or amendments to the Motions) tabled by the Government or the Opposition Front-bench. Thus (1) the subjects of such divisions are initiated by the front-benchers; (2) and the Members' names represent a *routine* response to (3) the exercise of the party Whip. But this same Order Paper also contains other lists of Members' names which stand in complete contrast. These are lists of Members who support various of the Motions tabled by private Members and technically known as Early Day Motions. For (1) these Motions are freely initiated by backbenchers on either side of the House (2) those who put their names down in support of such Motions do so spontaneously and (3) neither the tabling of the Motions nor the indication of support for them is subject to the party Whip. The Early Day Motions are *spontaneous un-whipped backbench manifestoes.*

Any M.P. has the right to table a Motion, but in the last forty years it has become increasingly common for those who agree with its sentiments to add their names in support. (Today, some such Motions attract as many as two or three hundred supporters.) They are put down on the Order Paper without any specific day having been fixed for their discussion and so appear under the heading: "For An Early Day": hence their technical name, Early Day Motions (henceforth abbreviated to EDMs). Thus the fiction is maintained that they are subjects for serious debate, and indeed every Thursday, when the next week's business is announced by the Leader of the House, he is subjected to goodhumoured and not very serious pressure to allow time for some of these Motions. But few if any are debated, and it is doubtful whether any but a small fraction are put down in the serious hope that they will be debated. They are today, essentially, a demonstration. Furthermore they are a backbench demonstration. If the front-benches on either side of the House seriously wish to debate a Motion they dispose of the ways and means to effect this. Thus the EDMs are backbench manifestoes; and correspondingly they are never signed by the Government and the Government Whips, and only very rarely by the Opposition Front-bench and its Whips.

Members are as free from the Whips in tabling or supporting a Motion as they are to put Questions. Between 1952 and 1959 the Labour party demanded that the Whips be "consulted" before Motions were tabled, and on the Conservative side the Whips always liked to be shown them (though without any power to exact this); furthermore, Motions shown to the Whips on either side sometimes meet with expressions of pleasure or of displeasure; but one thing appears to be quite certain, that on either side of the House the Whips cannot and do not prevent the Motions appearing and Members signing them. They are a backbencher's *right,* and are so regarded. Some of the Motions that appear are, therefore, critical of and very embarrassing to the leaders on either side: the notorious anti-American Motion, signed by 120 Conservatives on 27th November, 1956, during the Suez Crisis; the Motion of December 1959, signed by 178 Conservatives, demanding free N.H.S. drugs for patients attending private doctors; the Labour Motion, signed by 89 members on 9th June, 1959, opposing the transfer from France to Britain of American nuclear-weapon-carrying aircraft.

Between June 1955 and October 1958—some three and a half years—no less than 388 Motions or amendments were tabled. One hundred and eleven were cross-bench Motions; and 178 were party Motions, of which some two thirds came from the Labour benches, and one third from the Conservative side. We are not therefore limited, as we should be if we took free votes or floor revolts as our material, by its being sporadic or sparse. On the contrary; the Motions are numerous, frequent and accumulative. And they represent the spontaneous and unwhipped viewpoints of the backbenchers, sometimes in agreement with, sometimes in rebellion against, their frontbenchers' policies, and sometimes initiating policies all of their own.

This splendid mine of information on backbench opinion has never been systematically worked. This may seem surprising, but after reflection it is easy to see why. In the first place the correct interpretation to be placed on any particular motion may be difficult to establish. The reason for this is that EDMs are tabled for a wide variety of motives. An EDM may have been put down because the other opportunities for riding a private hobby-horse—chiefly Questions and adjournment debates—are so limited; or because the rules governing the admissibility of EDMs are much looser than those governing Questions and adjournment Motions; or because the Member tabling it wants publicity in his constituency or because a group of Members—e.g., the capital punishment faction—want national publicity for their view. Some EDMs are tabled to air the individual crotchets of an M.P.—a very effective way, since they are printed in the Order Paper and circulated to all Members; it is this which helps to account for the tabling, between June 1955 and October 1958, of 99 single-signature Motions. On the other hand, some EDMs are tabled in order to collect the general opinion of the party or of the House as a whole. Some such are designed by their sponsors to strengthen the hands of their leaders against the other side, by the demonstration of spontaneous, un-whipped support. Others are designed in just the opposite sense—as a hostile demonstration against the party leaders. Consequently the provenance of each EDM has to be established with some caution before it can be correctly assessed. However, this is not a difficult task though it may be time-consuming. And in any case, no matter what the private motives of the Member in tabling or supporting a Motion, one thing is constant: he has, by his signature, *freely and publicly committed himself to a particular point of view.*

Much more important is a second difficulty. If a Member *has* signed a Motion well and good—he may fairly be taken as being committed to that particular point of view. But what interpretation are we to place on the *absence* of the Member's signature from the list? For the collection of signatures to a Motion is a haphazard business. The promotors, usually with a clip-board in their hands, go the rounds to collect support—in the library, in the tea-room, in the corridors, or—a favourite place for collecting signatures—in the division lobbies. Quite often, also, a Member will read in the Order Paper or in the newspapers that a particular Motion has been put down, and may add his name to it without being asked. Now in these circumstances the number of names appearing on the list—and hence the presence or absence of any particular Member's name—depends on several quite different factors. Thrustful and businesslike sponsors, who make a considerable drive through the House, will collect more names than tepid or lazy sponsors. In any event, some sponsors do not want many names but certain particularly influential names—e.g., those Members who are, say, members of the National Parks Commission. Again, the number and character of the signatures may depend on the standing or personal popularity of the first names on the list; some of these may be unpopular or regarded as freaks or publicity hounds. Finally, some Members—like Sydney or Julius Silverman for instance—are generous with their signatures; others, like the late L. J. Edwards, are very reluctant to sign any Motion.

Suppose then that after counting, we find that Trades Unionist Members of the Labour Party are less inclined to sign pacifist Motions than Co-operators? It is possible to argue that this discrepancy is not due to the substance of the Motions but to the way in which the signatures have been collected or to the personal unpopularity of the sponsors. To put it another way: if identical Motions had been tabled on different days, with different or more energetic sponsors, it might have been found that the Trades Union Members signed *more* frequently than the Co-operators.

Doubts of this kind may well explain why this apparently rich source for the pristine opinions of M.P.s has been neglected. But these doubts are in no way conclusive. On the contrary they provide the starting point of a most fruitful inquiry. For there exists a standard statistical method for resolving them. Certainly, it demands laborious and systematic counting, and after that, time-consuming calculation. But, given this, it is possible in principle to establish just how probable or improbable it is that the support given by any type-class of Members to a certain kind of Motion is due to chance alone. If after counting and calculation it turns out after all that the degree of support may well have been due to chance, then in a sense one's labour has gone for naught. On the other hand, it may turn out that the degree of support is so large that the odds against this having occurred by chance are, say, 19 to 1; or 39 to 1; or even higher, say, 99 to 1.

In such cases one has done more than simply demolish the doubt that the distribution of signers and non-signers is haphazard. One has established that a particular type-class of Members—say the Trades Unionists—have a propensity to sign Motions of a certain kind. One has established an *association* between type-class and attitude.

The test by which this is carried out is technically known as the χ^2 *test*. It starts off by assuming that the collection of signatures has been quite random. On this basis it calculates how Members, in their various type-classes, would have distributed themselves between signing and non-signing. The numbers (frequencies) in each category are the "*expected frequencies*". These are compared with the actual (observed) frequencies (established by counting). The test is then applied to the difference between the *expected* (i.e., random) distribution and thc observed (i.e., actual) distribution. If these are sufficiently small the statistician will regard the actual distribution as the product of chance. If the differences are larger he calculates the probability of the actual distribution having come about by chance. He calls this the "significance level". A 10 per cent level of significance means that the actual distribution of names could have occurred by chance only once in every ten times: or, to put it another way, that the odds against the distribution occurring by pure chance are 9 to 1. A 5 per cent significance level means that the odds against are 19 to 1—and so forth.

The results of applying this test to the lists of names supporting the EDMs show that there *are indeed significant—in some cases highly significant—associations between the substance of a Motion and the type-class of Member supporting it*: for instance, that there are significant differences between the attitudes supported by Members with different occupations, different educational backgrounds, or (in the Labour party) with different political sponsorships. And from this it is possible to acquire a deeper insight into the nature and outlook of the two parliamentary parties.

THE NATURE OF THE INQUIRY

The statistical test described above is not the only test we have applied, and its operation is not always as straightforward as our description makes it appear. The problems of statistical method, and other problems of interpretation of the results are described in Annex 1.

All that remains to do here is to give a brief description of the scope and method of the inquiry. Basically, what we have done is this. On the one side we have established the type-classes of which each party is composed (e.g. the educational or occupational or age categories into which it can be resolved) and noted into which categories each Member fits. By "each party" we mean the backbenchers or each party because frontbenchers and Whips and a number of ex-Ministers do not sign EDMs. On the other side we classify the EDMs according to their subject matter, and for each topic, and so arrange them that they constitute a scale of possible attitudes. We then bring the two sides together to see whether, and how far, any particular type-class of Members tends to support one particular attitude rather than another.

For particulars, the reader may turn to the Annexes. However, it is useful to make certain points clear at this point also.

First, it must be repeated that the Members whose reactions we are testing are those who are in a constitutional and physical position to sign the EDMs. This means that frontbenchers, Whips, and ex-Ministers are excluded from the inquiry: and so also are Members whose late entry into the House of Commons means that they could not physically have signed all the Motions under discussion—and conversely, those whose death or retirement took them out of the House at an early stage. As a result, the inquiry reports on the attitude of, for instance, not the full 277 Labour Members, but only 236 of them. These Members were then classified according to various characteristics—not necessarily the same for either party—which are described in the chapters that follow.

Turning to the EDMs themselves, something must be said about the way we have "scaled" these. There are two methods of going about this and we have used either, whichever seemed appropriate. The first way is a "Qualitative" scale. For instance, on examining the many Labour EDMs on defence matters, it becomes clear that some of these are committed to a unilateralist position; others are committed to a multilateral disarmament position; and others express sentiments somewhere between these two. It is therefore possible to construct a "scale" of pacificism—ranging from unilateralism through to multilateralism. It is then possible to explore which type-classes on the Labour party backbenches show a preference for one of these attitudes rather than another; for instance whether Trades Unionist Members show a preference for the unilateralist or the multilateralist attitude.

The other method is applicable when we find a number of

EDMs all expressing more or less the same attitude; for instance there may be half a dozen Motions all expressing, in some shape or form, sympathy with colonial independence. None of the Motions is more extreme than the others. Here we have established a quantitative scale: the more Motions signed, the more intense (we assume) is the interest shown. It does not seem unreasonable to assume that those who sign a high number of Motions on a given topic are more interested than those who sign few and these in turn more interested than those who sign none. Admittedly, the presence or absence of clusters of habitual high-signers or non-signers might alter the picture. These, in principle, could distort the tables. In practice this does not appear to be so. The quantitative tables have been used, almost exclusively, for the Labour party; and here no single type-class of Member, consistently and irrespective of topic, signed more than the other type-classes. On the contrary: the signing rate of all the different type-classes varied up and down according to the topic, and a type-class with the highest signing rate on one matter would tend to have a low one, perhaps the lowest, on another.

These scales, qualitative or quantitative, are based on a complete survey of all the EDMs tabled between June 1955 when the new Parliament of Elizabeth II commenced, and October 1958: together with selected EDMs for the remainder of that Parliament. Where applicable, too, we have checked our results against the pattern of attitudes revealed by such free votes as took place in the House.

THE PATTERN OF THE BOOK

Any inquiry of this kind proceeds from various assumptions. Some of the statistical ones have been mentioned already. The construction of the scales is, obviously, a subjective exercise. Scholars may well wish to know these, possibly to question them. Furthermore they may be interested in details which the general public would find unenlightening or tedious.

To incorporate all these matters in the text would make it almost unreadable. The text, then, describes and comments on the most important findings. The assumptions made; the statistical techniques used; the way in which the scales have been constructed; and the detailed tables have been presented as Annexes.

Chapter 2 · The Labour Party

THE SOCIAL COMPOSITION OF THE LABOUR PARTY

Of the 277 Labour Members who took their seats in 1955, only 236 concern us here. These are the ones who could or did sign a fairly complete number of the EDMs tabled between 1955 and the end of 1958. The Whips, the members of the shadow cabinet, the ex-Ministers of senior status, together with a few Members who entered Parliament too late to be able to sign a complete train of Motions—all these, to the number of 41, have been disregarded.

These 236 can be classified in various ways. A classification according to the Member's majority would be interesting, to see if there was any relationship between attitude and the "safeness" of the seat. A pilot examination showed, however, that no such relationship existed, so the classification was abandoned. The classifications that seemed more fruitful were five: according to the occupation, the sponsorship, and the education of Members, and according to their age and their "intake", i.e., the year they first were elected.

Occupation means the Member's current occupation, or his last one previous to election. *Workers* includes Members who were full-time Union officials. *Professions* means, obviously enough, lawyers and doctors but also includes teachers, whether University or school teachers or full-time adult education teachers. *Business* is a small unsatisfactory classification which includes managerial staff as well as proprietors, though the bulk of this group were in fact proprietors of middle or small business. And the *Miscellaneous Occupations* group is just what the name suggests: a residuum of different white-collar jobs, including social workers, insurance agents, journalists, party publicists, party organizers and party research officers.

Education contains two categories that need some further description. The small category of *elementary/secondary+* comprises

Members who proceeded from elementary or secondary school to further formal training, in technical college, or teacher-training, or on to Ruskin College, Oxford. And *secondary* comprises not only those who attended secondary grammar schools (30) but also 7 public-school men: the two have been separated out, and the point noticed, wherever the occasion calls for it.

The way the party divides by occupation, sponsorship and education appears from Fig. 1. Occupationally, the party comprised three sections of roughly equal size—the Workers, the

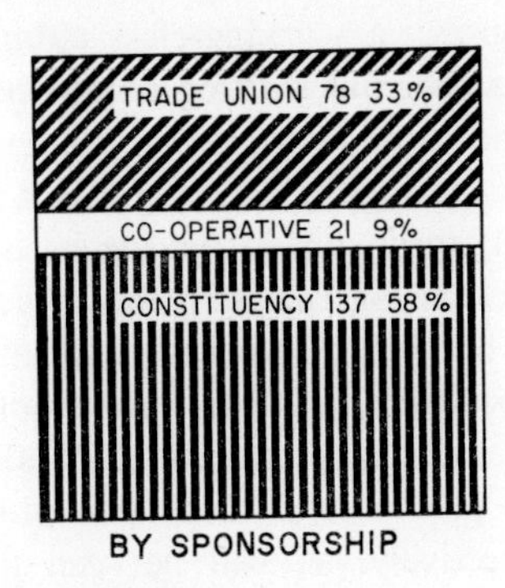

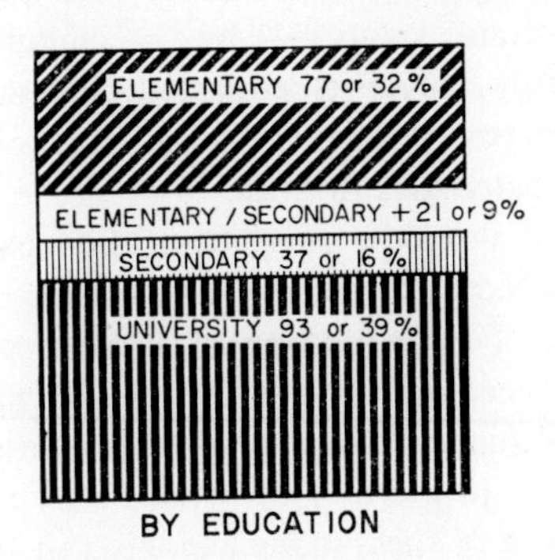

FIG. 1. *The composition of the Labour Party* 1955-59.

Miscellaneous Occupations and the Professions. Educationally, however, there were only two major blocs, the elementary school group and the university educated, roughly equal in numbers, with the remainder of the party forming a kind of detritus of elementary/secondary+ and secondary education. By sponsorship, there were two main blocs, grossly unequal: the Trades Union sponsored and the Constituency Party Members. Those sponsored by the Co-operatives formed a very small proportion of the party.

There is nothing new in this kind of analysis, which has been performed several times before. What is required is to know whether there is any overlap between these three categories. There is: and the striking fact emerges that the Labour party contains two groups whose occupational, educational and sponsorship attributes so fit together as to comprise, in effect, two distinct cultures: a working-class culture and a professional-class culture. Whatever our starting point—occupation, education or sponsorship—the result is much the same: there is a working-class wing and a professional-class wing with a miscellany in between.

Figure 2 starts from the basis of occupation. On the left are the Workers, on the right the Professions. The figure shows, to scale, the number of workers with elementary and university education respectively, and the number of professional men with elementary and university education. It also shows the numbers of Workers and professional men sponsored by the Unions or unsponsored, respectively. It will be seen that the two sides form an almost perfect mirror image. The Workers were predominantly from elementary school and sponsored by the Unions. The Professions were predominantly university educated, and were not sponsored. In between these two poles the Miscellaneous Occupations share some of the characteristics of both.

Figures 3 and 4 show the party from the basis of the Members' sponsorship—whether by Trades Union or Co-op, or whether not sponsored at all. The proportion of Professionals in each group rises from 9 per cent among the Trades Unionists to 44 per cent among the Constituency Party candidates, with the Co-ops half-way between. The proportion of Workers in each group declines from its 81 per cent of the Trades Unionists to 10 per cent for both the Co-operators and Constituency Party candidates. And Miscellaneous Occupations were, proportionately, most highly represented in the Co-operative group. Educationally (Fig. 4), the proportion of elementary-educated falls from the Trades Unionists, through the Co-operators to the Constituency candidates; while to almost equal degree, the proportion of the university-educated rises.

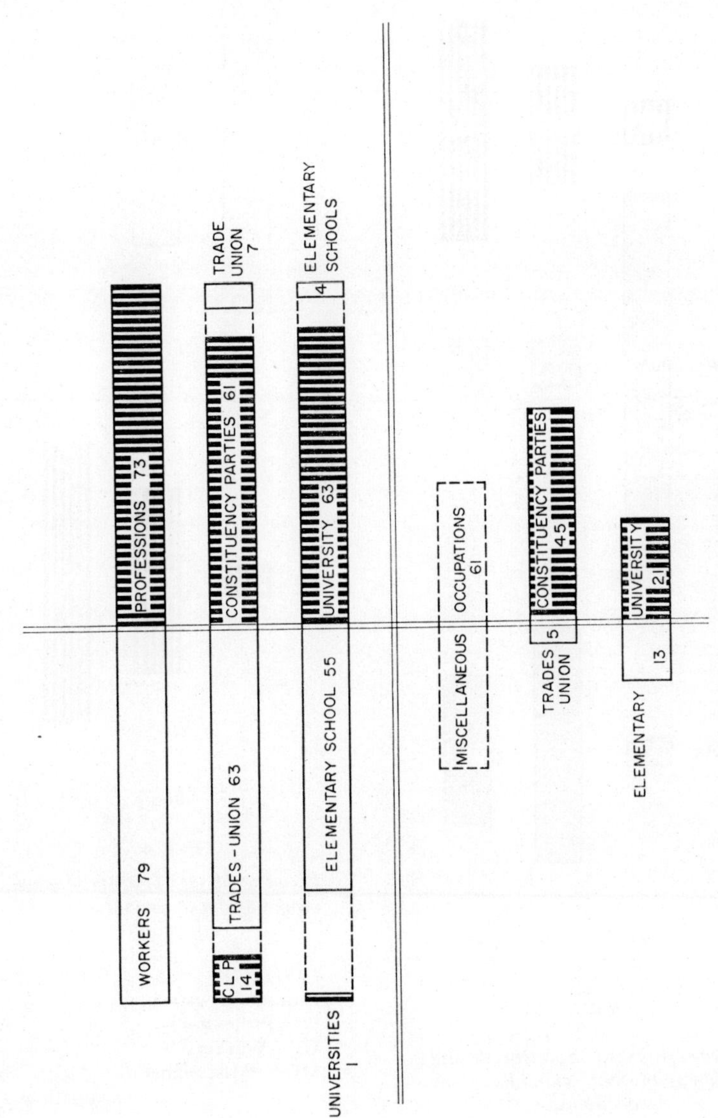

FIG. 2. *"Workers" and "Professions".*

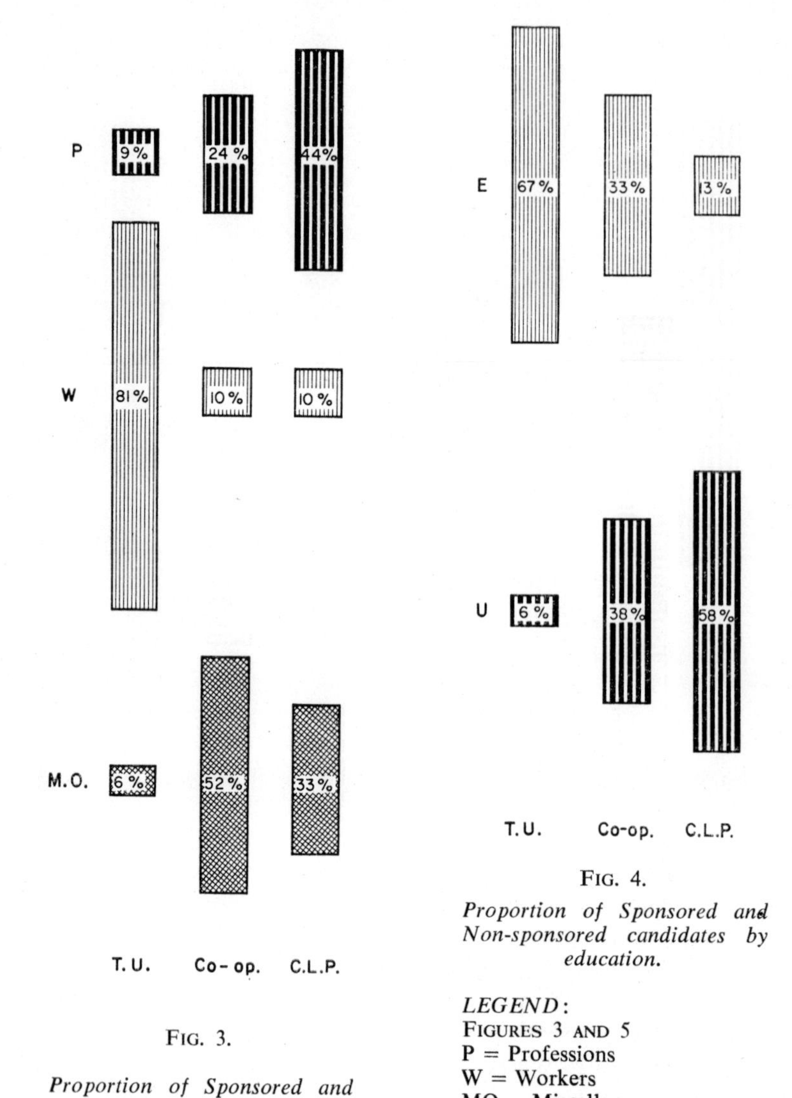

FIG. 3.

Proportion of Sponsored and Non-sponsored candidates by occupation.

FIG. 4.

Proportion of Sponsored and Non-sponsored candidates by education.

LEGEND:
FIGURES 3 AND 5
P = Professions
W = Workers
MO = Miscellaneous Occupations

FIGURE 4
E = Elementary School
U = University

The polarity of the party is most strikingly evidenced in Fig. 5, which shows the distribution of elementary, secondary and university education among the three main occupational groups. The distribution of the elementary school group is, so to speak, "equal

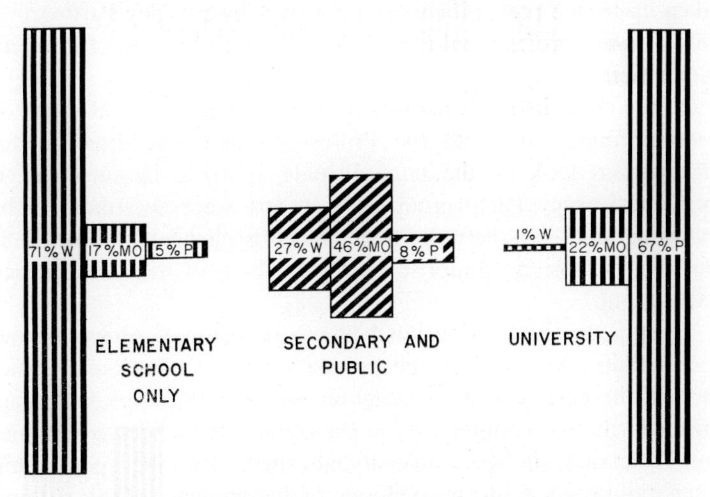

FIG. 5. *Educational distribution of the Labour Party. ("Business omitted")*

and opposite" to that of the university group: the two groups, one on the left and one on the right, form an almost exact mirror image of each other. The smallish secondary group, however, is most heavily concentrated in the middle occupational group, the Miscellaneous Occupations.

Since there is so considerable an overlap between the educational and sponsorship attributes of the Professions and the Workers, one would expect that attitudes associated with any one of these attributes would be associated with the other two also. Certainly there is a presumption that this would happen. However, the correspondence is by no means absolute, as the detailed figures show. For instance, of the 79 Workers 63 were Trades Unionists: moreover, there were 16 Workers who were not Trades Union sponsored, while 15 Trades Union sponsored members were not Workers. The difference is likely to be still more pronounced in the case of education. Fifty-five Workers had elementary schooling; but this means that 24 Workers went beyond elementary school, while another 22 Members, who had only elementary schooling, were not Workers by occupation.

Likewise the attitudes of the Constituency Party group would be linked to, but would not automatically follow from, the attitudes taken up by the professional class. Of the Constituency Party group only 61 were professional men and as many as 76 were of different occupations.

On the other hand, as another look at the figures would show: if it were found that both the Professions and the Miscellaneous Occupations took up the same attitude, it would be surprising if the Constituency Party group of members were not found to be following suit. For between them, the Miscellaneous Occupations and the Professions comprised the great bulk of the Constituency Party group.

To sum up the relationship between occupation, education and sponsorship: we find that the occupational and educational structures of the party roughly parallel one another, the Workers finding their educational counterparts in the elementary school group, and the Professions in the university-educated. But the sponsorship categories do not conform so closely to the symmetry of this pattern. True, the Workers are in large measure the occupational projection of the Trades Unionists, but the Constituency Party group reflects, not the professional class alone, but the combined Professions and Miscellaneous Occupation groups.

* * * *

The categories of age and of parliamentary "intake" cut across the three previous categories. Figure 7 shows how over 70 per cent of the party were over 50 and only 8 per cent under 41. It also shows that well over half the party consisted of the Members who came in in 1945.

The Trades Union sponsored Members tended to be older and to have come in earlier than other Members, but the association is not very pronounced. One would also expect a correspondence between age, and the year first elected; and certainly, the proportion of old Members tends to fall as the "intake" becomes more recent. Yet the correspondence is in fact a fairly loose one: the

FIG. 6. *Age and political seniority in the Labour Party.*

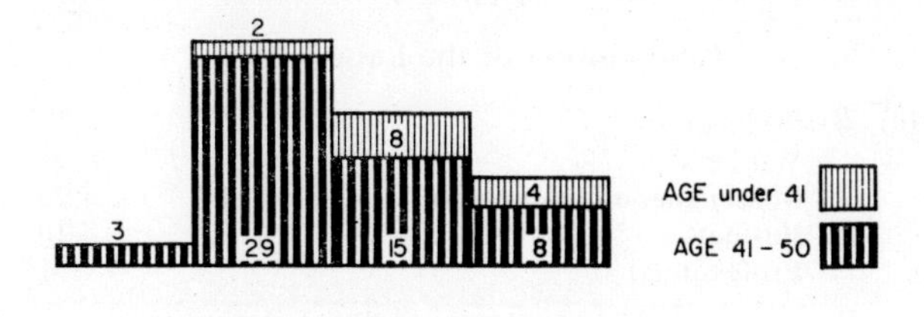

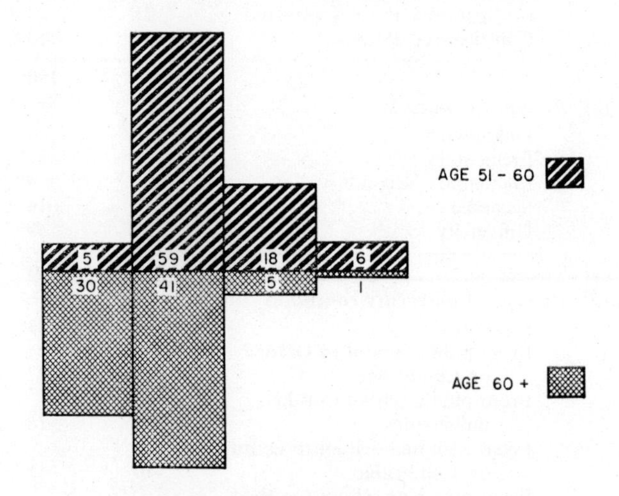

FIG. 7. *Age and year of first entering Parliament.*

party is so heavily composed of the over 50s that this age group is heavily represented in all the intakes, even among those elected in 1955 and afterwards. Consequently an attitude struck by a particular age group by no means entails a similar attitude by some corresponding intake group; or vice versa.

* * * *

The following tables contain the basic figures mentioned in the text, together with an analysis of the university educated group.

TABLE I

Composition of the Labour Party

(*a*) *By occupation*		
Workers	79	33%
Miscellaneous Occupations	61	26%
Business	23	10%
Professional	73	31%
	236	100%
(*b*) *By sponsorship of Members*		
Trades Union sponsored	78	33%
Co-operative Party sponsored	21	9%
Constituency Parties	137	58%
	236	100%
(*c*) *By type of education*		
Unknown	8	3%
Elementary	77	32%
Elementary/secondary +	21	9%
Secondary	37	16%
University	93	39%
	236	100%
(*d*) *By type of university education*		
Unknown	3	3%
From public school to Oxford or Cambridge	25	27%
From public school to other universities	15	16%
From grammar school to Oxford or Cambridge	10	11%
From grammar school to other universities	40	43%
	93	100%

(e) *By age*

Unknown	2	1%
Over 60, at Dec. 31st 1958	77	32%
51-60	88	37%
41-50	55	23%
Under 41	14	6%
	236	100%

(f) *Political seniority*

Elected before 1945	39	17%
Elected 1945-9	131	55%
Elected 1950-54	47	20%
Elected after 1954	19	8%
	236	100%

BACKBENCH ATTITUDES IN THE LABOUR PARTY

Through the medium of the EDMs, Labour backbenchers were able to express their individual opinions over a very wide range of issues. The most important of these were the H-bomb, foreign affairs, colonial matters, penal policy and civil liberties, and social welfare policy. Only on one important topic were the EDMs silent: nationalization.

The H-bomb, and pacificism

A pronounced feature of Labour policy—not merely today but throughout its history—is its revulsion from the use or even the threat of force in international affairs. In its most complete form this appears as pacifism, exemplified, for instance, by Mr. Emrys Hughes. But for the most part it appears in a qualified and conditional form which is more fittingly described as "pacificism": i.e., a desire to eschew as far as possible the threat or use of force.

The backbenchers' attitudes to the H-bomb constitute a kind of index, a barometer, of this pacificism. As opposed to the atom-bomb, the H-bomb—a far more destructive weapon—did not become a political issue in the party until the very eve of the 1955 Parliament. The U.S. exploded its first H-bomb in 1954. Russia followed suit very soon after. On March 1st 1955, speaking on the Defence White Paper, Sir Winston Churchill told the Commons that Britain, too, intended to manufacture its own H-bomb. A year later, in June 1956, Sir Anthony Eden announced that the weapon would be tested in 1957, and just over twelve months later the tests finally took place on Christmas Island. By then, however, the focus of attention was shifting from the nuclear warhead to the missiles that would deliver it. Russia demonstrated her unexpected superiority in October 1957 by launching Sputnik I, and a few weeks later sent up another with a live dog inside it. This alarming proof of her prowess was followed by the revelation that British and U.S. bombers were flying patrols over Britain in planes armed with hydrogen bombs: and hard on the heels of this, that the Government intended to provide British sites for ballistic missile bases.

Thus events moved very fast and very far in the lifetime of this Parliament, and the Labour party's official attitude tended to alter with the events. Broadly speaking, until April 1957 and Mr. Macmillan's announced determination to carry out the forthcoming tests on the British H-bomb, the official Labour party attitude (both at the Conference and in the Parliamentary Party) was in favour of manufacturing and testing the British H-bomb; against any unilateral renunciation of such manufacture and testing; in favour of British pressure for a *multilateral* negotiation between Britain, the U.S.A. and the U.S.S.R. to lead to multilateral nuclear disarmament under UNO. In April 1957, the Parliamentary Party split on this policy and subsequently agreed on a conditional unilateral *suspension* of the British H-bomb tests; should the U.S.A. and the U.S.S.R. continue their testing, Britain would be free to proceed. This policy was endorsed at the 1957 Annual Conference, where the unilateralists were heavily defeated. (They had wished to bind any future Labour government to renounce the testing, manufacture and use of the H-bomb.) After the Conference, the revelations about H-patrols and missile bases seriously perturbed large sections of the Parliamentary Party, and in March 1958 the National Executive Committee and the T.U.C. issued a joint statement on policy. This categorically opposed the H-bomb patrols; opposed the establishment of missile bases until further talks had taken place between Britain, the U.S.A. and the U.S.S.R.; and reaffirmed the policy of a temporary and conditional *suspension* of H-bomb tests.

This policy, or rather, succession of policies, had its dedicated opponents in the party; these favoured the unilateral renunciation of tests and manufacture. At the Margate Conference (1955) a resolution opposing British manufacture of the H-bomb and *all* nuclear weapons received 18 per cent of the votes.* At the Brighton Conference (1957), where Mr. Bevan opposed the unilateralists and made his famous speech about "going naked into the conference chamber", a resolution pledging the next Labour government to refuse to test, manufacture or use the nuclear weapon received 12 per cent of the votes.† This policy had its supporters and sympathizers in the Parliamentary Party; and it is through the EDMs that these can be identified. There are, however, two ways of doing this. Both have their interest.

(a) *Unilateralists and others.* At one time or another, 45 Members expressed themselves in favour of the unilateral renunciation of testing and/or of manufacture of the H-bomb. The unilateral renunciation of manufacture was contrary to expressed party policy throughout the whole of this period. The demands for unilateral abandonment of testing were made before the tests took place; at a time when the party line was that "we must be able to show an aggressor we have the bomb and the only way to do that is to show that it has been successfully tried out";‡ and when the abandonment of testing automatically entailed suspension of manufacture. Thus these 45 unilateralists expressed views which, at the time, were contrary to official party policy.

A second group, numbering 68, were less extreme. At no time did they express themselves in favour of unilateral renunciation of tests and manufacture of the H-bomb, but they did, at various times, express a high degree of alarm over, and hostility to, the H-bomb-plane patrols, and/or the provision of missile bases. Their line was neither official nor unofficial: but it is perhaps significant that the party's policy statement of March 1958, opposing the H-patrols and temporizing over the missile bases, appeared *after* and not before these M.P.s expressed their opinion.

A third group never expressed any of the opinions in the first and second categories mentioned, but did express themselves in favour of the official policy—the securing of general disarmament, with effective supervision under the U.N.

---

* Annual Conference of the Labour Party, 1955, Report, pp. 138–141; and p. 181.

† Annual Conference of the Labour Party, 1957, Report, pp. 180–181.

‡ Mr. G. Brown, *The Times*, April 1st, 1957.

Thus the party divided according to a rough "scale" of pacificism, the Left being the most pacifistic and the Right least so, thus:

Left:	Unilateral renunciation of tests and/or manufacture of the H-bomb	45	19%
Centre:	Those not in the category above, but opposing H-patrols and/or missile bases	68	29%
Right:	Those in neither of the above categories but favouring general disarmament under UNO and/or the strengthening of the U.N.	82	35%
Uncommitted:	Those expressing none of the previous attitudes	41	17%
		236	100%

(Forty-five is of course almost certainly an underestimate of the number of unilateralists in the party. Some Members no doubt could not for physical reasons have signed the unilateralist Motions. Others who could have done so might have been reluctant to flout so openly the party's declared policy. The list of unilateralists is therefore a minimum list—and largely a list of the more resolute.)

These attitudes were by no means equally shared throughout the party. On the contrary. Some were much more strongly supported by Members of a particular type than others. In statisticians' language, there was a significant association between attitudes, and the attributes of M.P.s relating to their occupation, their sponsorship, and their university background. In layman's language: Members with different occupational, sponsorship, and university backgrounds favoured particular attitudes on the scale and disfavoured others in so marked a fashion that the odds against this having occurred by pure chance were, in every case, equal to or greater than 19 to 1.*

The degree of pacificism expressed was significantly related to the occupation pursued by Members. The most pacific-minded

* 19 to 1 odds against the distribution having occurred by chance alone is described by statisticians as an *association significant at the 5 per cent level*. By the same token, then, odds of 39 to 1 against represent a significance level of 2.5 per cent: of 99 to 1 against, of 1 per cent. Statisticians usually take a 5 per cent (19 to 1) significance level as high enough odds to establish the association: and 10 per cent (9 to 1) as tentatively or provisionally suggesting one. We have followed their convention in this.

were the Miscellaneous Occupations. There was little difference in viewpoint between the Workers and the professional class, who were the least pacifistic.

There was also a connexion between the degree of pacificism and the sponsorship of Members. This was due to the distinctive attitude of the Co-operative group, which was much more pacifistic than either the Trades Union sponsored Members or those from the constituency parties—who behaved rather similarly.

There was, however, no connexion between the degree of pacificism and the kind of education which Members had received. Those educated at elementary schools, secondary schools or university all reacted similarly. There was, however, a most interesting relationship—extremely pronounced—between the attitudes expressed and the school-cum-university background of those Members who had attended university. The university educated did not, *as a whole*, react differently from those who had not been to university; but some types of university men reacted very differently from others. Those who went to any university from grammar schools were more pacifistic than those who went from public schools; and those who went from any school to universities other than Oxford and Cambridge were more pacifistic than those who went to the two older universities. There was a quite remarkable cleavage, therefore, between the attitudes of the group of 25 Members who had proceeded from public school to the older universities, and the 40 who had proceeded from grammar schools to the other universities. Of the first, 20 per cent supported the Left and Centre attitudes and 56 per cent the Right. Of the second, 70 per cent supported the Left and Centre attitudes, and 20 per cent the Right!

There may have been some connexion between attitude and year of entry into Parliament. It seems as though those elected in and after 1955 were more pacifistic than their seniors—but the conclusion must be regarded as tentative only.

(b) *The H-bomb.* Besides the 45 unilateralists referred to above, there were 34 Members who strongly pressed the Government to take immediate steps to secure an international agreement to ban H-bomb tests. They were much disturbed by the hazards to health arising from such tests. Though in no way contrary to official policy, their viewpoint struck a note of particular urgency. The 236 backbenchers might therefore be divided into the 79 who expressed their especial concern over the bomb, and the remainder. On this definition of pacificism, was there any connexion between the views expressed and the kind of Members expressing them?

As before the Co-operators were the most pacifistic of the sponsorship groups. The post-1949 entrants to the Commons showed a more marked degree of this kind of pacificism than they did under the previous definition, and the association was, statistically, an established one. There was, however, an interesting reversal of the roles played by occupation and education. Under the previous definition, attitude was connected with Members' occupation but not with their education. Here, however, the connexion between "special concern" and occupation is, at the best, tentative. On the other hand the connexion between attitude and education is particularly marked: the university educated were much the most pacifistic and the elementary school products much the least so: furthermore, among those educated at university, the type of university attended was not important, while the type of school from which the Member originated was. Those from the grammar schools were, as before, more pacifistic than those from the public schools.

The reason for these differences is interesting. The viewpoint of "the 34" was both conformist and humanitarian: and of these 34, the greater part came from the Professions and well over half from the university educated. The Professions who, on the previous definition, took up a right-wing stance almost identical with that of the Workers, took up under this new definition a middle ground between the Workers and the Miscellaneous Occupations. The previous sharp distinction between the attitudes of the Miscellaneous Occupations and those of the remainder of the party thus became blurred. By the same token however, the wider and more moderate appeal of the viewpoint of the 34 proved relatively more attractive to the university graduates, particularly from the older universities, and to the secondary school Members, than to any other educational group. Hence the relative preponderance of university graduates among the 79, as compared with the remainder.

Foreign Affairs

Germany. For the last decade, the future of Germany had been a dangerous divisive issue in the Labour party. In 1955 the official line was that Western Germany should be rearmed; that German reunification should take place through free elections; and that the reunited Germany should be free to decide whether to remain in NATO or not. By 1958 the party had retreated from most of these positions and had taken up a view not dissimilar from that of the 1955 critics of the official line. Its new policy was formulated in a pronouncement "Disengagement in Europe", published in April 1958 and adopted by Conference in the October of that year. Its five points were, briefly: the withdrawal of all foreign forces from West Germany, and from East Germany, Poland, Czechoslovakia and Hungary; internationally controlled armament levels in these countries; the reunification of the Germans by free election, the Germans themselves settling the ways and means; a four power security treaty to guarantee the frontiers of the countries in the zone; the withdrawal of West Germany from NATO, and of the satellites from the Warsaw pact.

As often happens in the Labour party, this policy statement was so drafted as to permit each different faction to put its own interpretation upon it. These views were expressed through the medium of EDMs, and from them it is possible to construct a scale of attitudes. (Substantially this derives from the Motions and countermotions tabled in February 1959 and referred to by *The Guardian* as the "battle of the Order Paper".) On the Left were those who interpreted the policy document as requiring the *de facto* recognition of the German People's Republic. On the Right were those who slurred over the requirement that a reunited Germany must leave NATO, by vaguely saying that she should, "in membership of the U.N., . . . play her full part in the maintenance of world peace and economic advancement". In the Centre were those who rallied to the leadership by reaffirming their support for the five points of the policy, without interpretation or paraphrase.

On the Left the Members numbered 37, plus 7 other Members who, led by Messrs. Zilliacus and Sydney Silverman, had expressed a very radical disengagement policy as long ago as 1955, when it was in flat opposition to the party's official policy. Thus the Left numbered 44. The Centre also numbered 44. The Right consisted of 70 Members to which may be added 16 others who had earlier expressed opposition to the nuclear armament of Germany and approval for the creation of a nuclear-free zone in Central Europe but had declined (or neglected) to make this view any more explicit. Thus the Right consisted of 86 Members. There were, in addition, 62 Members expressing no opinion on the matter.

The Right is, to a large extent, a mere residual category—those left after the Left and the Centre have been separated out. On pressure, or with further opportunities, many of its members would probably have joined the Centre. On the other hand it is most unlikely that any of either the Right or the Centre would have joined the Left. This, in the circumstances in which the Motions were signed represents a hard-core of opinion.

It has often been alleged that the Foreign-policy Left in the Labour party is a vociferous group of intellectuals and journalists. The more prominent and vocal Members—Messrs. Zilliacus, Swingler, Sydney and Julius Silverman—lend a certain colour to this view. In this instance, however, the Left was not dissimilar in composition from the rest of the party. Its viewpoint did not prove any more attractive to Members of a particular occupation, or education, or age, or intake-group than the Centre or Right-wing position. From this we can infer that views on German policy were not associated with any of the background characteristics mentioned. There was, however, a somewhat tenuous connexion between the view expressed and the *sponsorship* of Members. It is not sufficiently strong to be regarded as established, but not sufficiently weak to be treated as purely provisional. It suggests that the Co-operators were the most left-wing, the Trades Unionist the most right-wing, with the Constituency Party Members midway between the two.

It is quite clear, however, that there was a close connexion between extremism of views on Germany and the degree of pacifism as analysed above at pp. 23-28. Figure 8 shows that two-thirds of the pacificist Left were also members of the German Left: only 13 per cent of them were members of the German Centre and only 11 per cent, of the German Right. On the other hand, not one of the pacificist Right was a member of the German Left: only 27 per cent of the pacificist Right were members of the German Centre, and nearly one half were members of the German Right. This overlap is no coincidence. Indeed, the odds against this particular distribution having occurred by chance are 999 to 1.

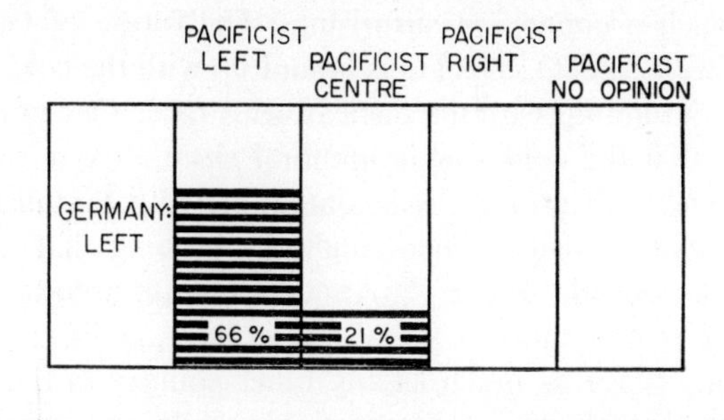

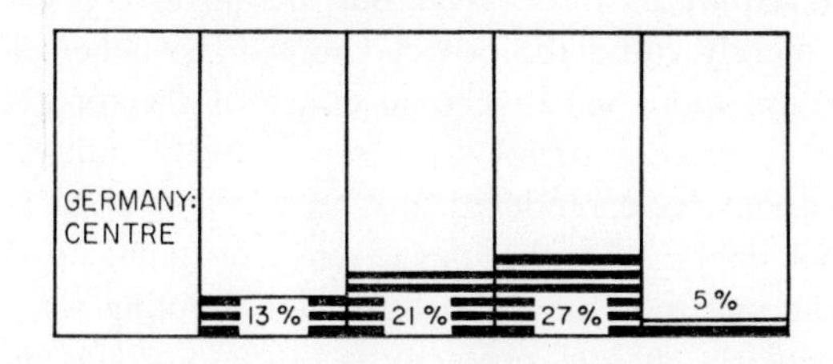

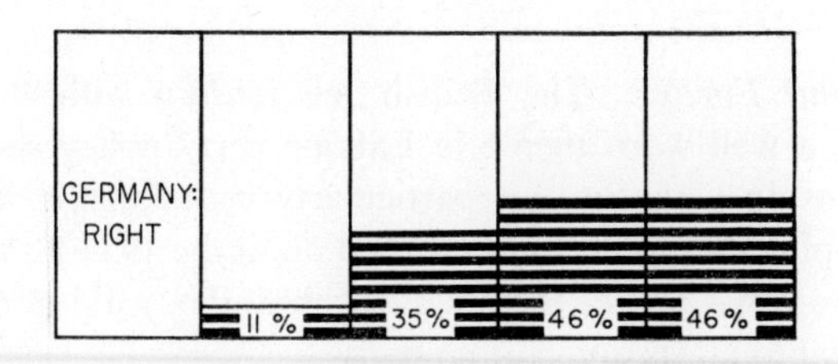

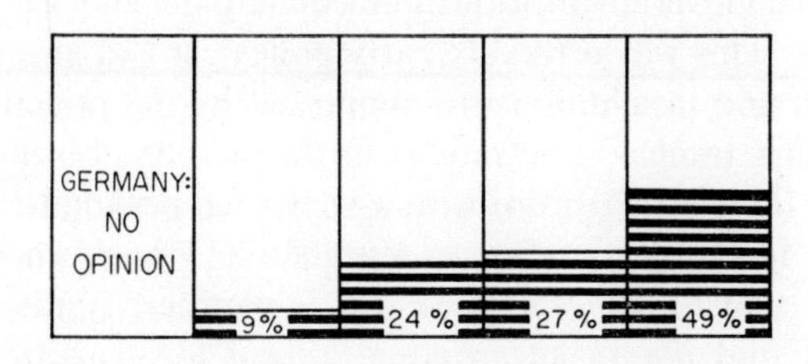

FIG. 8.
The correspondence between pacificist views and those on Germany.

Nor is such a connexion surprising. The future of Germany is bound up with NATO. NATO is bound up with the cold war. The cold war is bound up with the nuclear arms race. One group on the Left holds that the cold war is immoral since all war is immoral. "War," argues this group, "is incompatible with Socialism." This element explains Soviet armed might by arguing that "Russia is afraid of the outside world".* Another faction argues that "The challenge of Communism is social not military, and that the Soviet Union wants peace as much as any other country in the world."† On this showing all issues are negotiable while armaments are not merely not required by the West but are positively self-defeating since they merely cause the Soviet Union to arm herself likewise. A third group, more sensitive than either of the foregoing, argue that the cold war is pointless if not actively dangerous: that nuclear weapons have rendered any recourse to arms suicidal for all the contenders. As the most sensitive point in East–West relations, the one most likely to lead to a shooting war, Germany was a particularly anxious problem to all these groups on the Left; and a German policy acceptable to Russia a common objective of them all.

China and Europe. The British relationship with Communist China was a well worn theme in Labour party policy since 1950: the relationship with Europe, particularly with Europe of the Six, is a developing one. Both were touched on in the 1955-9 Parliament, and in a way that makes them comparable. They did not make an equal appeal to all sections of the party.

The China theme was expressed in a Motion, in 1957, which called on the Government to lift immediately the embargo on trade with China. This was orthodox party policy: it had anti-American undertones; and in addition was supported by the principal manufacturers' and traders' associations in the country. Furthermore, it was tabled (by Mr. Mikardo) with a view to appealing to all shades of opinion in the party, and no less than 113 backbenchers were induced to sign it. For this reason it is particularly interesting to note that it did *not* make an equal appeal to all sections of the

---

* *Annual Conference of the Labour Party, 1955, Report.* pp. 180-181.

† Ibid. pp. 141-2.

party, but was associated in a marked degree with the views Members held on the German question. Three quarters of the German Left signed as against one half of the German Centre and only 38 per cent of the German Right.

The European theme was also concerned with trade: following on the news (in July 1956) that the Six were about to create the Common Market, both Conservative and Labour backbenchers urged the British Government to negotiate. The Labour Motion, signed by 77 Members, urged the Government to negotiate agreement with the Six, though without detriment to the Commonwealth's interest. Unlike the China Motion, this view was equally attractive—or unattractive—to backbenchers irrespective of their sentiments towards Germany.

However, there were significant differences between the *kinds* of Members who gave support to one or the other view. Occupation and sponsorship played no part in either. But whereas the China Motion offered no special appeal to one type of university graduate rather than another, there was a provisional association between the European attitude and the university attended: the Oxford and Cambridge graduates supported it more strongly than those from other universities. Again, the China Motion proved equally attractive to all age groups: the European attitude was firmly associated with the age of Members, the under-41's being markedly more enthusiastic than their seniors, and the over-60's being markedly unenthusiastic compared with their juniors. On the other hand, the European attitude was quite unrelated to the year in which Members were elected. The China Motion most significantly was. It appealed far more sharply to those elected in and after 1950 than to those elected before that date.

The Suez period. The observer would scan the Order Paper in vain to discover signs of Labour disunity during the period of the Suez intervention and withdrawal. With the Conservatives, it is a different story. There, disunity did exist, and the traces of it can be found in the EDMs. But the Labour party was almost entirely united in opposing the despatch of troops and in demanding their unconditional withdrawal, and the few hardy spirits who did approve the Government's action were so buffetted by the gusts of passion in the party that they held their peace. Nevertheless, ignoring a number of minor Motions, there were three heavily signed ones which cast an oblique light on the state of the party during this tumultuous and indeed unique period of excitement.

Between the reassembly of Parliament on October 23rd 1956, and November 7th—during which period there had occurred the Israeli attack, the Anglo-French ultimatum and landings and the cease-fire—no EDMs were tabled on either side of the House. Attention then turned briefly to Hungary, where the Russian repression was taking place. From November 15th onwards, with the arrival of the U.N.E.F. in Egypt, the Opposition bent every effort to secure the immediate and unconditional withdrawal of British troops from Egypt, while the Government temporized in the hope of extorting concessions. Its efforts broke against determined American pressure which activated a wave of anti-American sentiment in the Conservative party and led to nasty but isolated anti-American incidents in the country; and also against the activities of the Afro-Asian bloc at the U.N., with which Mr. Krishna Menon of India was very prominently associated. His dedicated hostility, together with the relative indulgence with which Mr. Nehru judged the Russian intervention in Hungary, also aroused resentment on the Conservative side of the House.

Against a stormy background of this kind, anything that throws light on the inner feelings of the Labour party must be deemed of universal interest. Three EDMs, all well signed, illustrate the backbenchers' attitudes to the anti-American incidents, to the international role of India, and to the country which had sparked off the explosion—the State of Israel.

On December 11th, a group of Members from both sides of the House tabled a Motion deploring the anti-American incidents, with a view to securing all-party support. It ran as follows:

> This House views with concern the evidence that an irresponsible minority of British citizens has been and is, displaying an attitude of vindictiveness, hostility and prejudice towards citizens of the U.S.A. resident in this country; deplores the fact that in some cases punitive measures have been taken against Americans, such as evicting them from their homes and refusing them services readily available to British citizens ; and calls upon Her Majesty's Government to take such steps as may be necessary to bring to an end this regrettable manifestation of racial and national discrimination.*

Although the Motion's sponsors had hoped for an all-party demonstration, in the event the Motion received only 17 Conservative signatures as against no less than 97 Labour ones. Thus about two out of every five Labour backbenchers signed; but these were by no means a random sample of the whole backbench. There was, to begin with, a well established connexion between support for this attitude and views on German policy. The German Left contributed proportionately more signatures than the German Centre and Right, and to a degree that makes this phenomenon well beyond the reach of pure chance. Secondly, however, there was also a connexion—somewhat more marked—between support for this attitude and Members' zeal for civil liberties: the higher the attachment to civil liberties the greater the support for the Motion. The protest against what the Motion summed up as "racial and national discrimination" was thus part of a family of attitudes which included solicitude for civil liberties and an extremist view of disengagement in Central Europe. Nor was this all. The attitude appealed to certain types of Members significantly more than to others. The Miscellaneous Occupations favoured it much more than the Workers; the Co-operative Members more than the Constituency Party Members and very much more than the Trades Union sponsored group. The university, the elementary/secondary+, and most particularly those educated at secondary school, supported it more strongly than the products of the elementary schools. Those under 41 were by far the most favourable, those over 60 by far the least so.

The general implication is quite clear. Though the Labour Members and not the Conservatives gave extensive support to this generous expression of sympathy for Americans living in Britain, the working-class Trades Union sponsored element in it regarded it sourly as compared with those of the Miscellaneous Occupations, and with those educated at secondary school or university. Perhaps this was due to the well-known insularity of the Trades Union Members. Perhaps it reflects a general temperament, less tender and more matter-of-fact than that of the Miscellaneous Occupations and those with higher education: for it is at one with their comparative coolness towards pacificism and to humane penal legislation.

---

* EDM 26/1956.

Another Motion, tabled the day after the American one, was a response to the terrible events in Hungary. The Kadar government refused to admit U.N. observers, and intensified its terror. On December 10th the workers declared a general strike, but order was kept by Russian tanks. The Motion affords a vivid glimpse of the emotions struggling in the breasts of the Labour Members—their desire for peace, their misery over the events in Hungary, their yearning for friendship with the Soviet Union. It said that "recent events have demonstrated that violence can never solve the problems of modern society", and then, since "any nation attempting to impose its will upon any other nation can only endanger peace and freedom", welcomed the Government's decision to withdraw from Egypt. It continued, however, by "deploring the continued use of violence with its consequent bloodshed in Hungary". It wound up with the suggestion that the Government should invite Mr. Nehru "to secure a withdrawal of Russian military forces from Hungary and to use his influence to effect a reconciliation between Russia and the Western Powers which would make possible a new approach to a peaceful solution of world problems".*

This Motion would obviously appeal to the pacifists in the party, to the widespread sympathy with Hungary, even—in its suggestion of a reconciliation between Russia and the West—to the most determined fellow travellers. It is not surprising to find that it was massively supported by the German Left: no less than 86 per cent of their numbers signed it, as against only 43 per cent of the German Right. The correspondence is, statistically, a highly significant one. What is surprising however is that *one half* of the Labour backbenchers—118 Members—were willing to sign it. For, however well-intentioned, it appears a pious dream rather than a practical policy. A Conservative government could hardly be expected to rely on Mr. Nehru: his delegate, Mr. Menon, had ostentatiously voted against the U.N. resolution on Hungary on November 9th, and had abstained in the further votes on November 14th and 21st. Mr. Nehru himself had equivocated over Hungary, and both had actively supported the Afro-Asian bloc against Britain at the U.N. It is understandable that the Indian reactions

* EDM 27/1956.

were acceptable to the hard core of the Labour foreign-policy or anti-colonialist Left; but why to any others?

The reason lay in the intention of the sponsors—surely the most extraordinary use to which an EDM has ever been put! It was intended, and actually used as a petition to Mrs. Pandit, Nehru's sister and the Indian Ambassador to Britain, and intended for Mr. Nehru himself. Its sponsors made this clear to Members. Naturally, also, they made the greatest efforts to draw up support, while Members, in their turn, signed in large numbers because it appeared to have a practical object. In fact, once it was fully signed, a deputation did present it to Mrs. Pandit: it was "a very moving occasion and Mrs. Pandit received them with great warmth".* Nothing practical came of it; but that half the back-benchers could have signed it as a serious policy is the most striking testimony of their emotion and anguish. As we might by now expect, the Co-operators were much more heavily in favour than the Constituency Party Members and the Trades Union sponsored. Those with elementary/secondary+, or secondary school backgrounds were the keenest in support, and the elementary school group the least keen: and the junior Members, who had come in in 1955 and afterwards, were far more keen than any other intake group—particularly the old timers, who had first been elected before 1945.

The support given to this Motion contrasts strongly with that given to a third and final one, relating to Israel. During the intervention Labour Members had sternly condemned Israel's bellicosity while Conservatives had sprung to her defence. After the Anglo-French withdrawal came the turn of Israel. At the bidding of the U.N. she withdrew from all her conquests until she held nothing but the Gaza strip and the straits of Aquaba. From these she refused to budge, despite the distinct possibility, in January 1957, of U.N. sanctions backed by the U.S.A. administration, to compel her to do so.

Strictly speaking, the Labour party should have insisted on explicit Israeli compliance with the U.N. resolution. Mr. Gaitskell's line had been: "to say to the United Nations, 'We obey you, we accept whatever you say' "† In fact, the leadership did not take

---

* Private information supplied.

† *New York Times,* Nov. 25th, 1956.

this view. Mr. Bevan stated that the party's opinion was that "whereas it may not be a proper procedure for Israel to attach conditions for her withdrawal from the area, nevertheless guarantees about navigation for Israel and Jordan should occur simultaneously; and it would not be sufficient to ask Israel to withdraw and then wait and see what Egypt does". In reply, Mr. Selwyn Lloyd said that this was also the Government's view.* The next day an all-party Motion appeared, declaring that Israel ought to receive guarantees for the security of her Egyptian frontier and the freedom of the Gulf before she withdrew her forces from Gaza and Aquaba. One hundred and twelve Members, 42 Conservatives and 69 Labour, signed this Motion.

Unlike the two previous cases, the support for this Motion had *no* connexion with Members' "Leftness" or "Rightness" on the German problem; nor did the Motion appeal to any one category of Labour backbenchers rather than any other. The negative significance of these facts is of some importance. It used commonly to be thought that a pro-Israel and anti-Arab attitude was peculiar to the intellectual rather than the manual worker (although since Suez it has become fashionable for certain intellectuals, to take a pro-Arab and anti-Israel line). But an analysis of the signatures shows that support for Israel was derived from *all* sections of the party and was unassociated with any of the characteristics we have been able to observe. By contrast, the pacifistic, idealistic and anti-colonialist Nehru Motion was strongly associated with certain characteristics: with a left-wing attitude on German policy; with being a Co-operator rather than a Trades Union sponsored Member; with having had secondary rather than elementary or university education; with having been elected since 1950 rather than before.

Anti-Colonialism

The tradition of hostility to imperialism (now re-named colonialism) is, of course, of long standing in the Labour party. Since 1945, however, it was given additional point by the simultaneous rise of Asian and African nationalism and the decline of British military strength. In the last few years, as the country has

* *H.C. Debates,* Feb. 11th, 1957, col. 898. Cf. also *H.C. Debates,* Dec., 25th, 1957, col. 858.

grown more prosperous and relaxed, a fervid anti-colonialism has become an increasingly prominent trait of the young and radical Labour party member or supporter. Nineteen-sixty, it was proclaimed, was to be "Africa Year" for the party.

This anti-colonialism is a double-image. One of its aspects is a stress on the right of self-determination, and of the equal dignity of all men, just because they are men. The other is anxiety for the material welfare of the natives. Both aspects derive from a common morality, but they are not identical. Consequently they are not commensurable: it cannot be said that one aspect is more radical than the other. They must therefore be separated.

The backbenchers' views on the economic development of the colonies were not sufficiently numerous or distinctive to yield significant information. The case is otherwise with their attitudes on self-determination and the natural dignity of the native peoples. Here a fair number of Motions were tabled. None can justly be regarded as more radical than the others. It is possible to construct a "scale" of the intensity of Members' anti-colonialism, however, by assuming that a Member who signed more Motions than another was, to some extent at least, more concerned about the subject.

One Motion asked the Government to mediate in the Indo-Portuguese dispute over Goa so as to create conditions under which the Goans could "decide their own future": a straightforward plea for self-determination. A second, asking for an inquiry on Kenya, alleged racial discrimination between black and white in the administration of justice, and also protested about prison camp conditions and detention without trial; it stressed the equal dignity of all men. A third demanded the withdrawal of the Emergency Regulations in Cyprus (in November 1956), detailing their infringement of the civil liberties of the Cypriots. A fourth arose out of the French bombing of Sakiet in February 1958, expressing shock, and demanding British support for negotiations for a "just and peaceful settlement of the Algerian question". The final Motion, of 1959, was better supported than any of the previous ones. Signed by 178 Members, it demanded an inquiry into prison conditions in Kenya; a matter that had been vainly requested for years by the Labour party.

The most radical anti-colonialists, or Left, are those who signed three or more of the five possible Motions. There were only 28 of them. The Centre consists of those signing only two Motions—45 Members. The Right are those who signed only one Motion out of five: they number 103. Sixty Members expressed no opinion.

On this scaling of anti-colonialism, there were considerable differences between the attitudes of some classes of Members and other classes. Anti-colonialism was certainly not spread equally throughout the party as a whole. It was significantly linked with Members' occupation, sponsorship and age.

The Miscellaneous Occupations were distinctly more committed and more radical than the other groups: the Workers were the least committed and the least radical. The Professions came mid-way between the two. Likewise, the Trades-Union sponsored Members were markedly less anti-colonialist than the rest of the party. Interestingly—for this is the first case we have had to signalize—the Co-operators were not the most Left-wing of the sponsorship groups: their degree of anti-colonialism was the same as that of the Constituency Party members. Education had no bearing on anti-colonialism. Age, however, was significant. Those aged under 51 were more committed, and more committed to this self-determination aspect of anti-colonialism, than those aged over 51. A much higher proportion of the latter expressed no opinion whatsoever; and of those who did express an opinion, a higher proportion expressed views on economic development, to the exclusion of any view on political advancement.

In this instance it is wiser to note who were *least* radical, rather than who were most so: for it is really a case of the Workers and the Trades Union sponsored Members being markedly less committed and less anti-colonialist than the rest of the party. This partly accounts for the association of anti-colonialism and age: for the proportion of over-50's in the working-class and Trades Union element is far higher than for the rest of the party. And this in turn accounts for the fact that of the over-60's expressing an opinion, a higher proportion expressed views about economic and not political advancement than among the younger Members.

Civil Liberties

As in the previous case of anti-colonialism, so, in the present instance, we have equated intensity of attitude with the number of

Motions signed: the more Motions, the more intense the attitude. However, in the case of civil liberties it has been possible to put this assumption to the test. After a scale of zeal for civil liberties had been drawn up, based upon the number of Motions signed out of a total of six, a free vote occurred in the House of Commons on a civil liberties matter. It was possible to compare the scale with the votes cast. If the scale was correct, there ought to have been a correspondence between it and the division list.

The scale was as follows:

Left: (3 or more Motions signed) ...	27 Members
Centre: (2 Motions signed)	48 Members
Right: (1 Motion signed)	68 Members
Not Committed	93 Members

The free vote occurred on the Second Reading of the Street Offences Bill, 1959. Sixty-six Labour Members voted against this Bill and 12 supported it. Reference to the debate shows that the opposition was chiefly based on libertarian arguments—although some Members like Messrs. Paget and Silverman objected on wider social grounds as well.*

Figure 9 shows that the opponents of the Bill were proportionately most numerous on the Left and least numerous on the Right and among the uncommitted: and conversely that the Labour supporters of the Bill were proportionately least numerous on the Left and most numerous among the uncommitted. This correspondence could have occurred by pure chance less than once in 199 times. To this extent then, the evidence of the division list affords an important justification of this method of "scaling" the intensity of Members' attitudes. It also suggests, what is indeed implicit in this method of scaling, that the "Uncommitted" are in fact somewhat less zealous than the Right.

For the final analysis, a wider scale of seven Motions *and* the voting on the Street Offences Bill was used. Three Motions were concerned with infractions of liberty occurring under the penal system: one about the compensation due to innocent men who had

---

* *H.C. Debates*, Jan. 29th, 1959. Cols 1303: 1369: 1343.

been convicted and served sentences; another similar Motion arising from innocent men being convicted through mistaken identity at

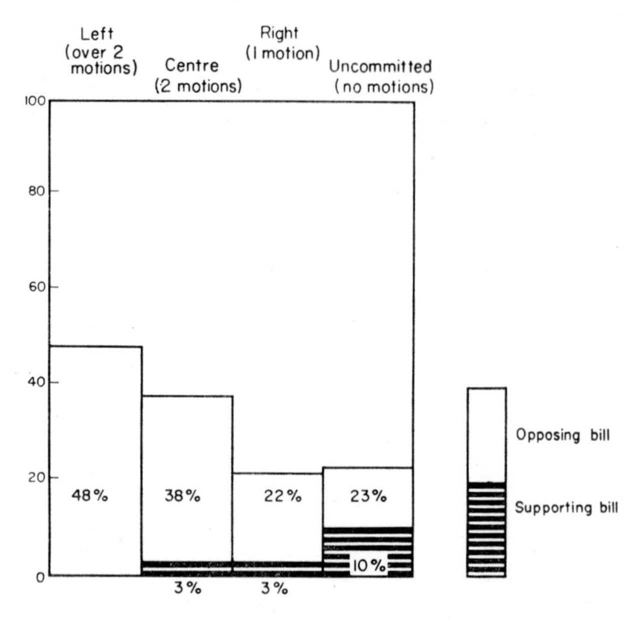

FIG. 9. *Association between number of civil liberties Motions signed, and voting on Street Offences Bill.*

identification parades: the third concerning a Mr. Hinds who had broken prison several times on the grounds that he was innocent, and suggesting that his case should be reinvestigated. A fourth Motion, demanded an inquiry into the allegation by the youth Waters, of Thurso, that he had been assaulted by the local police. The remaining three have a political flavour. One was a request for political asylum to a Spanish fugitive from the Franco regime—Joaquin Perez-Selles. The second protested at the dismissal by I.C.I. Ltd. of one of its employees, a solicitor named Mr. Lang, for security reasons, after the Government had made his dismissal a condition for placing a contract. The third went wider than this: it attacked the Report of the Privy Councillors on Security in the Public Service (Cmd 9715 of 1956) on the grounds that its proposals were "incompatible with the principles of a free democratic society". (The Government had appealed to this document as justification for its action on Mr. Lang). Finally, there are the votes against and for the Street Offences Bill.

On the whole there was little relationship between zeal for civil liberties and any of the observed characteristics of Members. There was a tentative (i.e., provisional) association between such zeal and education: it suggested that the least enthusiastic were those with elementary schooling, and the most zealous those from the narrow group of elementary/secondary+: the secondary school and university groups, similar in reaction, fell midway between the two.

There was, however, a firm association between attitude and the school-cum-university background of the university graduates. Irrespective of whether they went to Oxford and Cambridge or the other universities, those originating from grammar schools were more zealous than those with public school backgrounds.

Humanitarianism

Here again a quantitative scale was used: Members' humanitarianism was gauged by the number of Motions they signed out of a possible total of five. The first two amounted to support for the suspension or abolition of the death penalty for murder. The third, apparently an abstruse legal point (whether the Attorney General should have permitted a convicted murderer to appeal to the House of Lords) was in fact, a continuation of the abolitionist campaign. The fourth protested at the practice of punishing convicts by keeping their cells permanently lit. The fifth demanded that suicide should be removed from the list of criminal offences.

This produced a rank order, or scale, as follows:

Left: (4 or 3 Motions)	45 Members
Centre: (2 Motions)	84 Members
Right: (1 Motion)	73 Members
Uncommitted	34 Members

Humanitarianism, on this definition, was significantly related to the occupation, the sponsorship and the age of Members.

The most humane group were the Miscellaneous Occupations, followed hard by the small Business group. The least humane—and the least committed—were the Workers.

Equally significant is the association with sponsorship. As so often, the Co-operators were the most zealous and also the most committed, also. The Constituency Party Members were as well represented among the Left and Centre positions, but a high proportion expressed no opinions. The least enthusiastic and the least committed were the Trades Union sponsored Members.

As in the case of anti-colonialism, where the Worker–Trades Union-sponsored Members were also markedly the least enthusiastic, there was a close relationship between attitude and age; and probably, again, for the reason suggested there—the relative preponderance of the over-50's among the Worker and Trades Union groups. As in the case of anti-colonialism, the under-51's were more enthusiastic than the over 51's.

Social Welfare

Finally, we come to Members' attitudes on social welfare policy. Once again we have gauged the intensity of Members' feelings by the number of Motions they have signed. There were seven Motions available but the second and third have been treated as alternatives to one another, so that, in effect, intensity of attitude is ranked by the number of Motions signed out of a possible total of six.

These six Motions covered three different aspects of social welfare policy: the high cost of living, and government intervention in Arbitration Tribunals; social security benefits; and health and education. Conflated into a six-Motion scale, they yield Members' attitudes to what may be considered as social welfare generally; but since Members did not set the same value on all aspects of this social welfare programme, they ought also be considered separately.

The first Motion, of November 26th, 1957, attracted 75 names: it attacked the Government for trying to influence the attitudes of Arbitration Tribunals; the second, with 35 signatures, expressed alarm at the rise in the cost of living and blamed the Government: the third, (treated as an alternative to the second), signed by 104 Members, attacked the Government for failure to reduce the cost of living, and for its "jcopardization of industrial peace".

Then came the two Motions on social security payments. One hundred and thiry-five Members demanded immediate and substantial increases in old age pensions; one hundred and forty-seven demanded an immediate rise in the old age pensions to £3 a week.

Finally there were the two welfare services Motions. The first, signed by 91 Members, urged high priority for the building or modernization of hospitals, and increased grants to Regional Hospital Boards. The second protested against the Ministry of Education circular 334 (1958): it said it would cause irreparable harm to education, especially technical education, and demanded its withdrawal.

General.

The Members fell into the following ranks:

Very Keen (6 or 5 Motions)	45
Keen (4 or 3 Motions)	80
Moderate (2 or 1 Motions)	86
No opinion	25

Members' attitudes were significantly related to certain characteristics. In the first place there was a firm association between them and occupation. The Workers differed markedly from the rest of the party. There was little to choose between the attitudes of the Professions and Miscellaneous Occupations or Business: but the Workers stood apart as far more keen than all the others.

Likewise when we consider the sponsorship groups. The difference between the Trades Union sponsored Members and the Constituency Party Members was very considerable indeed with the former, of course, being the most keen and the latter the least so. The Co-operators stood midway between the two, but were, so to speak, broken into two: one half distinctly Keen and Very Keen, the other half distinctly Moderate.

This sharp polarization of the party into the Trades Union sponsored and working-class Members on the one side, and the remainder of the party on the other, was reflected in the educational dimensions. Eighty-four per cent of the Workers fall into the elementary and elementary/secondary+ category, but in the remainder of the party the proportion is only 20 per cent. Therefore it should cause no surprise that, by educational categories, the keenest were the elementary/secondary+ and the elementary school group (in that order) and the least keen by far, the university graduates. And among these there was a tentative association (significant at the 10 per cent level only) between both school background, and the kind of university attended. As we have perhaps come to expect, the university graduates with grammar school backgrounds were keener than those with public school backgrounds. In addition, those who attended universities other than Oxford and Cambridge showed themselves more enthusiastic than those who had graduated at these older universities. The tendencies met in those who went from public school to Oxford and Cambridge, and those who went from grammar school to the other universities. Between these two groups, the first being lukewarm, the second being enthusiastic, the differences were very marked.

Industrial arbitration and the high cost of living. It is only fair to point out that at least one of these Motions was couched in very provocative terms, and concluded with the cliché, no longer fashionable save in certain quarters, of "poverty in the midst of plenty". Without this warning the reaction of certain types of Members, e.g., university graduates, is not so easily comprehensible. Everything points to these Motions being Trades Unionist in conception, and possibly, in collection of signatures also.

Of the 236 Members, 53 signed both Motions, 81 signed only one, and 102 signed neither. The Workers, as one would expect, felt much the most strongly. The Professional class—and the Business group—felt much the least strongly. The Miscellaneous Occupations occupied the middle position.

These views were reflected in the behaviour of the sponsorship groups. By far the most keen were the Trades Union sponsored Members. The least keen were the Constituency Party Members. The Co-operators took up a midway view.

Since the Trades Unionist-cum-Worker *bloc* stems predominantly from the elementary school, both in absolute numbers and compared with the remainder of the party, there was an expected association between education and attitude. The greatest support came from the elementary/secondary+ group and the elementary school group. The least support came from the university educated, of whom 60 per cent expressed no views at all. Of these, those who went to Oxford and Cambridge were far less enthusiastic than those who went to other universities. Indeed, of the 25 Members who came to Oxford and Cambridge from public schools only *one* signed the full complement of (two) Motions and 21 signed neither!

More unexpectedly, there is a provisional association between attitude and the year of entering Parliament. There was a mild tendency for those elected in and after 1950 to be more enthusiastic than those elected before that date; but this is tentative only.

Social Security payments. These Motions were much more popular than the previous group. Seventy-seven Members signed both, 108 signed one or other, and only 51 signed neither. The Workers supported them in much the same numbers as before; but Members of Miscellaneous Occupations and of the professional class who had eschewed the previous cost of living Motions turned out in large numbers to support these social security Motions. Although the Workers were still somewhat keener than these other two occupational groups, the differences between their reactions were so reduced as to make it difficult to say that there was any significant association between type of occupation and attitude. What transforms the situation is the behaviour of the small and otherwise rather colourless Business group. These were far and away the keenest supporters of the social security Motions; even more so than the Workers.

Equally surprising, the most enthusiastic sponsorship group was *not* the Trades Unionists. On the contrary, there was little to choose between their behaviour and that of the Constituency Party Members. The most prominent supporters were the Co-operators. Furthermore, their behaviour cannot be ascribed to their occupational make-up. The occupational groups wherein their make-up differed from the Constituency candidates, were the Miscellaneous Occupations and the Professional; but these groups reacted in the same way. The occupational groups that reacted in an exceptional way were the Workers and Business groups: but these occupy the *same* proportions among both Constituency Party Members and the Co-operators.

Among the educational categories, the keener half of the party comprised the elementary and the secondary school groups. The elementary/secondary+ groups, and the university educated Members were the least keen. Compared with the cost of living Motions, therefore, the elementary/secondary+ group, which was in that matter the most enthusiastic of all, appears to have retreated. But this is an illusion. Its attitude was hardly less extreme for social security payments than in the cost-of-living question. The attitude of the elementary and secondary school groups, however, was even *more* extreme in the social welfare issue than in the question of the cost of living. The most important generalization from both cases is that the university educated were consistently the *least* interested.

Furthermore, among the university educated, both school and type of university were important. Those who originated from grammar schools were more enthusiastic than those from the public schools. Those who (irrespective of school) went to universities other than Oxford and Cambridge were more enthusiastic than those who had attended the two older universities.

Age may have been significant: but the association (at 10 per cent) is tentative only. It suggests that the keenest half of the party were the over-50's, the less keen the under 50's.

Health and Education. Here, 57 Members signed both Motions, 90 signed one or the other, and 89 signed neither. Enthusiasm in respect to these welfare services had no connexion with Members' occupation or education or age, or the year in which they first entered Parliament. It did, however, make a distinctive appeal to the Trades Union sponsored Members who were the most enthusiastic, contrasting in this with both Co-operators and the Constituency Party candidates who behaved similarly.

THE SYNDROME OF SOCIALISM

British socialism, unlike the Marxist socialisms of the European continent, does not and never has reposed on a single coherent and universalistic body of doctrine. It is much better described as a set of propositions or attitudes, which when all or many of them are simultaneously held, constitute "socialism", and the holder of them a socialist. It is true that a number of critics maintain that on the contrary, British socialism *is* founded on some coherent doctrine, or alternatively that of the six or seven basic propositions or attitudes, one or other is a *sine qua non,* or necessary condition for socialism —for example, Clause 4 of the Labour party Constitution. By implication, therefore, those who do not adopt this basic coherent doctrine—or that such and such an attitude or proposition is a necessary condition—are not socialists, but something else. This, for instance, is the root of the distinction which one of these, Dr. Miliband, draws between socialism and "Labourism"—which he characterizes as "tinkering empiricism". But when he or similar critics say that British socialism is founded on a coherent doctrine or the like, they do not mean "is", but "ought to be". For, historically, the variegated emphases of British socialism are open for all to see; while at the present moment, the only body competent to pronounce on whether a person is a socialist or not is the Labour party itself, and this—precisely because of its eclectic viewpoint—it is in no position to do so.

In consisting of a number of attitudes held conjointly, whether all or in great part, British socialism resembles movements like say, Romanticism, or nineteenth century European Liberalism, or Benthamism. The Benthamite, like the socialist, was recognizable by his holding a number of certain tenets simultaneously; and this meant that in certain individual cases where the number held was particularly small, he was barely identifiable at all. It also implies that in holding certain individual tenets they were at one, for purposes of practical politics, with other individuals who were certainly not Benthamites. Because their utilitarian views led them to desire a softening of the penal code, or the lunacy laws, or the abolition of slavery, they co-operated with persons as diverse as Romilly or Mackintosh, Lord Shaftesbury or the "Saints"—none of whom were Benthamites; because none of them held the remainder of the tenets which constituted Benthamism.

Similarly with contemporary socialism, although the simon-pure doctrinaires would disagree with this view on yet another point: that it admits the possibility that, in some matters, the British socialist may be indistinguishable from a partisan of any other British party. Identity and separateness are the hallmarks of those movements, like the Roman Catholic Church, or Soviet Communism, which are founded on a doctrine in which there is a place for everything and everything is in its place.

Even at the moment of writing, when the Labour party was split into pieces, each insisting on the rightness of its own version of socialist doctrine, it was not difficult to ascertain what the fundamental tenets were. Indeed, the reason for the factional disputes in the party is not due to a failure to identify or agree on these tenets: it is due to some party members laying peculiar or exclusive stress on one or some of these tenets, whereas other members wish to de-emphasize these tenets, or lay stress on others.

In the foregoing section we isolated five basic attitudes: pacificism (or peaceableness); anti-colonialism; zeal for civil liberties; humanitarianism; and the concern for social welfare policies. Within each one of these there was a wide span of practical application. For instance peaceableness ranged from unilateral disarmament to general disarmament under U.N.—but it reached its limit there; there was no faction demanding the retention of the H-bomb unconditionally. There are, in short, distinctions to be made between the basic attitude, its intensity, and its practical application in policy. British socialists differ from one another—as indeed the study has shown—in the intensity with which one or other attitude is felt, and they differ therefore in the practical applications of these attitudes which they are prepared to advocate. But the attitudes themselves are relatively few and are identifiable.

They can be established by comparing the attitudes implicit or explicit (usually the latter) in the following statements of Labour "values". They are derived from the 1959 policy document, *"The Future Labour Offers You";* Mr. Anthony Crosland's decalogue in his Fabian pamphlet "Can Labour Win?"; Mr. Gaitskell's seven point speech at the 1959 Conference; and "Victory for Socialism". *Pacificism* enters into all four; as "break the nuclear deadlock and lead the world to peace" (F.L.O.Y.); disarmament, international action and the rule of law (Crosland); enabling the peoples to live together in peace (Gaitskell); or unilateral nuclear disarmament (V.F.S.).

Anti-colonialism enters into all four and also the drive for greater *social welfare. Civil liberties* is mentioned but parenthetically in *"The Future Labour Offers You"* but is strongly mentioned by both Crosland and Gaitskell and the V.F.S. statement of aims.

Thus pacificism, anti-colonialism, social welfare, and civil liberties appear in all four sources. What appears in our own list and not elsewhere? Conversely what appears elsewhere, and not in our own list?

Humane penal legislation is the exception. It appears in our list but in none of the four sources. Yet it is connected with socialism. Mr. Roy Jenkins devotes attention to it in his "The Labour Case"; and the *New Left Review* (which is socialist by any definition) regards the Society for the Abolition of the Death Penalty as one of its "political roots".

On the other hand there are certain items which appear in the four sources but not on our list. By far the most significant is the belief in public enterprise and control of the economy. This must certainly be reckoned as a fundamental attitude of socialists, though both historically and actually it seems just to recognise—in the light of the Clause 4 controversy—that British socialists have and do differ in the emphasis they lay on it compared with the other attitudes, and on their practical application of it.

In addition both Crosland and Gaitskell speak of the desire to introduce a "socially classless society"; but that is because they no longer believe, or believe half-heartedly, in the existence of economic classes, and class warfare. V.F.S. and the *New Left Review* believe in the continued reality of both of these. All then, may be said to oppose a socially unequal society. This aspect also finds no place in our own list.

There are then, some seven basic attitudes which, in some degree or other, must be held simultaneously to constitute British socialism: pacificism, anti-colonialism, humanitarianism, zeal for the welfare services, libertarianism, a belief in the need for public enterprise and control of the economy; and the desire for social equality. These, held concurrently, make up socialism. They are the socialist *syndrome* (which is merely the Greek form of the word *concurrence*).

What then of "the Left"? Is this a body with a coherent and universalistic doctrine? Outside Parliament, and scattered throughout the party, there exist individuals who are consistent Marxists, though these are relatively few. There is the New Left group, certainly Marxist in approach, but differing in their style of Marxism, and also laced with the not always consistent attitudes of so-called socialist humanism, and thus forming their own socialist syndrome:—"If the *New Left Review* has any roots they will be *there.* Without C.N.D. supporters, Anti-ugly protesters, Africa demonstrators, Free Cinema, and the Society for the Abolition of the Death Penalty, we would be nowhere".* Outside Marxist circles Socialist theory is becoming increasingly dependent on the fashionable American social scientist of the day—first Wright Mills and latterly, J. K. Galbraith.

But inside the Parliamentary Party one would be very hard put

* *Universities and Left Review* No. 7, Autumn 1959, p. 2.

to find a group whose socialism constituted a coherent and complete system. There is certainly a small nucleus of Members who are always or nearly always found taking the extremer view over the whole range of questions, but these barely number a score. For the rest, there is a fluctuating membership "on the Left"—fluctuating through time and also according to the topic.

Until 1956 the Left might have been defined in terms of allegiance to Mr. Bevan; but as the *New Statesman* said after Mr. Bevan had disappointed his supporters at the Brighton Conference in 1957: "Deprived of [his] leadership, [the Left] was revealed as an army without much discipline or political coherence. Bevanism was a political mood as much as a movement."* This mood was satirized in 1952 by *Socialist Commentary*.

> Composed of anti-Americanism, of a belief that somehow we can stand apart from the U.S. in our island independence and give moral leadership to the world by adopting a "socialist foreign policy"; of a further belief that all our ills at home can be solved by "more socialism" by which is mainly meant more nationalization; and finally, of a conviction that war with Russia will be averted by developing the backward areas—†

This is a caricature. A more realistic appraisal suggests that the Left has a fluid membership which shares, albeit with varying degrees of fervour, many or most of the following attitudes.

There is, to begin with, a flavour of Marxism. The Left uses a number of stereotypes, or concepts, of Marxist provenance: a stereotype of capitalism, the concept of "economic power", the conception of class as an economic category; and with these goes the notion of a class-war and the belief that fundamentally all social relationships are determined by economic forces. In some instances, these notions are articulated together and held quite consciously, in a kind of Marxist system. In most cases, however, they are floating notions, hardly held together by any systematic philosophy—vestiges and residues of Marxism, often held unconsciously as presuppositions or assumptions.

Consistent with these attitudes or assumptions goes a pervasive mood of antipathy to America and sympathy for the Soviet Union. The dislike of America is rationalized under various forms: because the U.S.A. is capitalistic, because it is materialistic, because

---

* *The New Statesman,* Oct. 12th, 1957, p. 449.

† *Socialist Commentary,* Nov. 1952.

of its penetration of the British economy, because of its senior status in the Atlantic alliance, because of its hostility to Russia. Sympathy with the U.S.S.R. is ambivalent: there is hostility to its form of government, but a desire to co-operate with it on the international scene. There is always the assumption that, like Rousseau's General Will, the U.S.S.R. "may be deceived, but it is never corrupt". Its divagations from the democratic path and its apparent aggressiveness are supposedly due to its heavy but necessary task of rapid economic development, and its fears of armed intervention. With this goes a perennial optimism that whenever (as in 1936, or in 1953, or in 1956) the Russian leaders say that they have turned over a new leaf, they really mean what they say and that they have democratized their régime. This complex of pro- and anti-Russian sympathies is nothing new to the Labour party. Describing this as it was in 1924, Mr. Lyman writes:

> Within the world of socialism the British Labour Party fought the Communists; in the broader world of international affairs, Labour argued for the restoration of Russia to the European family, tended to discount unfavourable reports on Soviet affairs as anti-socialist propaganda, and urged that allowances be made for the difference between the task of a Russian government and that of a stable, democratically chosen British government.*

The semi-Marxist undertones help to reinforce another attitude of the Labour Left—the belief that African and Asian nationalism, and for that matter, Communism, is due to empty bellies. Thus the "plan for the Middle East" looks to an Economic Council "to fight poverty and ensure fairer distribution of oil profits". The plan for "World Mutual Aid" is defended on the grounds that "two worlds, one white and well fed and the other coloured and hungry, cannot live side by side in friendship."† And, again in a vulgarized version of Marxism, it sees war as an outcome of the attempt to retain and exploit the colonies.

But alongside these quasi-Marxist assumptions many members of the Left hold strongly pacifistic views. These are sometimes particularized as, for instance, in the demand for unilateral renunciation of the H-bomb: but in their most general form they take the shape of what Epstein calls "an aversion to force as an instru-

* R. W. Lyman, *The First Labour Government,* 1924, p. 185.

† Both views are now (1960) official party policy: *"The Future Labour Offers You"*, 1958, *"Peace"*.

ment of policy even as a means of keeping the peace—".* This again is not new. In 1924, when the Geneva protocol was under discussion some backbenchers were unwilling "to make the tremendous admission that Security and therefore Disarmament depends upon the organization of force—".† This pacificism reinforces the anti-NATO and anti-U.S. attitude, NATO being thought of as an aggressive alliance directed against the U.S.S.R., with the U.S.A. as its sponsor dragging a reluctant Britain with her into the arms race.

All these attitudes blend together to project a favourable image of India. India is ex-colonial: hence she is a tribute to the Left's policy of anti-colonialism. India is democratic. India's preamble to her second Five Year Plan states: "The achievement of a Socialist pattern of society has been accepted as the objective of our economic policy. This means that the basic criterion for determining the lines of advance is not private profit but social gain—"; so that a prominent member of the Labour Left can comment: "I would give three cheers if I could be sure that an official publication from a British Labour Government, while it is in power, would be equally clear in its avowals—."‡ And, finally, India is deemed pacifist. This stems largely from the memories of Ghandism and passive resistance: but it is noteworthy that during the passages of the speech in which Mr. Bevan was defending our retention of the H-bomb, at Brighton in 1957, voices were raised in protest, crying "Nehru has no bomb".§ In adulating India, pacificism, socialism, democracy and anti-colonialism find common ground; and these form the syndrome of "the Left".

But Members do not share these attitudes in equal degree, nor invariably apply them to the same concrete case. This can be seen quite clearly by taking four specific instances of left-wing" opinion. The first was the Bevanite abstention from voting for the official Labour amendment to the Government's defence Motion, in March 1952: 57 voted for Bevan's amendment. The second was the Bevanite abstention from the official Labour Motion on defence

* L. Epstein: *Britain—Uneasy Ally* (Chicago, 1954), p. 94.

† Lyman, *op. cit.*, p. 179.

‡ Jennie Lee: "Socialists can be proud of India" (*Tribune,* 29 June, 1956), quoted in *Tribune* 21 (McGibbon and Kee, 1958), pp. 270–272.

§ *Annual Conference of the Labour Party,* 1957, *Report,* p. 181.

in 1955. This time 60 Members abstained. The third was a public appeal, signed by 85 Members in January 1957, demanding fundamental changes and economies in Britain's military policy. The fourth was the letter signed by 32 Labour Members in July 1957 attacking the official policy of "Industry and Society", as a "policy of retreat".

Of the names on these four lists, 93 sat as Members throughout the whole period. Of these, however, 50 appear on only *one* or other of the lists; 23 appear on any *two* of the lists; 15 on any *three*; and only five appear on all lists. The fluctuating composition of the Left is apparent.

* * * *

Now it is possible to establish whether indeed, inside the Parliamentary Party, the attitudes of pacificism, humanitarianism, libertarianism, anti-colonialism and zeal for welfare services form a syndrome of the kind we have described. By talking of these as a *syndrome* we mean that, when one attitude is held, the others are also held.

This can be established by finding out whether Members who are enthusiastic on one matter tend to be enthusiastic on another; and vice versa. In statisticians' language this is termed a *correlation.* It compares the rank orders—the place on the scales—of Members, for each separate attitude. Members who are enthusiastic about one thing may be completely unenthusiastic about another. When *all* Members at the top of one scale are at the very bottom of the other scale, there is a complete *negative* correlation: this is expressed as -1. When all Members at the top of one scale are also at the top of the second scale there is a complete positive correlation. This is expressed as $+1{\cdot}0$. A value of $0{\cdot}0$ means *no* correlation. Anything higher than this, e.g., $0{\cdot}3$, means that there is a *tendency* for Members high in one scale to be higher in the other also. And by the same token, a value of $0{\cdot}3$ means that this tendency is greater than where we have a value of $0{\cdot}1$.

Table 2 shows the correlation between attitudes, and the first important point is that all are correlated together positively. There *is* a connexion between them all. It is highest in the correlation between Humanitarianism and Civil Liberties at 0.41. It is lowest

TABLE 2

Correlation between attitudes in the Labour Party

	Humanitarianism	Civil Liberties	Foreign Policy	Anti-colonialism	Pacificism	Welfare	Cost of Living	Health and Education
Humanitarianism	1·00	0·41	0·32	0·30	0·35	0·21	0·22	0·13
Civil Liberties		1·00	0·36	0·30	0·33	0·25	0·22	0·15
Foreign Policy			1·00	0·36	0·39	0·23	0·27	0·21
Anti-colonialism				1·00	0·32	0·19	0·20	0·09
Pacificism					1·00	0·34	0·19	0·21
Welfare						1·00	0·33	0·29
Cost of Living							1·00	0·33
Health and Education								1·00

between Anti-colonialism, and Health and Education; with a correlation of only 0.09. The values do, in short, constitute a *syndrome*; and to this extent they may be contrasted with the situation in the Conservative party where there is often no correlation at all between one attitude and another.

The second point is, however, that some of these attitudes are more highly correlated together than are others. There is a roughly equal degree of correlation between Humanitarianism and Civil Liberties as there is between Civil Liberties and Foreign Policy, and so on, down the table. The correlation between Anti-colonialism and Welfare is much lower however—but the correlation picks up again to the usual level (in the order of 0·3) when we consider the correlation between Welfare and Cost of Living and between Cost of Living and Health and Education.

Thus the table is arranged in *pairs,* each correlated by roughly the same amount. The pairs which are close together in the list are usually more highly correlated than those far apart. Humanitarianism is correlated with Civil Liberties at 0.41 but it is correlated to Health and Education at only 0.13.

Thus the table indicates a kind of scale. The nearer two attitudes stand together on this scale, the higher the probability that a Member who is enthusiastic in one attitude will be enthusiastic in the other—or vice versa; and the further apart they are on the scale the less will be the probability that there is a connexion between the intensity of one attitude and the intensity of the other. Thus there is some likelihood that a Member's intensity in one attitude will be matched by a like intensity in another; but the likelihood is greater in respect of some attitudes than of others. There is little likelihood that enthusiastic supporters of Health and Education will be enthusiastic anti-colonialists. There is a fairer likelihood, however, that they will be enthusiasts for higher welfare benefits.

The top attitudes on the list might be regarded as altruistic or ideological and the bottom as materialistic, thus:

Ideological	Humanitarianism Civil Liberties Foreign Policy (Germany) Anti-colonialism Pacificism
Material	Welfare Cost of Living Health and Education

If we could imagine Members placed at any given point on this scale, they would be more likely to sign the Motions near them than the ones that are far away.

Now, the position at which we ought to place them can be guessed by their characteristics. Co-operators would have to be placed at the top of this scale, Trades Union sponsored Members at the bottom. This would imply that the Co-operators were more likely to be equally enthusiastic about the attitudes near them at the top of the scale, and less and less enthusiastic as they moved down the scale, while the Trades Union sponsored Members acted in just the reverse order. And this is precisely what the synoptic table at p. 56 above suggests. Here is a correlation scale with the most enthusiastic supporters of each attitude:

TABLE 3

Scale of attitudes, and categories of support

Ideological	*Most enthusiastic group*
Humanitarianism	Co-operators
Civil liberties	—
Foreign policy	—

TABLE 3 (continued)

Ideological	*Most enthusiastic group*
Anti-colonialism	Co-operators / CLP
Pacificism	Co-operators
Material	*Most enthusiastic group*
Welfare Benefits	Trades Union sponsored
Cost of Living	Co-operators
Health and Education	Trades Union sponsored

Finally, all attitudes are correlated, on the average, to the degree of ·267. This means that Members tend to be equally enthusiastic —or unenthusiastic about *all* elements of the syndrome irrespectively. It is that group of Members who arc zcalous about all elements of the syndromc* that constitute the nucleus of the otherwise broader, fluctuating and inchoate Left. On this showing—and bearing in mind that only 236 of the total party is included in our survey—the Left consisted of the following Members:

The Fifty most Left Members

Royle, C.	Lee, F.	Hale, L.
Fernyhough, E.	Robinson, K.	Delargy, H.
Smith, E.	Silverman, S.	Swingler, S.
Slater, H., Mrs.	Owen, W.	Paton, J.
Allaun, F.	Parkin, B.	Cullen, A., Mrs.
Brockway, A. F.	Watkins, T.	Mikardo, I.
Plummer, L.	Pargiter, G.	Hastings, S.
King, H.	Hughes, E.	Warbey, W.
Reeeves, J.	Yates, V.	Lee, J.
Hughes, H.	Roberts, G. O.	Mellish, R.
Stross, B.	Hunter, A.	Butler, R., Mrs.
Davies, H.	Craddock, G.	Brown, T.
Thomas, G.	Monslow, W.	Taylor, H. B.
Silverman, J.	Weitzman, D.	Sorenson, R.
Mason, R.	Jones, T. W.	Jeger, L., Mrs.
Griffiths, W.	Lewis, A.	Hayman, F.
Oram, A. E.	Darling, G.	

To conclude. The five basic attitudes isolated here were supported, broadly speaking, by all Members and hence may be called

* N.B. "all elements". Some of the names in this list not usually classed as "left", qualify because of their heavy emphasis on social welfare matters.

a *syndrome*; Members tended to lay greater stress on some attitudes than on others; and the attitudes they stressed were significantly related to their characteristics. A core of Members supported all attitudes with maximum zeal. These form the permanent core of the otherwise fluctuating Left.

THE COMPONENT FORCES

A previous section defined the attitudes within the party, and showed the component groups with which they were associated. Each such component thus puts its own individual emphasis or counter-emphasis on the various items in the Labour syndrome. Out of the interplay of these emerges a viewpoint for the party as a whole. We must now look at each component, and relate its distinctive attitudes to that of its fellows.

In doing this, however, it is most necessary never to lose sight of two things. The first is that we are defining a pattern of *emphases*. One component feels *more* or *less* strongly than another on a certain matter; but that is all we can say. There is no absolute measure of the radicalism or moderation of the viewpoints expressed; and there is no way of saying, either, whether the radicalism of the most radical anti-colonialists is greater or less than that of the most radical pacificists. Some groups are more radical than others in the sense that they give disproportionate support to attitudes we have stipulated as being more radical than others. If *no* groups gave disproportionate support to any particular attitude, i.e., if they all gave equal support, there would be nothing for us to discern. But since for *some* attitudes *some* groups do give disproportionate support, the situation is much like that described in the silly joke on the back of a matchbox. "*Teacher*: 'Tommy, why are you always at the bottom of the class?' *Tommy*: 'Well, Miss, *someone's* got to be at the bottom, haven't they?' "

The second point is that although we talk of one group being more left or enthusiastic than another, we are talking only of a *tendency* within these groups. These groups or categories never acted as *blocs*. To say that the Constituency Party Members are more enthusiastic than the Trades Unionist sponsored Members means that a disproportionate number of them support the attitude as compared with the Constituency Members. There is always much "cross voting", i.e., Constituency Members among the moderate wing, and likewise Trades Union Members among the radical wing.

Indeed, it is this mixture of elements in each and any wing of the party, on any topic whatever, that makes it difficult for Members themselves to discern the different outlooks of the various sections of the party which we have outlined. They will notice that, say, the anti-colonialists consist of Trades Unionists, professional men and the like and draw the inference that therefore Trades Unionists are no less interested in anti-colonialism than professional men. They do not consider that the Trades Unionists there may be disproportionately fewer than their numbers in the party would warrant; and this is the crucial test.*

The Occupational Groupings

The reactions of the three main occupational groupings is diagrammatically illustrated in Fig. 10.

The Workers' position is clear: lagging on every ideological issue; leading the rest on every material issue. The Workers constitute, as has been shown, a separate culture world: elementary education, trade union sponsorship and occupation largely coincide. In all these respects, their "opposite number" is the Professional group—where occupation largely coincides with university education and absence of any kind of sponsorship. One might well have expected the viewpoints in the party to be sharply polarized between these two groupings: yet, as the diagram makes clear, this is not so. On all material issues, the Professions are indeed at the opposite end of the scale to the Workers: but this is not true of the ideological issues. On pacificism, despite the educational and occupational gulf that distinguishes the Professions from the Workers, they are at one. On the others they are somewhat more radical, but, in the context of the party as a whole, they occupy the centre, moderating position.

* One very prominent Member of the Labour party was quite certain that the unilateralists were "mainly Scots and Welshmen". Indeed he was so sure that he elaborated a long historical-sociological explanation for its being so. We thought there might well be something in this, and counted them (taking birthplace and/or place of education as our criterion). The number of Scots and Welshmen among the 45 unilateralists (see p. 26 above) turned out to be not more than 12—almost exactly the same proportion as they bore to the party as a whole!

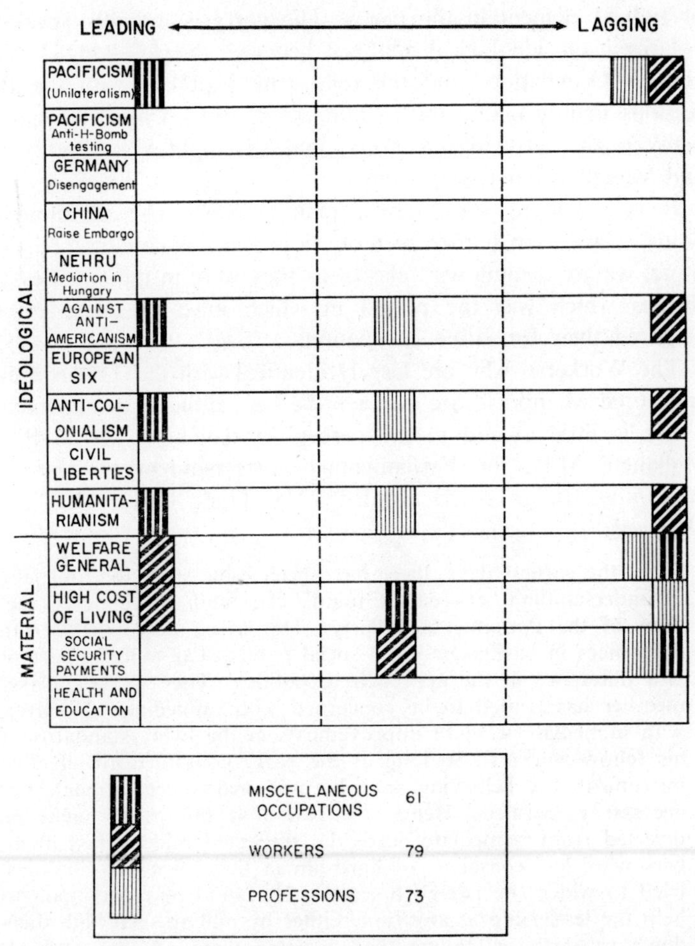

FIG. 10. *Attitudes of the major occupational groups in the Labour Party.*

No: consistently, the counterweight to the Workers' attitude is provided by the cultural "middle" of the party—the Miscellaneous Occupations. On the material issues they join hands with the Professions in counterbalancing the enthusiasm of the Workers; and the only apparent exception to this, their middle stance on the "high cost of living issue" is to be explained by the pronounced ideological content in the framing of the two particular Motions. On the ideological issues, they are, without exception the left-wing or radical element in the party. The party is, broadly speaking, polarized on ideological matters between the left-wing Miscellaneous Occupations and the right-wing Workers, with the Professions mainly taking the middle view: and on material matters between the left-wing Workers, and the right-wing Professions and Miscellaneous Occupations.

It is easier to say "how", than "why". The sociology of British classes has hardly been developed in this country. Furthermore, we are dealing with classes as they were in the twenties and thirties which was the period in which most of the Members acquired their formative occupation.

The Workers—who are largely identical with the Trades Union sponsored Members—are perhaps the least difficult to understand. There is little to add to the perceptive sketch of Mr. J. P. W. Mallalieu, M.P., the Parliamentary correspondent of *The New Statesman.* In an article entitled "The Trade Union M.P.",* he observed:

> From the earliest days, there have been some suspicion and lack of understanding between the middle-class and working-class sections of the Parliamentary Party. This arises only partly from differences in background and social habits. Far more important is a difference in the approach to politics. The "working-class" member has tended to be concerned with immediate objectives, with immediate if small improvements in the living standards of his fellow workers. So long as the party continued an effective instrument for achieving that he was acquiescent though not necessarily satisfied. Hence for fear that the party might be diverted from immediate needs, he suspected middle-class members who, less conscious of hardship in their own surroundings, tried to widen the party's horizons. He could be relied upon to help the leadership at any time, either by pulling such high fliers down to earth or, failing that, blasting them off the earth altogether. This difference in approach was accentuated by an uneasiness which some trade union members felt in trying to work with men whose upbringing provided them with a fluency which sometimes sounded like glibness and an assurance which often seemed like arrogance—

It is more difficult to account for the contrast between the Professions and the Miscellaneous Occupations. Education may be a factor. Nearly all the Professional Members received a university

---

* "The Trade Union M.P.", *The New Statesman,* 28 Nov., 1959, p. 736.

education and half of them a very protracted one—viz., the doctors and the barristers. Only one-third of the Miscellaneous Occupations had proceeded beyond the secondary level. There was a marked divergence of viewpoint between university and secondary school types, as far as ideological issues were concerned (see Fig. 12 below); and so the relatively high proportion of secondary school Members in the Miscellaneous group and of university people in the Professions must play some role in determining attitudes. The subject studied may also have had its importance. Left-wing radicalism in the thirties made its greatest inroads in the arts and sciences; medicine and the law seem to have been resistant. Most of the Professions are doctors and lawyers.

On the other hand, the family background of Members, especially in respect to wealth, might have been a factor. For the twenties and thirties, the type of school attended offers a rough index of family income: public school, secondary grammar school, elementary school spelt affluence, a very moderate income, poverty, in that order. As the following table shows, the proportions coming, in each case, from affluent ("public school") families were not widely different, but the proportions from elementary and elementary/secondary+ *were* very divergent.

TABLE 4

School Background of Members of the Professional and Miscellaneous Occupation Groups

	Elementary; elementary/ secondary+		Grammar Secondary;		Public school		Not known	
Miscellaneous Occupations	19	31%	21	34%	17	28%	4	7%
Professions	6	8%	37	49%	26	34%	4	9%

Perhaps the decisive factor, however, lies in the character of the work which Members of these two groupings performed. The Professions were principally lawyers (32), doctors and dentists (8) and schoolteachers (19); with three university teachers and four established adult education teachers. For lawyers, even attending the House is a part-time occupation: and all—lawyers, teachers and doctors—have an established profession into which they can slip back if at any time they quit the Commons. For them—in a word —becoming an M.P. is exchanging one profession for another. (Of course, this is less true of the schoolteachers.) Again, in their professional dealings lawyers and doctors, pre-eminently, are acting on *behalf* of other people, and must take full responsibility for them; added to which, the nature of their tasks demands great sobriety in judgment. In short, in their professional dealings, neither doctors nor lawyers "may answer for themselves". They are under restraints.

The Miscellaneous group pursue quite different occupations. One-third of them were in minor professions or white-collar avocations:—housewives, professional politicians, welfare workers, personnel officers, local government officers, insurance agents and the like. Two-thirds of them were journalists and publicists. Five were established professional journalists; seven were party publicists and journalists (e.g., "former editor, *New Leader*" or "former editor of a . . . Socialist weekly journal") and fourteen pursued a variety of tasks, often simultaneously, but were all part-time journalists. Finally, another fourteen were publicists, party organizers and party research workers. "Became a lecturer", runs the biography of one: "has been teacher, freelance journalist, labourer and insurance official", runs another. Two were organizers for the Co-operative party. Three were research officers of the Labour party or the Co-operative party.

For the great majority of this group politics was the great obsession, and once a seat had been obtained, the great profession. The occupations pursued were, for most, the means of preparing for the profession of politics or ways of making a living to support such a profession. Furthermore, very few of these occupations entail bearing a personal responsibility for a client, nor do they—like medicine and the law—demand controlled judgments. This group is at once, highly politicized and highly subjectivist. It largely corresponds to Leon Epstein's characterization of the Labour "intellectuals". "This category," he said, "did include some of the university teachers (and former teachers) who were active in the post-war Labour party, but 'left-wing intellectuals' were also, by definition, a more heterogeneous collection of white-collar socialists who customarily earned their living by journalism, lecturing, politicking, or any one of a large number of other journalistic activities. Although most of them were respectable participants in the life of the community they were rarely the holders of organizational responsibility either in government, business corporations, or trade unions."*

The Sponsorship Groupings

Attitude was associated with sponsorship more often than with any other kind of attribute. The attitude of each of the three

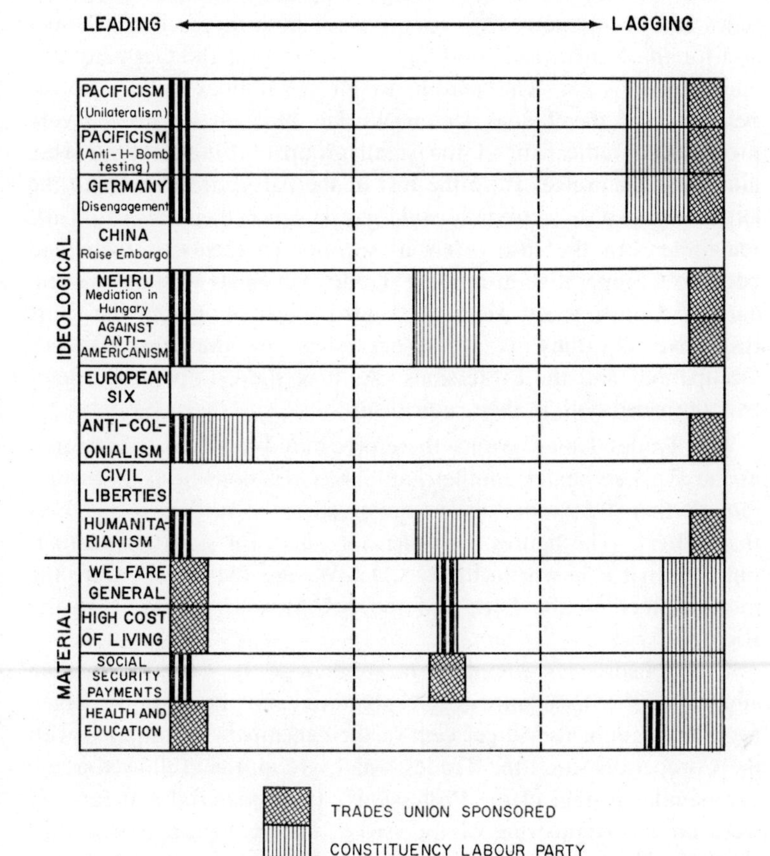

FIG. 11. *Attitudes of the sponsored groupings in the Labour Party.*

groups—Co-operators, Trade Union sponsored, and Constituency Party Members—is shown, diagrammatically, in Fig. 11.

The Trades Union sponsored group pursued a line similar to

* L. Epstein, *Britain—Uneasy Ally*, Univ. Chicago Press, 1954, pp. 78–9.

that of the Workers, i.e., lagging on all ideological issues, leading on all material issues except Health and Education. This is due to the fact that for the most part—to the tune of some 80 per cent—it is the same as the group of Workers. In that case, why was there an association between sponsorship and attitude in three cases, where there was no corresponding association between attitudes and occupation? This occurred for both the pacificism issues and for the Nehru mediation and—possibly—for the Germany disengagement issue. The reason, in all cases, does not lie in the behaviour of the Trades Union–Worker bloc. It lies in the very pronounced radicalism of the small group of Co-operators, who, launching themselves from the rest of the party, drew so far to the left as to open an extremely wide gap between themselves and the remainder. In the case of social security payments, if there had been no Co-operative group, the Trades Unionists would have led, and the Constituency Members lagged—thus occupying the same respective positions as the Workers do to the Miscellaneous Occupations and the Professions. As it is, the Co-operative Members outpaced both in their radicalism.

The Trades Union group, therefore, may broadly be considered as the Workers under another hat. Their reactions need no further remark than that some unions appeared to be further to the Left than others. The figures are much too small for statistical testing; but for what it is worth, the U.S.D.A.W. and the A.E.U. were the most inclined to the Left, and the N.U.M. and T.G.W.U. to the Right.

The Constituency Members may, likewise, be considered as an amalgam of Miscellaneous Occupations and Professions which together account for 80 per cent of their members. Compared with the Co-operators and the Trades Union group, they followed a line very similar to that of the Professions. In all material matters they were on the Right-wing of the party: on ideological issues, they shifted. They were indistinguishable from their Trades Union colleagues on pacificism and on Germany; balanced between the Co-operators and the Trades Unionists on the Nehru mediation, the anti-Americanism issue and humanitarianism; but, on anti-colonialism indistinguishable from the Co-operators. This was due less to a leftward lurch than to the backwardness of the Trades Union cum Worker bloc.

Thus both for the Constituency Members and for the Trades Union bloc, one needs go no further for explanation than to refer to their occupational composition. But in the case of the Co-operators, neither this nor the educational factor will do. The 21 Co-operative Members were a mixed bag both occupationally and educationally. Two were Workers. Three were involved in business. Five were professional people—two schoolmasters, a barrister, a doctor and an electrical engineer. Ten were Miscellaneous Occupations, mostly connected—by lecturing, organizing, etc.—with the Co-operative movement itself. One striking fact is the prevalence of Co-operative *apparatchiki.* Of the 21 at least 11 fell into this category, most of whom, as one would expect, were of the Miscellaneous Occupations. Thus one explanation of Co-operator radicalism lies in the high proportion of persons for whom politics was their vocation. Incidentally (though no statistical significance attaches to the figures, which are tiny), the *apparatchiki* were more radical than the other Co-operative members.

The explanation for the Co-operators' record must be sought, surely, in the *type* of candidate nominated by the local Co-operative parties, approved by the party's Executive, and selected by a constituency party (to which the local Co-operative parties or societies may be affiliated and on whose selection panel they will be represented). All these bodies clearly choose candidates who are completely different from the Trades Unionists. Practically none were "Workers"; two-thirds had progressed beyond the elementary school; and two-fifths were under 51 (as against only 13 per cent among the Trades Unionists); and, as is obvious, their political attitudes were widely different. Not too far removed from the Trades Union emphasis on welfare services, they were ideologically always on the Left.

It has been suggested that this type of candidate is nominated, at the local party level, by the influence of the Women's Guilds. These sections are often markedly internationalist in viewpoint. Another suggestion is that the movement's political thinking has been powerfully permeated by the rather distinctive flavour of Co-operative education. Indeed, the two matters may be connected, since, the education committees of the local societies consist to the extent of 45 per cent, of women. The high proportion of *apparatchiki* suggests other avenues for being nominated, and being centrally approved. One Member was the party's research officer; another, the former head of the research and information centre of the C.W.S.; two more were education officers; one was the secretary to a large local society; another, a member of the Co-operative Union's Executive Committee, was a former lecturer and propagandist for the movement. Such people almost suggest themselves for nomination and for approval by the Central Executive Committee.

Nor is it difficult to understand why Co-operators should be selected, in preference to Trades Unionists, by certain constituency parties. It is not due to the Co-operative party being more lavish in the financial and other help which it gives the Constituency Party;* nor to Co-operative party pressure at the selection conferences of the constituency Labour parties. It is simply that the Co-operative candidates have tended to be more loquacious, more energetic, more doctrinaire and more youthful than the usual run of Trades Unionist candidates.†

The Educational Groupings

The most influential groupings, because of their size, were the elementary school and the university groups. Together they accounted for 170 of the 236 Members.

The elementary school group pursued a similar pattern to the Trades Unionists or Workers, as is to be expected owing to the overlap between these three categories. They were consistently on the Right on all ideological matters, but to the Left on all material issues.

The university group, however, was less predictable.

It helps to remember, however, that it largely overlaps the Miscellaneous Occupations and the Professions. As was to be expected, it was on the right on all material issues. On ideological issues, however, it showed important variations. It was far to the left of the party, in opposition to the testing of the H-bombs. This reaction has already been described at p. 28 above. It was a humanitarian reaction, largely influenced by the health-hazards of radiation.

---

* Cf., Smith and Ostergard: *Constitutional Relations between the Labour and Co-operative Parties*, Hansard Society, 1960, pp. 17–22.

† *Ibid., loc cit.*

The Nehru-mediation Motion found it firmly on the Right. It will be remembered that, sponsorship-wise, the Co-ops were on the Left, the Constituency Members in the Centre and the Trades Unionists on the Right. Figure 12 shows, in effect, a division among

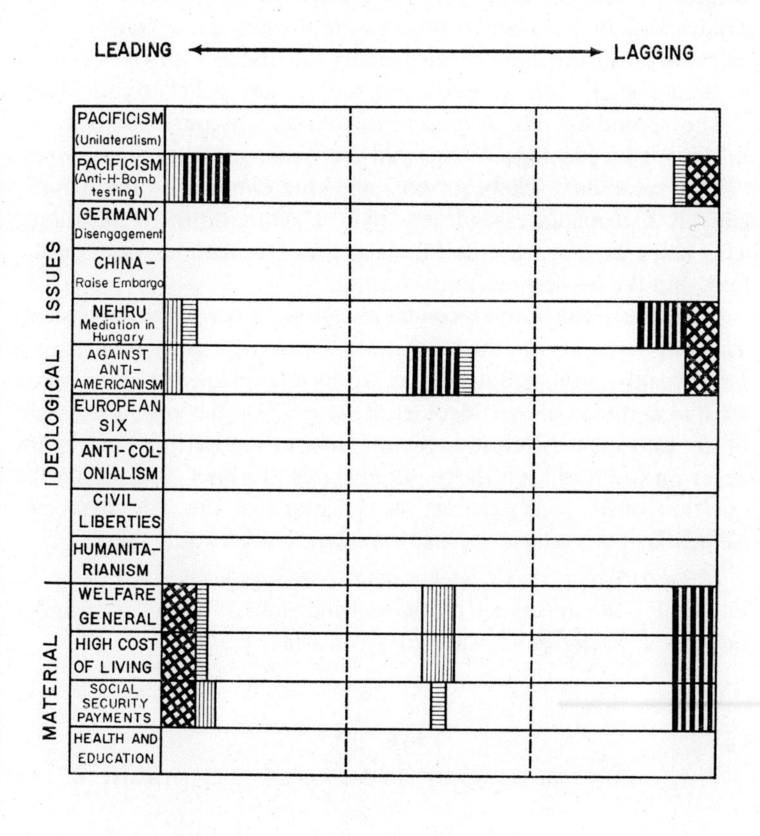

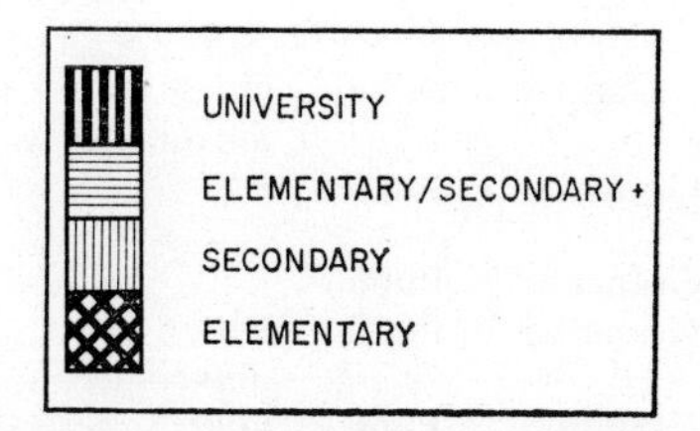

FIG. 12. *Attitudes of the educational groupings in the Labour Party.*

the Constituency Member bloc: the university Members of this bloc pulled Right, its elementary school and secondary school Members pulled Left—hence it wound up in the middle.

Similarly with anti-Americanism. There, as before, the Constituency Members were midway between the Co-operators and the Trades Unionists. Such Members were divided education-wise, the university trained and the elementary/secondary school+ took a moderate stand, the secondary school group pulled to the Left.

The secondary school group also pursued a consistent pattern: to the left on ideological issues, in the centre on the material ones.

This secondary school group represents *one-half* of the Miscellaneous Occupations—and less than a tenth of the Professions. This helps explain why the Miscellaneous Occupations were on the Left, and the Professions in the Centre.

Even the elementary/secondary+ group were fairly consistent. The one anomaly in their behaviour was their right-wing stance on H-bomb testing. But this, as we have explained, was as much an humanitarian as an ideological issue. For the rest, they were to the Left on the Nehru mediation, and to the Left or Centre, but never on the Right, on the material issues. In brief, apart from the question of H.-bomb testing, the positions of the secondary and elementary/secondary+ groups were never very far apart.

University and school backgrounds. Among those educated at the university, the reactions of those with similar school, or similar university, backgrounds showed a consistent pattern.

TABLE 5

Attitudes of University Graduates in the Labour Party

	By type of school			By type of university		
	Leading		*Lagging*	*Leading*		*Lagging*
Pacificism (unilateralism)	Grammar	*v.*	Public	Other universities	*v.*	Oxford Cambridge
Pacificism (anti-H-bomb tests)	Grammar	*v.*	Public		—	
Civil liberties	Grammar	*v.*	Public		—	
The high cost of living	Grammar	*v.*	Public	Other universities	*v.*	Oxford Cambridge
Social security payments	Grammar	*v.*	Public	Other universities	*v.*	Oxford Cambridge

In every case, grammar school Members were more radical than the products of public schools—irrespective of the universities they attended: and likewise, Members from universities other than Oxford and Cambridge were, irrespective of school background, more radical than those who went to the older universities.

The radicalism of the grammar schools is almost certainly accounted for, principally, by the relatively narrower and poorer homes from which the Members sprang. Those families who could afford to send their children to public school must have been tolerably well off. However, the professions followed may also be a factor. The public schools produced 14 lawyers and only two schoolteachers (out of a total of 50); the grammar schools produced 14 lawyers, but also 14 schoolteachers (out of 50). There is some evidence to show that on all matters except humane penal reforms, the lawyers were less radical than the teachers. Thus the relative radicalism of the grammar school graduates may be partly due to a considerably higher proportion of teachers. The exigencies of the profession would lead lawyers to be more cautious and responsible than teachers, especially when most of the lawyer M.P.s were practising part-time and the teachers had cut entirely loose from their profession. On the other hand, the apparent radicalism of the teachers as opposed to the lawyers might itself be a reflection on the home circumstances; for in the thirties few but the wealthy took up law as a career, while schoolteaching was a favoured course in humbler homes.

The relatively right-wing attitude of the Oxford and Cambridge graduates also probably reflects affluence at home. In the thirties, even on a full scholarship grant, a grammar school boy needed some parental support to keep him at Oxford and Cambridge. Another factor may be the mellowing influence of the traditions in the older universities. There is possibly a third factor, however —the condition of labour or socialist university clubs in the thirties, outside London, Oxford and Cambridge. At these last, left-wing radicalism made great strides, and it was fashionable to belong to the Left—fashionable and easy. Elsewhere it was unfashionable, and rather uncomfortable. Paradoxically, therefore, the young socialist students of the provincial university would tend to be more radical than those from Oxford, Cambridge and London.

One final factor may be relevant. The public school products were practically all English. The grammar school products were, roughly, half English and half from Wales and Scotland. Again, the Oxford and Cambridge Members were only one-sixth Scottish as against five-sixths English. The Members who attended other universities, however, were one-third Scots and Welshmen.

Age

The pattern of the relations between age and attitude is, as Fig. 13

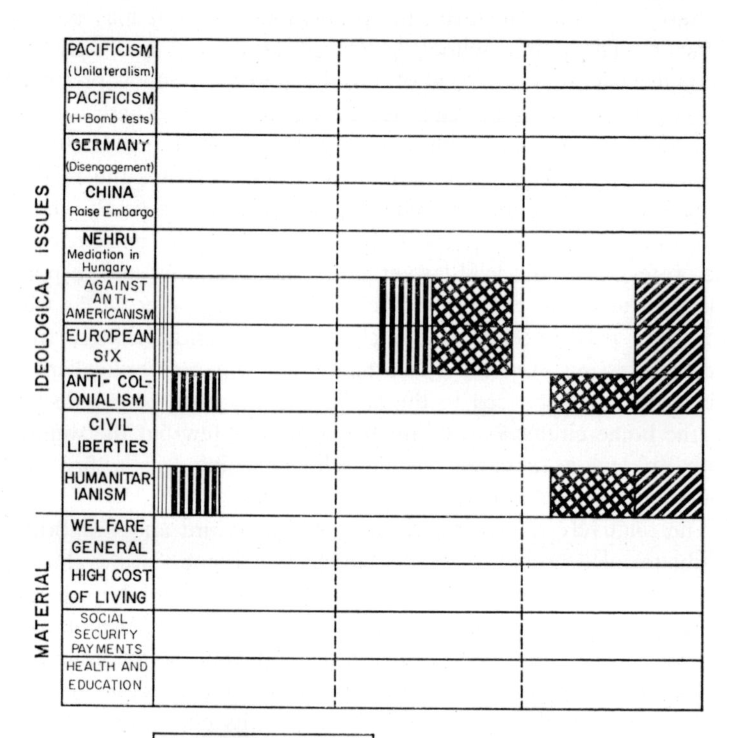

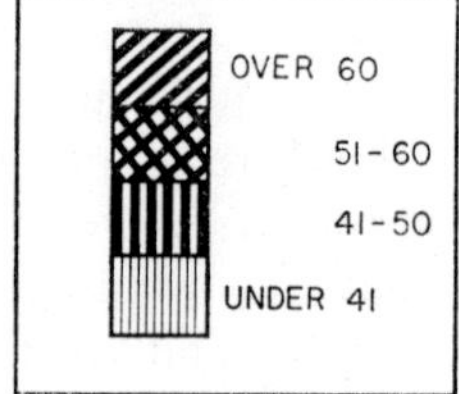

FIG. 13. *Attitudes of Labour Members by age.*

shows, uncomplicated. Age was not a significant factor on any of the material issues. It was significant only for a limited number of ideological matters. And it had no connexion with any of the defence or foreign policy issues—with one exception, the problem of the European Common Market.

Where age was significant, the younger were the more radical. The differences were most pronounced over anti-Americanism and the Common Market: but the great bulk of the party, the 41–60 group, were firmly in the middle. On anti-colonialism and humanitarianism, however, the line of division was between two more equally matched groupings.

Age and "intake" are the most significant pointers to the future behaviour of the Labour party, since these are the factors that are bound to change most drastically with each succeeding Parliament. The pattern of age differences suggests that two important elements of the Labour syndrome—pacificism and the welfare services—are unlikely to alter with changing age structure. On the other hand, two others—humanitarianism and anti-colonialism—are likely to receive more stress.

Year of Election to Parliament

The year in which Members were elected might be supposed to be connected with the successive re-interpretation of socialism as the party presents it, from one election to another. Some attitudes are up and coming: others, becoming obsolete. Which then were the ones followed by the more recently elected Members as opposed to the senior ones?

TABLE 6

Attitudes of Labour Members by Year of first entering Parliament

	Leading		*Lagging*
Pacificism (anti-H-bomb tests)	Elected after 1949	*v*.	Elected before 1949
China—Raise embargo	Elected after 1949	*v*.	Elected before 1949
Nehru—Mediation in Hungary	Elected after 1949	*v*.	Elected before 1949

Again the pattern is uncomplicated. As in the case of the age-factor, so here: there was no connexion between year of election and material issues; the intake year was related only to ideological matters and here it *complemented* the pattern of age-preferences.

The post-1949 generations were affected, as the age-groups were not, by pacificism and neutralism. In every case, the rather small post-1949 generation (rather more than a quarter of the total backbenchers) was more pacificistic than its seniors.

As the proportion of the under 40s increases, and the proportion of pre-1949 Members decreases, one might therefore expect to see an ideological move towards the Left.

CONCLUSION

British socialism is a syndrome of attitudes, some idealistic, some materialistic. Two of the attitudes, egalitarianism and public ownership, do not figure in this analysis. Both, incidentally, have an ideological as well as a materialistic aspect. In the light of the story so far, it would not be surprising if on these issues the two chief occupational blocs, the Miscellaneous Occupations and the Trades Union cum Worker bloc, joined hands.

Leaving aside egalitarianism and public control, however, on which we have no information, it is possible to discern the balance of forces in the party.

On the knife and fork questions, the impulsions came from the Trades Unionists, the Workers, the elementary and elementary/secondary+ groups. If all these are conflated together, they total 120 Members—one-half of the backbenchers. But this represents the outside limit of this bloc. Its hard core consists of only those who were, simultaneously, Workers and Trades Unionists with elementary or elementary/secondary+ education. This hard core amounts to 55 Members.

On the ideological side, this bloc of 55 Members represented the right-wing force in the party. It opposed and was opposed by the Miscellaneous Occupations, the Co-operators and to some extent the secondary school group and Members who had proceeded from secondary school to provincial universities. The size of this group, when all are conflated, is 85 Members. Here the attitude of the Professions has proved decisive: sometimes siding with the working-class bloc (as with unilateralism), sometimes against it (as with anti-colonialism).

Thus the various parts of the party key into one another. Miscellaneous Occupations, Co-operators, and the secondary schools form the ideological vanguard: the Trades Unionist cum working-class cum elementary school Members hold them back. The latter bloc form the materialistic vanguard: the Miscellaneous Occupations, the Professions and the university graduates constitute the inertia.

Now, in the usual way, one would expect the two extremes to cancel. But these forces are part of a parliamentary party, whose effectiveness, in opposition no less than in power, depends exclusively upon its solidarity. The extremes, in such a case, do not cancel out: they add up. Following its Trades Unionist and elementary schooled colleagues, the whole party presses for improved material standards for the workers. Following the lead of its ideologically inclined Miscellaneous Occupations, its Co-operative group, its secondary, and secondary-cum-provincial university Members, the whole party plunges towards pacificism, humanitarianism and anti-colonialism.

And all of this takes place in the context of Members' age and year of election. The younger Members and the more recent Members are at one with their elders and seniors on the welfare services. They are ahead of them on the ideological issues of pacificism, humanitarianism and anti-colonialism. Irrespective of the occupational or educational balance or the balance of sponsored membership, as old Members drop out and seniors decline to stand again, so the ideological tone will move leftwards. The failure of the Labour party to win the 1959 election only checked the replacement of the old and the senior by the young and newly elected; it happened more slowly than in the conquering party—but, to an extent, it did occur.

Furthermore, as it occurs, so will changes in the educational system influence the party. The occupational balance is at large—nobody can predict what will happen here. The balance of sponsorship looks as though it will remain steady for some time to come since both Co-operators and Trades Unions are loath to retreat from their present proportions of Members.* But the educational balance is bound to change. The elementary school and the elementary/secondary+ types belong to a past age. They will be increasingly replaced by secondary school, and university Members: and this will reinforce the ideological drive to the left.

---

* A large increase in the number of Labour M.P.s, however, would probably mean a reduction in the *proportion* of Trades Union sponsored Members.

Chapter 3 · The Conservative Party

THE SOCIAL COMPOSITION OF THE CONSERVATIVE PARTY

The fierce disputes within the Labour party are well-known, despite the strict formal discipline which is imposed in the division lobbies of the House of Commons, but amongst the Conservatives there are few disagreements conducted as dramatically, or with as much heat; yet even in the Conservative party there are differences of emphasis and in priorities, and sometimes there are deeper fissures as well. Disagreements are found in the realms of foreign affairs, of penal reform, and less obviously, in the fields of financial and social policy.

Since the object of this study is to see whether differences of

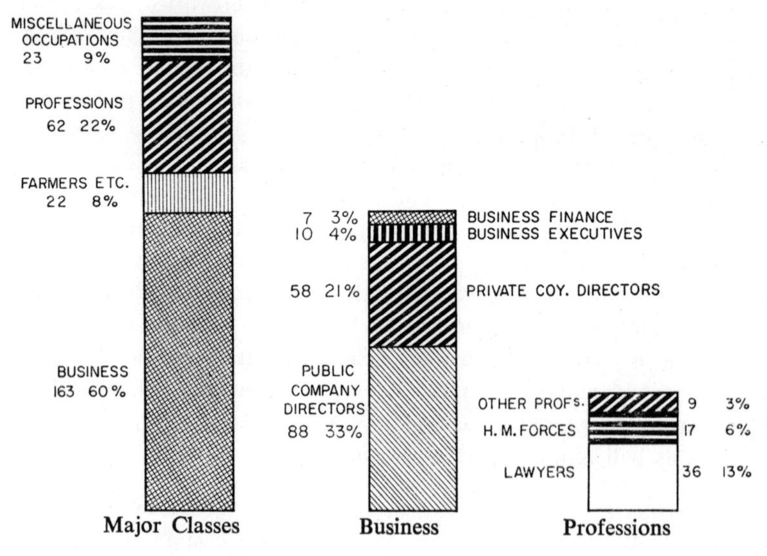

FIG. 14. *The Conservative Party: occupational distribution.*

opinion and attitude were related to any recognizable characteristics of the Members themselves or of the constituencies they represented, the first step is to decide which background factors should be selected for study, and secondly, to classify Members according to their characteristics.

Members of the Government, and M.P.s who were on the back benches for too short a period to sign a complete train of EDMs on any one topic, were excluded altogether. This left 270 M.P.s and a few of these Members were excluded from particular counts for reasons described in detail in Annex 2.

The Parliamentary Conservative party was analysed by seven different criteria:

First of all, Members were divided into four major *occupational* classes: viz. Business, Farmers, Professions and Miscellaneous Occupations. The Business class comprised all company directors, business executives, brokers and underwriters: the Professional class, all members following a recognized profession. Miscellaneous Occupations covered journalists, publicists, political organizers, administrators (other than those employed in business), housewives and a few Members who lived on private means.

The Business class was broken down into four sub-categories, and the Professions into three. The distinction between the two largest business groups, directors of public companies* and directors of private companies† corresponds very roughly to the division between big business and medium or small business. Business (executives) and business (finance) were two small residual groups of Members who held no directorships but who made their living in business.

The Professional class was composed of regular officers, lawyers and other professions.

Secondly, Members were divided into four *school* categories: Clarendon Public Schools, Other Public Schools, Non-Public Schools, and the Rest. The Clarendon Schools are the nine traditional English public schools and include the most expensive and exclusive public schools. Four-fifths of the Members in this category went to one of the three leading schools—Eton, Harrow and

* Defined here as companies whose shares are quoted on the London Stock Exchange.

† Defined here as companies whose shares are not quoted on the London Stock Exchange.

Winchester; and more than half came from a single school—Eton.

The Other Public Schools category contained those M.P.s educated at any other recognized British public school. The Non-Public School group was a diverse class consisting of all Members (other than the "Rest") who had not had a public school education. Some had attended private schools, some had been to old-established grammar schools and others were educated at secondary or elementary council schools.

The Rest was a residual class containing the seven women M.P.s and six Members who were educated in the Commonwealth.

Next came the five *University* classes: Oxford, Cambridge, Other Universities, Sandhurst and None.* The Other Universities group comprised Members who were educated at provincial, Scottish, Irish or overseas universities. The None* category included Members from military, naval or air-force colleges other than Sandhurst, as well as those who went straight from school to a job.

Two further methods of classifying Members—according to *age*

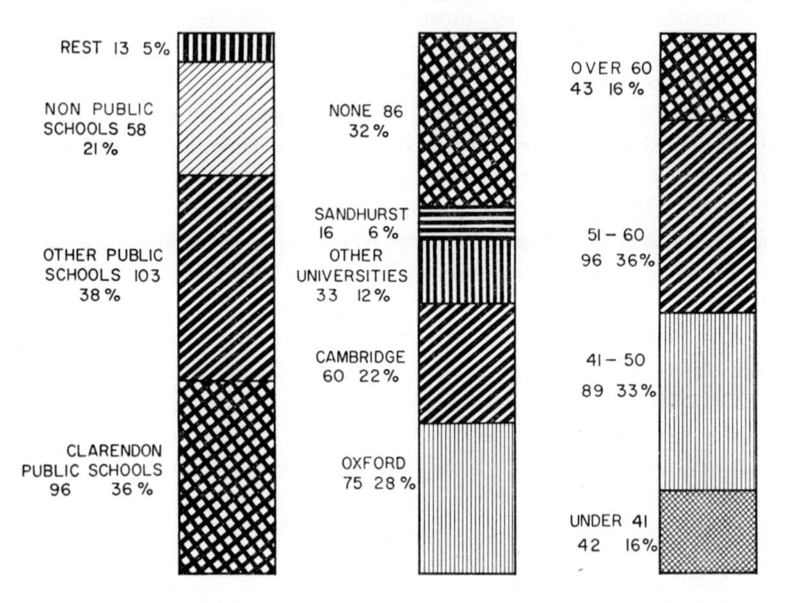

FIG. 15. *The Conservative Party: age and educational distribution.*

* Usually referred to as non-graduates.

and *length of Parliamentary service*—require no elaboration. *Size of majority* afforded a further method of classification. Members were divided according to their majorities at the 1955 General Election. The reason for this classification was to see whether Members' views were related to the size of the Conservative vote in their constituencies. Moreover, the size of the Conservative majority probably bore a rough relationship to the social composition of the area. (For instance, most marginal constituencies had a majority of working-class electors.) Differences in the social make-up of constituencies may have been reflected in the political viewpoints of their M.P.s.

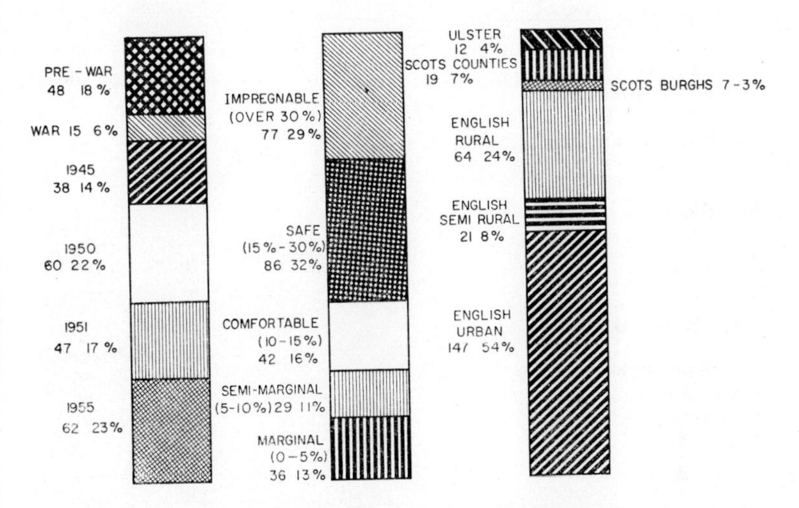

FIG. 16. *The Conservative Party: year of first entering Parliament, size of majority and type of constituency.*

* * * *

Finally, Members were classified according to the *types of constituency* they represented, whether they were Urban, Semi-rural, or Rural.

A regional breakdown was made, but there were no significant variations in the behaviour of Members from different areas.

These categories are shown in the following tables.

TABLE 7

Composition of the Conservative Party

(*a*) *By Occupation*

Business	*No.*	*Percentage*
Public Company Directors	88	33
Private Company Directors	58	21
Business Executive	10	4
Business Financial	7	3
All Business	163	60
Farmers	22	8
Professions		
Lawyers	36	13
H.M. Forces	17	6
Other Professions	9	3
All Professions	62	23
Miscellaneous	23	9
Total	270	100

(*b*) *By Schools Attended*

	No.	*Percentage*
Clarendon Public	96	36
Other Public	103	38
Non-Public	58	21
Rest	13	5
Total	270	100

(*c*) *By Universities Attended*

	No.	*Percentage*
Oxford	75	28
Cambridge	60	22
Other	33	12
All Graduates	168	62
Sandhurst	16	6
None	86	32
Total	270	100

TABLE 7 (continued)

(*d*) *By Age*

	No.	*Percentage*
Under 41	42	16
41–50	89	33
51–60	96	36
Over 60	43	16
Total	270	100

(*e*) *By Year of First Entering Parliament*

	No.	*Percentage*
1955	62	23
1951	47	17
1950	60	22
1945	38	14
War	15	6
Pre-War	48	18
	270	100

(*f*) *By Size of Majority*

	No.	*Percentage*
Marginal (0–5%)	36	13
Semi-Marginal (5–10%)	29	11
Comfortable (10–15%)	42	16
Safe (15–30%)	86	32
Impregnable (Over 30%)	77	29
	270	100

(*g*) *By Type of Constituency*

		No.	*Percentage*
England and Wales :	Urban	147	54
	Semi-Rural	21	8
	Rural	64	24
All England and Wales		232	86
Scotland:	Burghs	7	3
	Counties	19	7
All Scotland		26	10
Ulster		12	4
Total		270	100

None of the overlaps are as striking as those which were found in the Labour party: in that party, Trades Unionists were sharply differentiated from other groups by virtue of both education and occupation. Nevertheless, in the Conservative party there were some important cross-relationships.

The most important inter-relationships occurred between occupation, education and age. There was a pronounced contrast in the educational background of public and private company directors. By any criterion, the public company directors were drawn from higher educational circles than the directors of private companies. More of the former had been to exclusive public schools, and fewer

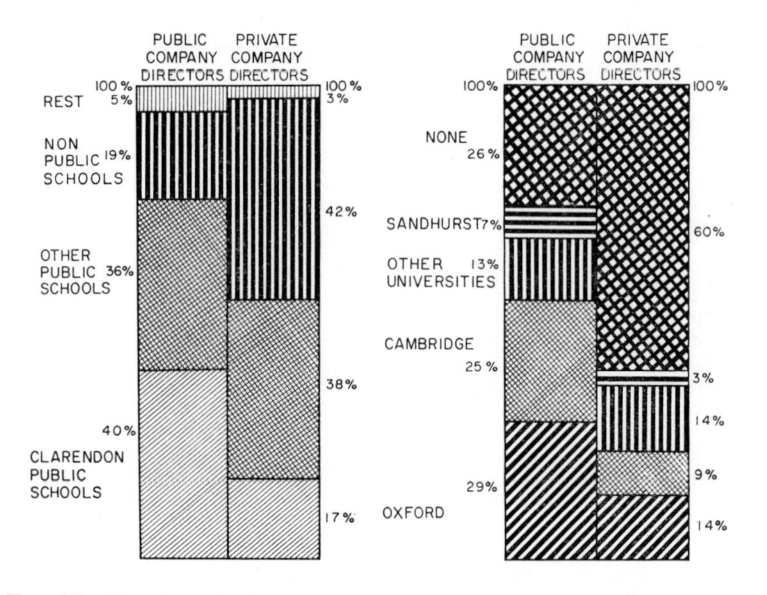

FIG. 17. *The Conservative Party: public and private company directors by school and university.*

to private or local authority schools. More of them had gone to either Oxford or Cambridge, and more of them had had some kind of university training. Public company directors also tended to be older, and most of them had entered Parliament before 1951.

As might be expected, there was also a marked overlap between the school and the university categories. Non-graduates were drawn to a disproportionate extent from the Non-Public School

M.P.s. Nearly all of the Clarendon School M.P.s however, and two-thirds of the Other Public School class, had been either to a university or to Sandhurst. Clarendon School M.P.s and Members from the newer public schools differed sharply in their choice of university. Twice as many of the Clarendon School M.P.s went to Oxford as went to Cambridge; the Other Public School group went predominantly to Cambridge.

Age was related to school background. The Clarendon School M.P.s were considerably younger than the Non-Public School group. There are two possible reasons for this. Conservatives with an Eton and Oxford background may have found it easier to be selected for winnable seats when still young, than men with a secondary school and non-university background; and men from a non-public school background may have preferred to postpone their entry into politics until they had established themselves in their careers. Secondly, Ministers were necessarily excluded from this enquiry and the Government tended to recruit its Ministers largely from the older Clarendon Members. This would have had the effect of diminishing the proportion of Clarendon School M.P.s amongst the older backbenchers.

Similarly, there were connections between the type of school attended and the size of majority. Non-Public School M.P.s came in disproportionately large numbers from marginal seats, but relatively few came from the safe and very safe seats. Rural constituencies favoured M.P.s from Clarendon Schools.

There was naturally a close connection between age and the year of first entering Parliament. More than half of the under forty-ones were first elected in 1955 or at subsequent by-elections. Most of the over-sixties had entered the House before 1950.

The relationship between age and size of majority was less regular, but the group of under 41's contained more M.P.s from marginal seats, and fewer from impregnable seats, than any other age group. On the other hand, a high proportion of the oldest Members sat for very safe constituencies.

So much, then, for the more important overlaps between different groups. There were other and less well-marked relationships: the reader may follow these himself by referring to Annex 2.

The most significant feature was the nature of the business group. It was not a homogeneous class. Directors of public and private

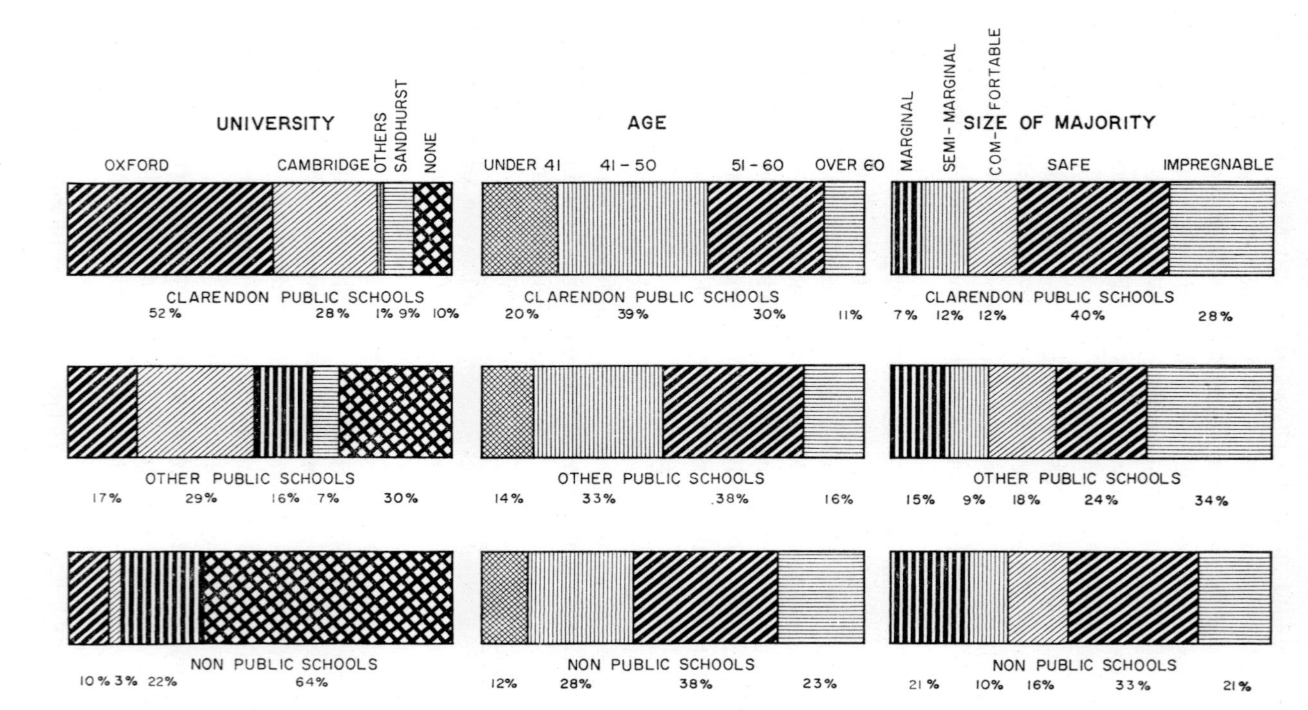

FIG. 18. *The Conservative Party: School backgrounds by university, age and size of majority.*

companies differed not only in some of their attitudes, but in the sort of schools they went to, in their university backgrounds, their length of Parliamentary service, and in the kind of constituencies they represented. Directors of public companies were in every sense a better entrenched and more well-established group within the party.

The Business class, comprising over half of the Parliamentary Party, turns out on inspection to have been a highly variegated group of Members. In itself, this fact suggests that we are unlikely to find a distinctive "business" point of view within the Conservative party at Westminster. The preponderance of this large and heterogeneous category, coupled with the smallness of the Miscellaneous Occupations group, suggests that occupation is unlikely to play the important role within the Conservative party that it often plays in the Labour party.

There is another feature, of perhaps equal, though negative significance. In the Labour party, we found that there were two distinct cultural groups, the Workers and the Professions, with a miscellany in between. Educational and sponsorship divisions largely coincided with the occupational boundaries. We find no counterpart to this in the Conservative party. Such inter-relationships as we find, between, say, different occupational and educational classes are much less pronounced. In short, particular educational and social characteristics do not cumulate as markedly as they do in the Labour party, but blend and combine to produce a relatively undifferentiated and integral party.

BACKBENCH ATTITUDES IN THE CONSERVATIVE PARTY

Foreign Affairs and Commonwealth Policy

The Conservatives have not been beset, since the war, by internal disputes as deep and as prolonged as those which have bedevilled the Labour party. Few of their divisions reflected any differences of outlook or ideology as profound as those which prompted the Bevanite struggle. The Conservatives often seem to enjoy a spontaneous and unforced unity, but on foreign affairs especially, there are important differences of approach and emphasis, which at moments of crisis may lead to acute and bitter disagreement. The Suez crisis affords a good example: both the original decision to evacuate the Canal, and the subsequent attack on Egypt, provoked sharp internal conflicts.

Nevertheless, there has been no *fundamental* dispute within the party about Britain's foreign policy. There has been no serious opposition to Britain's role in the cold war, or to her membership of NATO and little to her reliance on American friendship. The Soviet challenge has imposed certain ineluctable policies upon British governments, whatever their colour. Within the assumptions of the cold war and the western alliance, however, Britain has had some scope for an independent policy. Difficult choices have been posed; there has been the question of Britain's attitude to her colonial empire; there has been the problem of the Middle East; there have been the strains and problems imposed by Britain's membership of the United Nations; and, a signal cause of conflict, underlying most other controversies of foreign policy, has been the issue of national sovereignty: how far should Britain relinquish her freedom of action to the United Nations or other international bodies?

Many politicians and commentators have spoken of post-war British foreign policy as an essay in reconciling the claims of the four overlapping associations of which Britain is a member—Western Europe, the Atlantic Alliance, the Commonwealth and the United Nations. To a considerable extent, the policies imposed by membership of these four groupings are consistent with one another. But there are potential divergences, which may lead either to concealed disagreement or open schism. Moreover, membership of each of these bodies carries with it, either in form or substance, a limitation of British sovereignty and obligations that may clash with Britain's own interests. There are occasions when onerous choices or unwilling compromises have to be made. Each decision is likely to find its own partisans and opponents within the Conservative Parliamentary Party. A decision to expand trade with Europe at the expense of the Commonwealth countries may provoke the anger of the imperial preference group. Concessions to America on Middle Eastern policy, in the interests of the Western alliance, may incur the enmity of those who believe in a firm and independent British policy. Any move to relinquish British sovereignty may mean opposition from those who see themselves as the champions of British power and prestige. In turn, to ignore Europe's call for

British support may antagonise her sympathisers within the party. To pursue a policy conceived in the narrowest terms of British prestige, without regard for allies or international obligations, may incur the criticism of the more internationally-minded. These differences, though latent and often unobserved, are nevertheless real, and may lead to violent struggles within the party at moments of crisis.

Europe and the Commonwealth. Since the beginning of the European movement there have been keen disagreements within the Conservative party about British attitudes to Western Europe and to the Commonwealth. Britain's dual position as the mother-country of the Commonwealth and as a leading European power has compelled an ambivalent attitude. British governments have consistently refused to take any step towards closer association with Europe that would limit the United Kingdom's freedom of action, injure her own interests or damage her relationship with the Commonwealth. Within the Conservative party are many who would like to see a closer liaison between Britain and Western Europe; but the cause of European unity is a recent and exotic bloom, whereas the tradition of imperialism in the Conservative party is old and deeply rooted. Amongst the Commonwealth group are some who would welcome British association with Europe so long as it does nothing to imperil relations with the Commonwealth; and there are also those for whom European unity has little, if any, appeal and whose international interests are almost wholly absorbed by the Commonwealth.

The differences between the European and the Commonwealth wings of the party are strongest over economic policy. Since the turn of the century a large section in the Conservative party has laid stress on increased Empire trade, both for its economic benefits and as a means of preserving and strengthening the ties between the nations of the Commonwealth. In greater Commonwealth trade and investment is seen a means of sustaining the links between Britain and her former empire. Economic bonds take the place of formal political unity. For this section of the party, the flag follows the cargo-ship.

Most of the proposals for European co-operation have been primarily economic or have had economic implications; some of them have conflicted, or have appeared to conflict, with the cause of increased Commonwealth trade and investment. Greater economic co-operation, such as entry into the Common Market or the abortive Free Trade Area might, unless accompanied by special concessions, endanger Commonwealth development and the expansion of Commonwealth trade. Moreover, closer ties between Britain and Western Europe might impair those special diplomatic and political links still remaining between Britain and the Commonwealth. Political involvement, in the form of Britain's entry into a federal or quasi-federal Western Europe, could compromise Britain's role as leader of the Commonwealth.

This dilemma is not absolute. The partisans of European unity find it politic to make some acknowledgment to the Commonwealth ideal, and many members of the party look for some mutually satisfactory arrangement which will associate the Commonwealth with Europe. Some members of the Commonwealth lobby regard the Commonwealth and Europe as natural allies in the effort to save the world from domination by America and Russia. Thus, Mr. Braine, an Empire man spoke in the House of Commons of the fear that a divided and fragmented Europe would be "a prey to the great dollar and rouble imperialisms".* To some degree, closer ties with Europe, whether economic or political, may be compatible with the preservation and growth of Britain's Commonwealth connection, but much depends on the exact form which the new political and economic institutions take. This need to find some synthesis between the claims of European co-operation and the Commonwealth tie has often been emphasized by the Conservative leaders.

It nevertheless remains true that on many occasions and at many points, the claims of Western Europe will conflict with those of the Commonwealth. There are not two opposing and irreconcilable sides within the Conservative party: but there are differences of emphasis. There are many who would like Britain to give a strong lead towards European unity; and there is a strong and vocal group which is much more concerned to sustain Britain's Commonwealth ties, even if it means that Britain must be lukewarm or hostile to new European involvements. At the popular level, the ideas of the latter group find their most extreme expression in the Beaverbrook Press. While the debate in the Conservative party

* *H.C. Debates,* March 26th, 1958, Col. 7.

may not be conducted with the same passion or bitterness, the apostles of the Commonwealth with the party are still determined and articulate.

Backbench motions in European and Commonwealth relations were of three kinds. The "European" Motions expressed support for closer British association with Western Europe. The "Empire Moderate" Motions called for increased Commonwealth trade and investment; and there were the "Empire Stalwart" EDMs which demanded either an extension of imperial preference or an unequivocal declaration that the expansion of Commonwealth trade would take priority over closer relations between Britain and Western Europe.

Members fell, according to the Motions they signed, into two blocs, "Europe" and "Commonwealth". The "Commonwealth" bloc was subdivided into two groups, the "Empire Moderates" and the "Empire Stalwarts".

It would be wrong to imagine that all of the Empire Stalwarts were indifferent to the cause of European co-operation. Many showed their concern by signing the European Motions: but they also made it clear that their first loyalty lay with the Commonwealth. On the other hand, within their ranks, there was also a tiny group of eight Members, headed by Major Legge-Bourke, who explicitly rejected any federal or quasi-federal relationship with Europe.

There were 104 Europeans. The "Commonwealth" bloc consisted of 127 Members—63 of whom were classified as "Moderates" and 64 as "Stalwarts".*

These figures do not purport to give an accurate picture of the strength which the pro-Commonwealth and the pro-European factions could muster if a crisis occurred, and a definite choice were posed. The "Europeans" have been regarded as leaning towards Europe, for the Empire Motions which most of them signed were consistent with putting Britain's European commitments on at least an equal footing with her Commonwealth obligations. Yet if Britain's relations with the two prove incompatible, it is unlikely that all those Members classed as Europeans will choose Europe in preference to the Commonwealth. The most that can be said is

* The total of Members classified falls short of 270 because some Members were uncommitted, and others were excluded from this count. For each count, it was necessary to exclude some Members. See Annex 2.

that these backbenchers were more sympathetic to Europe, and less committed to the Commonwealth, than the Members in the Commonwealth bloc. Within the Conservative party there were substantial pressures on both sides. Any policy that is ultimately chosen by a Conservative government must take into account the numbers, influence and the strength of feeling of these two blocs.

Now these different attitudes clearly appealed to distinctive groups of Members. The conflict between the Europeans and the partisans of Commonwealth trade and development was primarily a contest between two Parliamentary generations. Members who entered Parliament in 1950 or before were predominantly Empire-minded. With the intake of 1951 there came an abrupt change. The Members who entered the House in that year split almost equally between the two blocs. This movement towards Europe was confirmed and accentuated in 1955: among the Members who won their seats in the election of that year the Europeans outnumbered the Empire men by nearly two to one.

Age and the date of entry into Parliament are closely connected factors: it is not surprising, therefore, that the youngest Members were preponderantly European minded, and that the over-sixties were overwhelmingly pro-Commonwealth.

There was a similar connection between the year of entry and the size of majority: Members from safe and impregnable constituencies, most of whom had entered the House before 1951, proved to be predominantly pro-Commonwealth. The M.P.s from the more marginal seats inclined towards Europe.

There was no significant difference of attitude between university graduates and non-graduates, but among the graduates there was an important divergence between Oxford and Cambridge. Among the Oxford Members there was a European majority, while Cambridge graduates were heavily pro-Commonwealth. So too, were the Sandhurst M.P.s. The reaction of the Sandhurst men is easy to understand: but the marked disparity in the attitudes of Oxford and Cambridge graduates is puzzling. A similar but less striking contrast between Oxford and Cambridge Members was found on most issues.

Occupation was of minor significance; but within the Professional group there was one noteworthy contrast. The lawyers were preponderantly European: the regular officers, like the Sandhurst group with whom they so largely overlapped, leaned strongly to the Commonwealth.

The position of British agriculture has often been cited as a justification for Britain's aloofness from Europe, yet the rural constituencies mustered proportionately as many pro-Europeans as the towns. Within the Commonwealth bloc there was, moreover, a sharp urban-rural split, the rural Commonwealth men being distinguishable by their moderation. An overwhelming majority of them were Empire Moderates but a high proportion of the urban Commonwealthers were Empire Stalwarts.

Thus, attitudes to Europe and the Commonwealth were closely associated with a complex of related characteristics—the date of first election, age, and size of majority. The older Members with long Parliamentary experience and representing safe Conservative seats were mainly pro-Commonwealth: the younger, more recently elected Members from less secure constituencies, were preponderantly European. The date of first election seems to have been the key factor.

Independent of this complex of related attributes was the contrast between Oxford and Cambridge. Occupational differences were of little, and regional variations of no, importance.

Suez. The Suez operation was an event which aroused the most passionate feelings amongst both supporters and opponents. On both sides of the House it provoked a spate of Motions and of other demonstrations of opinion.

On the basis of these Motions one could discern four groups.

First, there were the Diehards, the Right-wing, the heirs of the old "Suez Group" which had opposed the evacuation from the Canal Zone in 1954. They were in favour, after the withdrawal from Port Said, of more vigorous action to protect British rights in the Canal. They numbered 37.

Then there were the "Anti-Americans",* a large right-centre group which supported the Government's intervention in November, 1956, fiercely resented the conduct of the United States during the crisis but acquiesced without visible protest in the Government's

* So called, because they signed the well-known EDM of November 26th, 1956, criticizing the attitude of the United States during the Suez imbroglio. Members who also signed the Diehard EDMs have, of course, been classed as Diehards, not as "Anti-Americans".

policy after the withdrawal of British forces. There were 85 of these Members.

The smallest group, the Suez Critics, consisted of 24 Members who seem to have been hostile to, or to have had misgivings about, the British intervention.

Finally, there was a large residual group, the Uncommitted, consisting of 102 M.P.s. None of its members signed any Motion directly relevant to the Anglo-French action, or to the control of the canal. Most of them may be regarded as pro-Government backbenchers, supporting both the intervention and the subsequent withdrawal.

It is difficult to draw statistically impressive conclusions about the opinions of Conservative Members on Suez. For this, there are several reasons. Two of the groups—the Diehards and the Critics—were small. Many Members were uncommitted. And the differences in attitude between the various classes were minor.

Indeed, attitudes to the Suez campaign were associated with only one identifiable characteristic: the university background. There was no distinction in the behaviour of graduates and non-graduates, but amongst the university Members, Oxford was distinguished by the high proportion of Critics who came from its ranks. Cambridge and the Other Universities were barely represented amongst the Critics: and not a single Sandhurst man was found amongst them. Oxford was, in addition, sharply polarized: though it supplied a disproportionately large number of Critics, it contributed as many Diehards as Cambridge. This one relationship apart, the relationship between attitudes and the university attended, each opinion group was very much a miniature of the whole party.*

The Suez intervention provoked the most serious crisis within the Conservative party since 1940: but apart from the behaviour of the Oxford Members, backbench reactions do not seem to have been related to any recognizable background factors. Changes in the social, geographical or educational composition of the Conservative party are not likely to cause any important shift in attitudes towards issues such as those raised by the Suez campaign.

The United Nations. Any step which involves the surrender or abridgment of national sovereignty will provoke an angry reaction

* Even this association is not fully established, the significance level being only 10%.

in some quarters of the Conservative party. Because of these fears about national sovereignty some Tories look with suspicion upon the United Nations and other international organizations. Other Conservatives, however, feel the need for close international co-operation so strongly that they are willing, if need be, to accept certain limitations of national sovereignty. There are a number of active European federalists, and others who look forward to some kind of world government. Members like Martin Maddan, John Foster and Sir James Pitman are vocal and persistent advocates of an international authority which transcends national boundaries.

This cleavage underlies many of the Conservative disagreements about foreign policy. It plays some part in the controversy about European and Commonwealth relationships. One reason why many Conservatives favour greater collaboration with the Commonwealth, if necessary at the expense of co-operation with Europe, is that the Commonwealth is an association of sovereign states. Membership does not formally entail any loss of individual freedom of action, and the member countries would refuse to contemplate any such restrictions. Although the European organizations to which Britain at present belongs do not impair British sovereignty, the more ambitious plans for European unity certainly would. Those Empire men who welcome closer relations with Europe insist that it must take the form of co-operation between sovereign states and must not place any fetters upon Britain's capacity for independent action. Their motto is consultation between equals, not subordination to a federal government.

The same emphasis upon national independence and sovereignty played a conspicuous part in the Suez crisis, and was reflected in the bitter anti-American and anti-United Nations mood prevailing in some sections of the party.

This division of opinion was reflected in the Motions tabled and signed by Conservative backbenchers. About 60 M.P.s expressed support for the United Nations: some wanted the United Nations to undertake specific and restricted functions, such as the creation of a permanent international police force, while others went further and sought the transformation of the United Nations into a world government with limited powers. On the other side, there were approximately 30 M.P.s who, without opposing Britain's membership of the United Nations, rejected the proposal for a world authority, insisted that international co-operation be based on national sovereignty, and made, by implication, some sharp criticisms of the present role of the United Nations. Among them were Members such as John Eden, Paul Williams and Lord Hinchingbrooke.

More than half of the party were uncommitted and the views of these backbenchers can only be surmised. Estimating the numerical strength of the "internationalists" and the "nationalists" in the full Parliamentary party is therefore extremely hazardous. Furthermore, the small number of Members expressing an opinion severely limits the conclusions which can be drawn.

There are again some signs, however, that Oxford Members took a distinctively internationalist stand. Cambridge graduates, and Members from Sandhurst, were the most hostile to the United Nations. The association is again not fully established, the numbers of the committed being too few, and the disparities between the different classes too small, to support a clear association; but the results are consistent with the variations of opinion on the Europe/Commonwealth question.

There is also some evidence that occupation was related to Members' views. Lawyers were by far the most internationalist group whilst the Miscellaneous Occupations class—the journalists, publicists and professional politicians—were the least friendly to the United Nations. Amongst the businessmen, too, there was some evidence of disagreement: big business, represented by the directors of public companies, was more friendly to the United Nations than the private company directors. Neither of these associations, however, is firmly established.

The sharpest cleavage appeared between town and country. Rural backbenchers were more sympathetic to the United Nations than urban Conservatives. The grounds for this are not easy to discern; but the coolness of the urban Conservatives towards the United Nations may have been connected with the dogmatic Commonwealth sentiments avowed by some of their number.

Home Affairs

Penal Reform and Civil Liberties. The rank and file of the Conservative party, both in Parliament and in the country, have been traditionally opposed to any relaxation in the penalties for crime. The Conservative leadership has met strong resistance whenever it has attempted to mitigate the severity of the law. When Lord Templewood, as Home Secretary, tried to abolish corporal punishment as a judicial penalty in 1939, he met with strong resistance from his own backbenchers and from Conservative supporters in the constituencies. More recently, proposals to re-introduce flogging and birching have been embodied in Conservative Private Members' Bills, in backbench Motions and in resolutions submitted to the Conservative Annual Conference. Conservative Members have provided most of the opposition in the House of Commons to the abolition or limitation of the death penalty.

Despite this, there has often been a minority within the Conservative party in favour of a less rigorous treatment of offenders. Joseph Chamberlain was a lifelong opponent of corporal punishment. The predominantly Conservative National Government tried to abolish birching in 1932 and was baulked only by the House of Lords. Within the last few years, there has been the paradox of a Conservative House of Commons voting to abolish the death penalty and of a Conservative government introducing a drastic limitation of capital punishment.

Penal reform played an important part in the backbench Motions of this period. The cry from some sections of the public and the press for sterner penalties was echoed within the Conservative party. Nevertheless, at the same time, the call for the abolition or restriction of the death penalty found unexpected support in the Conservative ranks.

The number of Members who signed any of the relevant Motions was small—less than a third of the total. Twenty-three Members, opponents of capital punishment, were classed as *Humane*: and forty-nine M.P.s who demanded the reintroduction of corporal punishment, or the extension of the death penalty, were styled *Severe*.

Fortunately, there were several free votes on issues of penal reform; these free votes raised questions similar to, though not exactly in the same form as, the issues posed in the EDM scale. By analysing some of these free votes, it has been possible to check and to supplement findings based on the admittedly small numbers of Members signing Motions on this matter.

On penal issues the sharpest division occurred between graduates and non-graduates. The birching lobby in the Conservative Party consisted predominantly of men without a university education. Non-graduates were heavily and persistently in favour of both capital and corporal punishment. Graduates were much more hostile to the death penalty. There may also have been significant divisions between graduates of different universities. Some of the evidence suggests that Oxford graduates were more humane than Members from Cambridge and the Other Universities. This difference was particularly marked in the vote on Mr. Ede's amendment to suspend the death penalty, in February 1956.

The division between the university educated and the non-graduates was reflected in a similar but less striking distinction between public school and non-public school Conservatives. In each school group, the Severe outnumbered the Humane: but the Severe Members were weakest in the Clarendon School group and strongest amongst the Non-Public School men. This association is not fully established, and is merely a projection of the University Non-Graduates division; most of the M.P.s who went to university had been to a public school; most of the non-graduates, however, came from private and local authority schools. The Motion to suspend the death penalty was carried, not on the playing fields of Eton, but in the cloisters of Oxford.

The youngest and the most recently elected Members were more humane than their seniors. When Mr. Ede's amendment to suspend the death penalty was carried there was widespread comment that the numbers against capital punishment had been swollen by the votes of young Conservatives who had won their seats in 1955. But it was the younger M.P.s, rather than the class of 1955 as such, who helped to carry the suspension of the death penalty. Older men who won their seats in 1955 were as severe as their predecessors. This is a distinction of substance, for it implies that the strong support for abolition amongst the 1955 class was a reflection of the views of the younger generation of Conservatives seeking adoption as candidates, rather than a sign of increasing liberalism amongst Conservative selection committees.

The zeal of younger Members for penal reform seems to have been confined to university men: younger graduates were more humane than older graduates, but amongst the non-graduates there was no difference between the generations. Older Members and those with no university training were consistently and markedly severe; support for penal reform was strongest amongst younger graduates and, more doubtfully, among Oxonians.

Civil Liberties. In both parties, the cause of civil liberties has its zealots. The Labour party has inherited part of the tradition of nineteenth century radicalism, a tradition which tempers Labour's collectivist policies with a bias against authority. As for their opponents, there was a time when Conservatism saw its chief duty as the defence of the prerogatives of the Crown against the encroachments of Parliament and people. But with the growth of a collectivist and bureaucratic society the role of the Conservative has changed; the balance has swung in favour of the executive, and he now sees himself as the champion of the little man and the defender of individual liberty against the encroachments of an impersonal state.

Nearly 90 Conservatives displayed a special concern about personal liberty and official malpractices. They have been called "Libertarians". However, this concern was evenly spread throughout the party.

Libertarianism may be related to the year of entry into Parliament, for the 1950 class were conspicuously more libertarian than other groups, but there was no regular trend. Similarly, there is evidence that rural Members showed more concern than urban Conservatives, but the association is not fully established.

Social Policy. Since the Conservative victory of 1951, there have been few overt signs of major disagreement about social policy within the party. Conservative governments followed, with some changes, the measures of their Labour opponents. The gloomy forecasts of the Labour party were not fulfilled. There was no assault upon the social services and there was little unemployment. Working-class living standards rose as production increased. Some welfare services were cut, but others expanded considerably; there were several increases in old age pensions, insurance benefits and national assistance payments. There were some changes in the pattern of social welfare: the Conservatives laid more stress upon discrimination in the distribution of social benefits; the food and housing subsidies were reduced for instance, whilst family allowances were raised. But there was no drastic disturbance of the welfare system itself. Wage-earners kept intact the gains they had made in the the war and post-war years.

The Conservative party showed itself responsive to working-class claims. Quite apart from any inner reluctance to impair working-class living standards and conditions they had to obey the facts of electoral life. A party which depended for half of its votes on working-class electors had to pay heed to their wishes. At the same time, the Conservatives did not ignore the demands of their middle-class supporters. The maintenance of full employment was accompanied by concessions such as the removal of restrictions on private building; the improvement of the social services was matched by cautious tax-reliefs.

In the economic field the Conservatives stopped further nationalization and restored two industries to private ownership. The Government put their faith in market forces and monetary discipline and gradually dismantled the machinery of physical controls which had been assembled during the wartime and Labour administrations. The party even shed much of their traditional protectionism.

These policies were accepted by the rank and file in Parliament with little apparent dissent. During the first four years there were misgivings at the slow pace of denationalization, and there was more prolonged disquiet about the control of these industries which remained in public ownership. There were sporadic calls for heavy cuts in public expenditure and occasional complaints about the Government's willingness to satisfy working-class demands and to conciliate the trades unions. The renewed inflation of the years 1955 to 1957 led to a Cabinet disagreement which culminated in the resignation of the Chancellor of the Exchequer, Mr. Thorneycroft. But at no stage was there a major dispute within the Parliamentary party. The Conservative party has not yet had to face a domestic Suez.

The party is nevertheless often depicted as suffering from latent disagreements over social policy. Contemporary journalism often portrays a "progressive" wing of the party which has eagerly accepted the Welfare State and all its implications. The members of this wing are the guardians of the Conservative social reform tradition, the heirs of Shaftesbury and Disraeli, of Joseph Chamberlain and Lord Randolph Churchill. They march under the banner of the "Industrial Charter"* and to slogans such as "a property-owning democracy". They have been in the ascendant since the late forties; from their ranks were drawn the new Conservative leaders—men such as Harold Macmillan and Sir Walter Monckton, R. A. Butler and Iain Macleod. In terms which are commonly used but are perhaps inappropriate to the Conservatives, they form the Left of the Conservative party on social matters.

There has, however, been no audible challenge to the policy of domestic moderation, except perhaps for Mr. Thorneycroft's resignation. Sir Waldron Smithers and Sir Herbert Williams left no obvious heirs as the antagonists of the Welfare State. The Social Right of the Conservative party, if it exists at all, is a submerged body. Indeed, some observers assert that differences within the party about the size and scope of the social services or the level of taxation are much less important than disagreement about economic method. In so far as there are divisions, it is said that they lie chiefly between the partisans of the market economy and those who wish to protect existing sectional privileges by state action.†

Since the General Election of 1959, disagreement about the level of government expenditure on social services has become sharper. A small knot of Members centred around Lord Hinchingbrooke and Mr. John Eden have adopted an explicitly right-wing policy. They have called for vigorous retrenchment in expenditure, and greater reductions of taxation. Differences about social policy were publicly expressed after the 1960 Budget.

It is probably true that Conservative Members look on the Welfare State with varying degrees of enthusiasm. Some show a genuine desire to carry on the tradition of Tory reform; others are more sensitive about high taxation. Some show a close and detailed interest in the development of the social services and the welfare of industrial workers. Others are more concerned about the interests of property owners and taxpayers. There may be no deep cleavage on social policy but there are variations of interest and emphasis which might reveal themselves if a choice had to be made

* A document drawn up by the Conservative party, after its defeat in 1945, which adumbrated an industrial code for the protection of the workers.

† Cotton, agriculture and monopolies are examples where this issue is relevant.

in a moment of crisis, or if, over a period of two or three years, tax reductions failed to match improvements in social welfare. These nuances are potentially important.

The backbench Conservative Motions which were put down in this period afford no evidence of violent disagreement on social questions. No direct issue between say, more welfare and less taxation, was posed. However, several Motions, espousing the claims of wage-earners or allied groups were selected as being "Left" in character; and there was one Motion, and an amendment, sponsoring the demands of property owners, which was regarded as "Right".

Members were distinguished as Left, Centre or Right according to the kind of Motions they signed. The Right consisted of 73 Members: backbenchers who showed their sympathy for the demands of property-owners but who were apparently indifferent to lower-middle and working-class demands. Then there was the Centre, 40 strong; this group consisted of Members who balanced moderate support for the claims of wage-earners with sympathy for property-owners. The Left, of 50 Members, comprised those whose sympathy for working-class concessions was either strongly marked, or else more pronounced than their enthusiasm for the right of property owners.

Again, a warning must be registered: these figures do not pretend to measure the absolute size of the Social Left, or the Social Right. It is not possible to identify *blocs* of Members who think alike on social questions and act together in the House. All that these figures purport to show is a spectrum of political attitudes: there were 73 M.P.s whose opinions, on the evidence of the EDMs, lay to the right of their colleagues; there were 50 M.P.s who were more Left-wing in their approach to social problems, than their fellows: and 40 M.P.s came between these two bands.

The deepest rift again occurred amongst *graduates.* The Oxonians behaved once more in a distinctive manner; but on this question, and in contrast to their views on foreign policy and penal reform, they were to the *right* of the Cambridge graduates. The Other University Members were the most Left-wing of the university categories.

The remaining differences were minor. Opinions on social policy seem to have been related to school backgrounds. The Clarendon

School M.P.s, the men who had been educated at the most expensive and exclusive public schools, were the most right-wing group. The Non-Public School Members stood well to the left. In between, came the Other Public School M.P.s.

These divisions between Members from different school backgrounds underlay a similar but less clear division between public company and private company directors. The public company directors contained a high proportion of Clarendon School M.P.s; whereas the private company directors contained a high percentage of Members from state and private schools. These educational differences were reflected in their attitudes to social policy: the public company directors inclined to the Right, the private company directors to the Left.

Not unexpectedly, these backbench attitudes on social policy were also related to the strength of Conservative support in the constituencies. Members from marginal, predominantly working-class seats were more sensitive to working-class demands than the rest of the party. But there was no completely regular or fully established relationship between the size of the Conservative vote and Members' opinions. Broadly speaking, however, the safer the constituency the more right-wing the Member tended to be.

These results, modest though they may be, are offered tentatively and with more hesitation than the findings on foreign affairs and penal reform. The difficulty lies in the raw material of the EDMs. How far can these expressions of opinion in favour of specific social reforms be taken as proof of a *general* left-wing orientation in the field of social policy? The left-wing Motions embrace several disparate topics. Support for any one or two of these demands does not furnish conclusive evidence of a general left-wing bias, for a belief in the security of employment does not necessarily entail support for increased expenditure on the social services; nor does a zeal for the wider dispersion of property necessarily carry with it a reforming ardour about working conditions. Nor indeed is sponsorship of the claims of property owners incompatible with sympathy for wage-earners and the beneficiaries of the social services. It is possible to press both claims simultaneously and many Conservatives do so.

Thus, the "Social Left" in the Conservative party may well have been segmented into several distinct groups: some Members may have interested themselves in health and education, others in employment problems, others in pensions and yet more in individual property ownership.

Although the Conservative Parliamentary Party is fairly homogeneous it relies on a variegated electoral support: it has to cater for the business interests, for the professional classes, and for a large lower middle and working-class electorate. Within these broad categories are a number of distinct groups with special problems and claims for whom the Conservatives have a traditional regard. The claims of each of these groups must be satisfied, partially if not wholly.

The Conservative party, in framing their policy about taxation and the social services, have a more difficult task than Labour. They have to reconcile diverse and often disparate demands: a task that the Labour party, with its huge working-class support, does not have to face. The retired professional man living on a small fixed income, and the rising young executive; the suburban clerk, and the well-to-do doctor; the prosperous business-man and the industrial wage-earner; the old age pensioner and the owner-occupier: each of these groups furnishes the Conservative party with indispensable support, and the allegiance of each of them must be acknowledged in party policy.

It is hardly surprising, therefore, that the attitudes of Conservative M.P.s on social policy cannot be fitted into a simple Left–Right mould. To attempt to do so is to impose a pattern, borrowed from the Labour party, which is not appropriate to the Conservatives. The picture is rather one of a succession of specific, unrelated, pressures by different Members on behalf of a number of distinct groups. Furthermore, it is often misleading to define these claims as either Left or Right. Into which class, Left or Right, would one put the demand for the provision of free drugs to patients using private doctors; the demand for the abolition of the Schedule A Tax; the resolutions calling for an easing of the earnings rule for pensioners; the call for improved pensions for regular Service officers; or the demand that the letting of council houses should be restricted to persons in need?

At one extreme, then, there were a small knot of Members dedicated to a reduction of government expenditure, and cuts in taxation; on the other, a small group of self-consciously radical

Tories, who appointed themselves as the guardians of the tradition of Tory democracy. On neither side, however, is it possible to distinguish any large group of Members espousing a coherent social philosophy and pressing consistently for measures that can be termed a left-wing or right-wing Conservative programme.

Yet it probably remains true that some Conservatives cherished a special affection for the Welfare State, whilst others were more concerned about the weight of taxation and the extent of government interference in industry. Only rarely were these differences of outlook made articulate. Despite all these qualifications, however, the validity of the Left–Centre–Right scale, based on the EDMs and used in this study, has been borne out by external evidence; this evidence is the free vote on the Office Charter Bill of 1959. The highest proportion of backbenchers who turned out to try and destroy the Bill came from the Right; the lowest proportion from the Left. There was no sharp cleavage between "reactionaries" and "progressives", but there were vague and largely dormant tendencies, some attuned to the demands and claims of employees and their dependants and others more responsive to the wishes of the middle and well-to-do classes.

With rising affluence and with the increasing diffusion of pros-

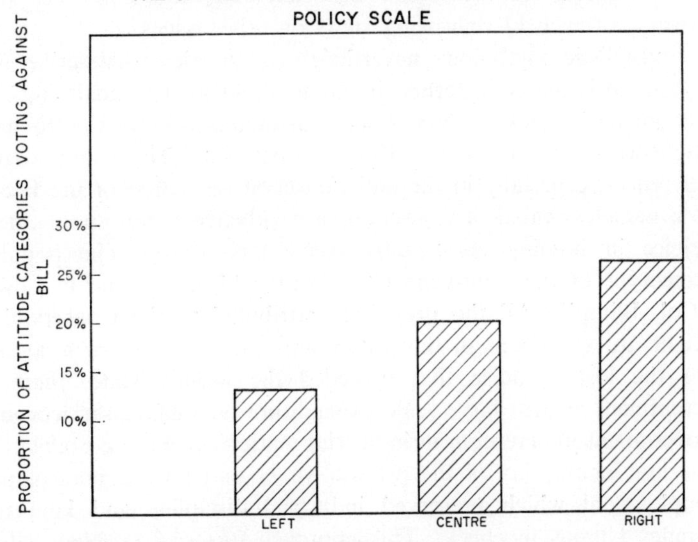

perity, the lines between "Left" and "Right" may become even more blurred than they are; issues of social welfare will become less urgent and the demands of various groups more differentiated; in the absence of a severe economic crisis, or a middle-class revolt against the burden of taxation, differences between Conservatives on social questions may become even less pronounced than they are now.

Analysis of the EDMs suggest that these nuances of opinion are associated with school backgrounds, and (though less clearly) with the political character of constituencies: amongst graduates, they are clearly related to the university attended. Except amongst graduates, the differences between the various classes were not marked.

THE CONSERVATIVE SYNDROME

It is hard to distinguish any clear-cut Left–Right division in the Conservative party even within the relatively narrow field of social policy but over the whole range of policy such a task becomes impossible. When used to analyse the structure of the Conservative party, the terms "Left" and "Right" are misleading and dangerous.

There was little tendency for groups of Members holding "right-wing" or "left-wing" views on one question to hold similar views on other issues. There were few correlations between one attitude and another. Members who held left-wing views in one controversy often held right-wing views on other issues.

Journalistic mythology nevertheless often tries to describe the Conservative party in terms similar to those used in analysing the Labour party; and just as Labour is divided into Left-, Centre- and Right-wings, so must the Conservatives be. There are vague references, especially in the anti-Conservative section of the Press, to a nameless cabal of Conservative backbenchers whose members rejoice in holding consistently reactionary views. The popular stereotype of the right-wing Conservative M.P. is found in Low's "Col. Blimp". All the prejudices attributed to the Conservative Right are embodied in this caricature. At home, there is a sigh for the lost paradise that preceded the welfare state; there is resentment against large scale expenditure on welfare services and government intervention in industrial matters; there is nostalgia for the low income tax of the pre-war years, and for the pool of unemployment which preserved industrial discipline and kept the Trades Unions in check. This approach to social problems, it is alleged, goes hand in hand with a penal philosophy summed up by the birch and the rope, and with a predisposition to support traditional authority against the individual dissident. These attitudes are in turn coupled with a belief in the domination of subject peoples, scepticism towards the United Nations, and a vigorous insistence on a firm and independent British foreign policy. These beliefs comprise the right-wing syndrome, allegedly held by a substantial wing of the Conservative party in Parliament, and *a fortiori,* by the fierce majors and tweedy women who are said to be the backbone of the Conservative organizations in rural and seaside constituencies.

On the other side is the image of the progressive Conservative, who appears as the incarnation of a moderate, humane, intelligent and forward-looking Conservatism. This modern Conservatism, often identified with the Bow Group, agrees with the abolition of capital punishment, and opposes the re-introduction of flogging. It seeks to co-operate with the Trades Unions, and favours generous welfare services and a high measure of government regulation in industry.* It accepts the demand of colonial peoples for self-government, and carries belief in international co-operation to the point of advocating limitations on British sovereignty.

Now this division of the Conservative party into Left and Right, progressive and reactionary, moderate and diehard, finds no warrant in Conservative history. There have been groups, to be true, which have taken a progressive or diehard stand on particular issues; but it is difficult to find any substantial and important group which took a consistently right-wing or left-wing position on all the questions of their day. Indeed, one of the most important historic strains in British Conservatism combined social reform at home with bellicose foreign and colonial policies abroad. The emancipation of the Trades Unions was accompanied by the annexation of the Transvaal; Workmen's Compensation, by the subjugation of the Sudan.

Today there are few Tory M.P.s who take a right-wing stand in every controversy. The right-wing syndrome, i.e., a complex

---

* Some members of the Bow Group in fact take a distinctly right-wing line on the social services, and on economic questions generally This merely re-inforces the view that terms such as Left-wing and Right-wing cannot usefully be applied, *in a general sense,* to the Conservative party.

of uniformly "reactionary" views, barely exists. There is no general conflict, not even a suppressed one, between "Left" and "Right" in the Conservative party; such disagreements as arise are struggles between *ad hoc* groups of Members who may be "left" or "right" on specific questions; but as new controversies break out the coherence of the former groups dissolves, and new alignments appear, uniting former enemies, and separating old allies.

Nevertheless, there were some correlations between certain of these attitudes, as is shown in Tables 8 to 12. First there was a correlation between opinions on social policy and civil liberties. The Social Left and the Social Centre showed more concern about infringements of personal liberty than the Right. Secondly, there was also a small positive correlation between attitudes to the Suez crisis and penal reform. Right-wing views on Suez tended to be linked to right-wing views on penal reform.

The chief complex of related views, however, was displayed in the sphere of foreign affairs. The Empire Stalwarts section of the Commonwealth bloc formed a distinctive group; and they overlapped to a significant extent with the Suez Diehards and the anti-internationalists. We can only infer that belief in imperial preference and a deep conviction of the significance and value of the Commonwealth tended to carry with them an emphasis on national sovereignty and belief in a robust and independent Middle Eastern policy. This group of backbenchers may be termed the Foreign Policy Right.

Yet even in this field, the coincidence between the different groups was far from perfect. The Suez Diehards included several ardent Europeans; indeed, one effect of Suez was to increase support in the Conservative party for British participation in the new Western European community. Moreover, there were almost certainly sharp differences within this group on colonial policy. Many of the most ardent Empire men have accepted the full logic of a multi-racial Commonwealth. Men such as Nigel Fisher are keen opponents of racial discrimination, and enthusiastic supporters of colonial independence. In the eyes of such men, the Commonwealth can only survive if Britain comes to terms with the emergent nationalisms of Africa and Asia. But other members of the group seem to have been more sympathetic to small European communities such as the Rhodesian whites.

TABLE 8

Attitudes to Suez and Penal Reform

	Humane	*Uncommitted*	*Severe*	*Total*
Critics	5	15	—	20
Uncommitted	7	76	14	97
"Anti-Americans"	6	58	20	84
Diehards	4	17	15	36
TOTAL	22	166	49	237

$^{*}\tau c = 0 \cdot 18$. Significant at 5%

There was a clear tendency for Members who believed in the reintroduction of corporal punishment to take a right-wing line on the Suez operation. But more striking than the correlation were the exceptions: a substantial number of abolitionists signed either the "Anti-American" or the Diehard Motions.

TABLE 9

Attitudes to Civil Liberties and Social Policy

	Social Left	*Social Centre*	*Social Right*	*Social Policy Uncommitted*†	*Total*
Libertarian	25	21	19	16	81
Uncommitted	21	17	47	49	134
TOTAL	46	38	66	65	215

$\tau c = 0 \cdot 25$. Significant at 2·5%

Concern about civil liberties went hand in hand with views on social policy. The Social Left and the Social Centre were much more committed to civil liberties than the Social Right. This correlation strengthens the belief that the Social Left included a large

* For an explanation of this correlation coefficient see Annex 1.
† Social Policy Uncommitted were excluded from the calculation.

number of Members who re-acted against specific injustices rather than adhered to a comprehensive philosophy of social reform.

TABLE 10

Attitudes to Europe/Commonwealth Relationships and to Suez

	Diehards	*"Anti-Americans"*	*Uncommitted*	*Critics*	*Total*
Europeans*	—	9	11	6	26
Europe & Empire	14	24	30	7	75
Empire Moderates	4	21	31	5	61
Empire Stalwarts	16	21	22	1	60
TOTAL	34	75	94	19	222

$\chi^2_9 = 15 \cdot 42$. Significant at 10%

* Those signing European EDMs, but not signing any Commonwealth EDM. (See Annex 6.)

TABLE 11

Attitudes to Europe/Commonwealth Relationships and to the United Nations

	Pro-U.N.	*Uncommitted*	*Anti-U.N.*	*Total*
Europeans	8	11	1	20
Europe & Empire	21	41	9	71
Empire Moderates	9	46	2	57
Empire Stalwarts	11	27	20	58
TOTAL	49	125	32	206

$\tau c = 0 \cdot 21$. Significant at 5%

TABLE 12
Attitudes to Suez and to the United Nations

	Pro-U.N.	*Uncommitted*	*Anti-U.N.*	*Total*
Diehards	2	15	15	32
"Anti-Americans"	19	50	9	78
Uncommitted	25	60	8	93
Critics	10	10	—	20
TOTAL	56	135	32	223*

$\tau c = 0 \cdot 23$. Significant at 1%

These figures demonstrate the close identity between the Empire Stalwarts, the Suez Diehards, and the Anti-U.N. group. Nearly half of the Diehards also belonged to the Empire Stalwarts; but only one of the Critics did so. Moreover a third of the Critics came from the small group of Europeans who displayed no interest in the Commonwealth. Turning to the Europe/Commonwealth and United Nation tables, we find that two-thirds of the Anti-U.N. group were also Empire Stalwarts, compared with less than a quarter of the Pro-U.N. group. Nearly half of the small European group were Pro-U.N.; only one of them signed the Anti-U.N. amendment. The behaviour of this group suggests that their abstention from the Empire Moderate Motions was deliberate, not fortuitous.

Finally, Table 12 shows the close overlap, at the high significance level of 1 per cent, between the various Suez and United Nations categories. Nearly half of the Diehards were Anti-U.N.; only two of them were Pro-U.N. On the other hand, half of the Critics were overtly sympathetic to the United Nations, while not a single one of them supported the Anti-U.N. amendment.

Again, the exceptions were almost as important as the connection. Eleven Empire Stalwarts had internationalist sympathies; and so did nineteen "Anti-Americans", almost one quarter of the total.

The right-wing complex covers a narrow range of attitudes, largely confined to foreign policy. No correlation was found between views on social policy and foreign policy.

* Differences in the totals for Tables 8 to 12 arise because some Members were excluded from particular counts. See Annex 2.

It would seem that the Conservative party acts or thinks as unrelated, *ad hoc* groups of Members, groups whose members join together to contend for one specific objective, and then fall apart once the goal has been attained or has been by-passed by events.

This picture is confirmed by ordinary observation. The old Suez Group of 1954, which resisted the British evacuation of the Suez Canal base, included two keen partisans of world government—Sir James Pitman and William Rees-Davies. Several Members of the Suez Group such as Montgomery Hyde, Lord Hinchingbrooke, Angus Maude, Enoch Powell, Reader Harris and Julian Amery were conspicuous opponents of the death penalty.

Similarly, two of the sharpest right-wing critics of Mr. Heathcoat Amory's last budget—Sir Henry D'Avigdor-Goldsmid and Albert Cooper—voted for the abolition of the death penalty. Two of the strongest Conservative backers of Roy Jenkins' "Obscene Publications Bill" which sought to relax the stringent obscenity laws, were Hugh Fraser and Viscount Lambton, both prominent foreign policy Right-wingers. The small group of Conservatives who criticized the Rent Act included two former members of the Suez Group—Sir Ian Horobin and William Rees-Davies. Sir Thomas Moore, the leading advocate of the restoration of corporal punishment, voted for the implementation of the Wolfenden Committee's recommendations on homosexuality. Gerald Nabarro, a Right-winger on economic and social questions, or foreign policy and penal reform, championed Mr. Benn in his fight to stay in the Commons.

Occasionally it is possible to identify a small group of Conservative backbenchers who acted together on one issue and maintained their unity on other questions. Thus, there is a small knot of Conservatives centred around Lord Hinchingbrooke who press jointly the claims of the Commonwealth national sovereignty, and a reduction of government expenditure. On penal matters the coherence of the group breaks down: witness the votes of Lord Hinchingbrooke and John Biggs-Davison against the death penalty. The old Suez Group of 1954 retained some of its unity when a number of its adherents defied the Whips and voted against the Coal Industry Bill in 1956. Nevertheless, these cases are exceptional.

The unstable character of backbench, anti-leadership alignments in the Conservative party, can be illustrated by two quotations from Conservative M.P.s—one a private Member, the other an eminent

Minister. Thus William Shepherd, a Conservative critic of Eden's intervention at Suez wrote, "The genesis (of the underlying reasons for the Suez action) lies in the years since the war, and particularly in the virulent criticism to which the party and the leadership have been subjected by those people who resent the broad pattern of social change in the past decade or so. To these must, I think, be added those who can think of national greatness and prestige only in nineteenth century terms. It is an interesting reflection that they are not necessarily the same people". (Letter to *The Observer,* January 6th, 1957.)

A similar point was made by Mr. Iain Macleod, speaking at a Conservative Summer School.

" . . . the terms "Left" and "Right" have little relevance in our Party. Many of you, for example, know Angus Maude well. He is a prominent Member of what has been called the Suez Group. Is he then on the right of the Party? But he was also Director of the C.P.C. co-editor with myself of *One Nation,* a passionate believer in the abolition of the death penalty, and one of the most informed students of the social services in general and of education in particular in our Party. Does this mean then that he is on the left? The truth is that these phrases are meaningless and the Party is the stronger for it."*

Another feature of the Conservative party is that so many of its Parliamentary representatives seem to have no distinctive personal viewpoint on any major issue of policy. At least, they express none. With many of the backbenchers we know that they are Conservatives; beyond that we know nothing. If they have any marked opinion or hold any special dogma which deviates from the current ministerial line on any important and enduring political controversies, we rarely hear of them.

Any competent political observer, acting on the basis of published speeches and questions, let alone EDMs, could accurately assign at least a half of the Labour M.P.s to their place in the political spectrum. Relatively few Conservatives can be labelled and classified in this way. We may know that Commander X speaks for the pig-farmers, that Mr. Y is a Commonwealth preference man, and that Viscount Z is a naval specialist. But each

* *The Future of the Welfare State* (C.P.C. Lectures delivered at Oxford Summer School, 1957).

of these topics is tangential to the great political conflicts of the day. We probably do not know, except by negative inference, how any one of these men stands on questions such as the scope of the social services, the extent of government intervention in the economy or the pace of political advance in the colonies.

This inability to classify Conservative M.P.s arises not so much because Conservatives conduct their disputes more discreetly than the Labour party (though they do) but because so many of them do not know where they lie, in a general sense, within the party spectrum.

The average Conservative M.P. does not approach political problems from a prepared emotional or intellectual position. As one former Conservative M.P. put it:

> "In general, we find it difficult to arrange our colleagues in neat categories. . . . I could see no pattern emerging which would enable one to classify the heterogeneous mass of the House of Commons according to their opinions or their backgrounds. We do not think in these terms. We weigh up our colleagues according to their abilities, energy and political prospects much more than by the trend of their ideas."*

The Labour party often resembles a coalition of parties, and each party or wing possesses a general outlook which conditions its reaction to any particular event. The Conservative party, by contrast, is a collection of evanescent pressure-groups existing to promote or impede some highly specific, concrete policy. As an empirical party, their task is to adapt themselves to, and to influence, an environment which has been shaped by external forces. They try to make adjustments, as they are needed, to this environment; and the quarrels within the party are largely over the timing, pace and detail of these adjustments. As a party of empiricists they are not plagued by ideological disputes about party dogma.

Within the Labour party, a clear division was found between the attitudes of different occupational and sponsorship classes, and to a lesser extent between different educational groups. On ideological questions, the Miscellaneous Occupations took the most extreme, and the Trades-Union/Worker group the most moderate, view; the Professions followed a middling line. On material issues, the Trades-

* Private information.

TABLE 13

Attitudes and Backgrounds—Synoptic Table of Significant Associations (with level of significance obtained)

	Europe/ Common-wealth	*Suez*	*United Nations*	*Penal Reform*	*Civil Liberties*	*Social Policy*
Occupation (Major Classes—)	—	—	(Professions vs. Misc. occupation) 10%	—	—	—
Occupation (Business)	—	—	Pub. Coy. Dirs. vs. Pte. Coy. 10%	—	—	(Pte. Coy. Dirs. vs. Pub. Coy. Dirs.) 5%
Occupation (Profession)	Lawyers vs. H.M. Forces 0.5%	—	—	—	—	—
School	—	—	—	Clarendon vs. Non-Public 10%	—	Non-Public vs. Clarendon 5%
University Attendance	—	—	—	(Graduates vs. Non-Graduates) 0.5%	—	—
Graduates University Attended	Oxford vs. Cambridge 2.5%	(Oxford vs. Cambridge) 10%	Oxford vs. Cambridge 10%	* Oxford vs. Cambridge 1%	—	Other Univs. vs. Oxford 2.5%
Year of Entry	(1955 vs. 1945) 0.5%	—	—	(1955 vs. others) 5%	1950 vs. pre-1945 0.5%	—
Age	Under 41s vs. Over 60s 5%	—	—	(Under 41s vs. Over 50s) 0.5%	—	—
Size of Majority	Less safe vs. More safe 1%	—	—	—	—	Marginal vs. Others 5%
Type of Constituency Town or Country	—	—	Rural vs. Urban 5%	—	Rural vs. Urban 10%	—

(The category displaying the most "left-wing attitude" is shown first; the category showing the most "right-wing attitude" is shown second. Brackets indicate that the attitude in question may only be held by committed M.P.s; where no brackets are shown it is presumed that the attitude extends to the whole. "Vs." is used here in a layman's sense. For details of the statistical tests, see Annexes).

* On Death Penalty Division 16.2.56.

Union/Worker group took the lead, the Miscellaneous Occupations and the Professions lagging behind.

The pattern in the Conservative party was much less simple: indeed, it is difficult to speak of a pattern at all. One reason for this absence of pattern lay in the homogeneous, relatively well-integrated character of the Parliamentary Party.

With the Conservatives, the social dividing line tended to shift according to the nature of the issue. On Europe/Commonwealth relationships the dividing line was length of parliamentary service: on social policy it was school backgrounds, which in turn probably reflected social class; on penal questions, the controversy followed a University/Non-Graduate and age versus youth division; on the United Nations, the dispute was to some extent a divergence between town and country; and running through almost every controversy, was the division between Oxford on the one hand, and Cambridge and the Other Universities on the other.

The most persistent, though not the most acute differences, were found amongst graduates. On all issues of foreign policy, Oxford graduates were more liberal than graduates from other universities and there is some evidence that this Oxford liberalism was carried over into the field of penal reform. On social questions, however, Oxford graduates were predominantly Right-wing.

This ambivalence is not hard to explain. Historically, there has been a vein of Conservatism which combines an imperialist foreign policy with domestic social reform, a tradition of which Disraeli and Joseph Chamberlain were the most notable exponents. This tradition may have been blurred by the growth of a self-consciously radical Conservatism; but in so far as it still exists, it is not surprising that those classes which inclined to the Right on foreign policy, should have leaned to the Left on domestic questions. Moreover, belief in a resolute and independent foreign policy may lead naturally to a positive social programme.

What is surprising is the infrequency with which the more obvious social and educational divisions were associated with differences of attitude. Between graduates, as a class, and non-graduates, differences arose on the question of penal reform and no other. Differences between public school M.P.s and the non-public school men appeared only over social policy, and even on this question were slender. The rift between town and country was narrow, and took an unexpected course. The Right-wing, anti-United Nations lobby was strong in the towns and weak in the countryside. The Conservatism of the shires was if anything more forward-looking and less parochial than the Conservatism of the towns and suburbs.

Between the major occupational groups differences were slight. One reason for this is that each major group consisted of two diverse classes. The Business category comprised the public and private company directors with their divergent educational and constituency backgrounds: and the Professions included both lawyers and regular Service officers, whose opinions sometimes cancelled one another. Even within the occupational sub-groups the differences were rarely pronounced.

OUTSTANDING PROBLEMS

Convincing and sometimes obvious reasons can be discerned for some of the associations of attitude and background.

Support for social reform was strongest amongst the Non-Public School M.P.s and least amongst the Clarendon School M.P.s. The more exclusive the Member's school the less responsive he tended to be towards working-class demands.

It is easy to sketch out a plausible explanation for these tendencies. The reason for the contrast probably lies in the social backgrounds and future careers denoted by different kinds of school. Members brought up at very exclusive public schools would have been more insulated than their colleagues from working-class contacts and working-class needs. Most of them went on to Oxford or Cambridge. Company directorships, private means or landowning would have come the way of many. Others would have followed law, a profession which would have done little to increase their knowledge of industrial conditions. Many of them would have entered Parliament in their thirties, and whilst this would have enabled them to acquire Parliamentary experience at an early age it would have done little to bring them into direct contact with the needs of industrial employees.

M.P.s educated at the newer public schools would have had a wider and more varied experience. Over a third of them did not go on to university. Many of them would have entered the service of relatively small family firms, perhaps nurturing a tradition of paternalism and of close relations with their employees. Others would have made their way as business executives or in management. The office of a family firm, or a career in the executive ranks of a large public company, would have been less remote from day to day working-class experience than the board rooms of one of the great corporations. Similarly, Members from secondary or elementary schools would have had an even closer knowledge and perhaps first-hand experience of lower middle-class and working-class circumstances; and in their working lives, they would have come into a closer relationship with rank and file employees.

This explanation is admittedly conjectural: but what we know of the careers of Members coming from these different kinds of school suggests that the Other Public and Non-Public School M.P.s did have a wider and more variegated experience than the Clarendon School Conservatives. Both the Other Public and Non-Public School groups contained higher proportions of private company directors than the Clarendon School group; they tended to be older, and were less likely to be chosen for safe seats. They were a less privileged group, representing a more democratic Conservatism, and more in touch with the wants and trouble of ordinary people.

It must be conceded that this particular distinction between Clarendon School and non-Clarendon School M.P.s is denied by some observers who aver that, paradoxically, the greatest support for the tradition of Tory Reform comes from aristocratic Etonian circles, and the least from the self-made men. This proposition, however, is based on casual observation: possibly it may owe something to the vociferous right-wing views which have been expressed by a few individuals of the self-made man type.

It is easy to account for the left-wing standpoint of the M.P.s from marginal seats. Members from these constituencies, lately won and vulnerable to counter-attack, would have emphasized their adherence to welfare policies. Conservative selection committees in such areas would have been more likely than associations in residential suburbs or seaside resorts to choose candidates with a vigorous social programme. Nearly all marginal seats would have contained large working-class electorates, and in most, working-class voters would have formed a majority. Backbenchers from these constituencies would have been more conscious of the pressure for better social services, and more in touch with working-class problems, than Members from safe Conservative areas.

On penal reform, there were two clear dividing lines: education and age. The first of these differences is probably accounted for by the personal qualities connected with and fostered by different kinds of education. The self-made man of Conservative views tends to rely on "instinct" and "commonsense": he distrusts statistics and sophisticated argument and likes to obey his intuition in matters such as penal reform. Moreover, coming from a less favoured home background he may have had greater personal acquaintance with criminal violence. Graduates, by their training, tend to take a more detached view, and to be more susceptible to arguments based on scientific enquiry and criminological research, however implausible such arguments may seem at first sight. Younger graduates will be naturally more receptive than their seniors to modern theories of punishment.

This difference in outlook between graduates and non-graduates may obtain throughout the party.* At Conservative conferences it has been the representatives of University Conservative Associations who have resisted demands for the retention of the death penalty and the restoration of flogging. The contrast was epitomised at the 1956 Conservative Conference in a debate on a resolution calling for the retention of capital punishment. The cause of the death penalty found its most extreme champion in Mr. Beaman, a railwayman from Crewe, who declared that he was frankly disgusted with the Conservative M.P.s who had yielded "to sloppy sentimentalism" in voting to abolish hanging.† From the other side of the educational barricade, the challenge was taken up by Mr. Beaumont of the Federation of University Conservative Associations, who opposed "this revolting motion" and went on to add:

"I am proud to say that in nearly every university in this country wherever this motion is debated there is frequently a strong majority in favour of the abolition of this barbarous act."

The contrast between the European views of the newer Members, and the Commonwealth bias of their seniors is easy to

---

* The *Daily Telegraph* made a similar point. "Judged by this standard, the demand for flogging is the very reverse of Right-wing since it is supported by the great body of people and opposed only by the privileged few, who, by reason of superior education think they know best." *Daily Telegraph,* November 18th, 1959.

† Report of Conference of National Union of Conservative Associations, 1956.

explain. The older generation of Conservative M.P.s, those elected before 1951 and especially those elected before 1950, had had their political apprenticeship when the emphasis in foreign economic policy lay on the Empire. The Ottawa Agreements of 1932 saw the long-deferred fulfilment of Joseph Chamberlain's dream of imperial preference. That year also saw Britain's repudiation of free trade, and the erection of commercial barriers against continental countries. European unity, whether economic or political, was a meaningless phrase and Britain, for her part, tended to stand aloof from Europe. Economically, she sought to repair the damage of the depression by cultivating her Empire. The political and economic climate of the thirties was more favourable to the mystique of empire than to the European idea.

The war, however, saw the birth of the movement for European unity; at the same time the climate of economic thought changed. The depression-charged atmosphere of the thirties had been protectionist; the expansionist environment of the fifties was liberal. To many the preferential trading club of the Commonwealth became increasingly irrelevant.

Events in the Commonwealth had also, perhaps, some effect. Post-war colonial emancipation and the emergence into full nationhood of countries alien in race, language and traditions impaired the unity of the Commonwealth. These changes have had a dual influence: the champions of the Empire have made a remarkable adaptation to the changed character of the Commonwealth. They have accepted its multi-racial character. But at the same time the effect of these changes upon their colleagues may have been to lessen the significance and reality of the Commonwealth, and to sharpen interest in Western European unity.

The post-war Conservative leadership had shown an early interest in European unity and displayed more benevolence to the cause than did the leaders of the Labour party. This perhaps had some influence on the new generation of Conservative candidates and M.P.s The political thinking of the older candidates had been shaped in the nineteen-thirties. The emerging generation, whose political outlook was still being formed, were more responsive to the pleas from the continent for British interest and participation.

The attitudes of rural Members and the persistent contrast between Oxford and Cambridge are less simply explained. The rural Commonwealth men were much more moderate than their urban partners. Possibly, this was because the rural constituencies had little to gain from an extension of Commonwealth preferences. Moreover, whatever arrangements may be made to protect British agriculture for the time being, New Zealand and Australian producers are potential competitors. The development of the colonial empire, however, offers little menace to the livelihood of the British farmers.

There may, nevertheless, be a more profound reason for this contrast. Support for imperial preference in the Conservative party tended to be linked with a distrust of internationalism. Rural Conservatives were not only inclined to eschew imperial preference: they were also more sympathetic towards the United Nations. Possibly, men with the syndrome of views marked by a belief in Commonwealth preference and dislike of internationalism were more acceptable to Conservative selection committees in the towns than in the countryside. Why this should be so is not clear.* What is clear is that there are no grounds at all for identifying the more reactionary sections of the Conservative party with the representatives of the rural areas. On the question of internationalism they were more liberal than the urban Members, and on no issue were they significantly more right-wing than the representatives of the towns.

An authoritative explanation of the division between Oxford and Cambridge, and between Oxford and all other groups, would require prolonged research. The difference was persistent, and sometimes marked. On every question, except that of civil liberties, Oxford Members behaved differently from the rest of the party. Nor does this difference seem to have been caused by the idiosyncratic attitude of one particular generation; within each age-group, so far as can be ascertained, Oxonians were more European, more internationalist, and more humane than their opposite numbers from Cambridge. If these divergences of opinion are connected with

---

* It has been suggested to us that the strength of the old League of Nations Union lay in the countries rather than in the boroughs and that this may have led to an overlap of officials and voluntary workers between the local branches of the Union, and Conservative Committees. If so, this would account for the rural preference for internationally-minded candidates.

factors within the universities, these factors are not temporary and accidental, but permanent and inherent.

A number of hypotheses may be mentioned. The intellectual influences at Oxford and Cambridge are dissimilar. The importance of different subjects varies: Cambridge is noted for science, Oxford for Greats and P.P.E. The difference might be linked with separate religious traditions: Cambridge has a strong evangelical strain, Oxford a High Church tradition. More simply the contrast may be due to different interpretations of Conservatism, handed down over the decades through the political clubs.

Another explanation is that the differences are not connected with the universities themselves, but with the families from which students at the two universities are recruited. Oxford drew many more of its members than Cambridge from the Clarendon Public Schools. Possibly families with a tradition of political leadership tend to send their sons to Oxford rather than Cambridge. This would support a picture of an aristocratic, detached, sophisticated and internationally-minded Conservatism associated with Oxford, compared with a more popular, more nationalist and blunter Conservatism from Cambridge.

Whatever be the truth of these hypotheses, some observers confirm the existence of two distinct veins of Conservatism. Oxford, with no single coherent tradition of Conservatism, accommodates several rival strains, among them internationalism, humanitarianism and domestic *laissez faire*. Cambridge, it is said, has inherited Disraeli's synthesis of imperialism and social reform, and cherishes a nostalgic affection for empire, prestige and national sovereignty.

Conclusion

When discussing the Labour party, we suggested that the extremes did not cancel each other out, but "added up"; left-wing parties in Britain are obliged, by reason of the tacit agreement which holds them together, to press strongly the particular crotchets of each of their component groups. The old Liberal party was constrained to advocate temperance legislation along with limitation of the hours of labour in the coal mines, Welsh disestablishment along with Irish Home Rule, free trade side by side with the removal of barriers to Trades Union activity. Similarly, the modern Labour party has to pursue all the special enthusiasms of its various sections. But where the differences are qualitative, rather than quantitative, it is not possible to indulge in log-rolling of this kind. On an issue such as defence the party can go unilateralist or it can stay rigidly in favour of the independent deterrent. What it cannot do is to run the two opinions in harness.

To some extent, the Conservative party resembles the Labour and former Liberal parties in being able to satisfy the various sections of which it is composed by catering for the special interest of each. For a long time, it could placate those whose primary interest was Commonwealth unity along with those whose first consideration was the maintenance of free enterprise. So long as prosperity continues, and production expands, it can reconcile the demand for tax reductions with the expansion of the social services. But some of the differences in the Conservative party are qualitative ones; these differences may be variations of emphasis, but they are variations which point in opposite directions. At some stage, it may be logically impossible to reconcile the claims of Europe and the Commonwealth; at some point it becomes clear that you cannot simultaneously maintain national sovereignty and promote supranational authorities; you cannot both invade and not invade Egypt; and if production should cease to expand, it will not be possible to combine reductions of taxation with the development of the welfare services. But the greater resilience of the Conservatives should enable them to survive these difficulties. When the Labour party has to resolve qualitative differences, it is driven to the verge of collapse; the Conservative party is able to restore itself within a term of months, as it did over the Suez and death penalty crises.

Chapter 4 · Reflections and Forecasts

THE CONSERVATIVE PARTY

THE Conservative party has, save at rare intervals, maintained its cohesion with little formal machinery for penalizing open dissent or resolving disagreements: the Labour party, however, has been unable to preserve its unity, despite the existence of elaborate procedures for discovering and enforcing the will of the party. This analysis suggests some reasons for the contrasting experience of the two parliamentary parties.

The two parties are strikingly dissimilar in their composition. The Conservative party is much more homogeneous than the Labour party. Most Conservative M.P.s come from the same social and educational circles. More than three-quarters had been to public schools. More than half of them were businessmen, and nearly all of them were drawn from the upper or upper-middle classes. The Labour party is educationally and socially far more diverse: Labour boasts that their party is a much better cross-section of the nation than the Conservative party: but this may be a source of considerable weakness, for different social groups may bring with them distinct values, and their approach to political problems may be coloured by dissimilar experiences. Moreover, the tensions between different social and educational groups in the Labour party are exacerbated because the occupational boundaries so largely coincide with educational and sponsorship boundaries. The Trades Unionists largely coincide with the workers, and the elementary educated; the professions with the university graduates. The effect is to reinforce occupational distinctions by educational divisions: the three main occupational groups—the Workers, the Professions and the Miscellaneous Occupations—suffer a sort of cultural segregation. Amongst the Conservatives occupational and educational frontiers do not coincide to the same extent. Admittedly, there were differences in the school, university and constituency backgrounds of public and private company directors; there were also differences in the characteristics of the three school categories; but these divisions were not marked. The Conservatives were a much better integrated party.

Moreover, divisions of opinion rarely corresponded with important social distinctions. The most persistent dissenters were the Oxford Members, who almost always differed from the rest of the party, and from fellow graduates from other universities. The rivalry between Oxford and Cambridge is usually keen, always good-humoured and never serious. Political tensions between Members from rival universities, even if recognized to be such, are unlikely to acquire the same force as tensions between people from differing social classes. There were, moreover, few differences between public and non-public school Members, few between business and the professions: there was no contrast between Members from the two ancient universities, as a class, and graduates from the new universities: and difference between graduates and non-graduates arose only on penal reform.

The differences that were associated with various background factors were usually small; in only eight instances was the significance level as high as 2·5 per cent. In the Labour party, however, this level of significance was reached in 20 cases.

Finally, the Conservative party is not divided into wings, with each wing espousing a line or tendency of policy affecting all departments of national life. This alone goes far to explain the resilience and unity of the Conservative party. By their very nature, the internal quarrels of the party are temporary. They subside as the issues which gave them birth are resolved. The absence of two clearly drawn camps means that the man who deserts on one issue may be a staunch party man on another: the Member who agitates against his front-bench in one dispute may be a valued friend of the leadership in some other controversy. Alternatively, a dissident Member may deviate from the party line in several directions at once. The Member who takes a dangerously radical stand on one question, may be gratifyingly Right-wing on another. If Lord Hinchingbrooke and Mr. Montgomery Hyde provoked misgivings by their support for the abolition of capital punishment, they were able to re-assure their colleagues by their hostility to the evacuation of the Suez Canal base in 1954. Political disagreements are temporary and specific, and are therefore never invested with the dangerous personal bitterness that is found in the Labour party. The task of the Conservative leadership is made easy: there is no permanently alienated faction to contend with. It knows that the opposition of any group is limited to a solitary issue, and that today's critics may be next week's allies.

Two trends of future development can be discerned. Support for British association with Europe is likely to grow, and the party is likely to become more sympathetic towards penal reform, unless the movements of opinion amongst the younger and more junior Members are checked by a sustained reaction from the constituency selection committees. As older Members retire, the adherents of imperial exclusiveness will diminish, and will largely be replaced by young, pro-European candidates. Similarly there is likely to be increasing support for humanitarian penal policies: on the other hand this may be slowed down if, as seems likely, the proportion of non-graduates rises significantly.

There has been virtually no change in the proportion of Oxonians amongst the newcomers of 1959, and the number of non-public school men has risen but slightly, so that little change in Conservative attitudes to the United Nations or social policy is portended. There was no tendency for younger Members to be more internationalist than their seniors: and in recent years, young recruits to the internationalist section of the party have been balanced by an infusion of young and articulate apostles of national sovereignty—men such as Paul Williams and John Biggs-Davison.

Retirements and deaths have not substantially altered the balance of forces. Not unexpectedly, the change has been greatest in the Europe/Empire distribution. The Commonwealth wings have lost twice as many Members as the Europeans. The four Suez categories have lost roughly the same proportion of Members—the losses amongst the Critics being rather higher, because of the failure of two or three of them to obtain re-nomination. More surprisingly, the Social Left and Centre have suffered heavier losses than the Social Right.

There were few important and controversial Conservative EDMs in the first session of the new Parliament. Two half-hearted demonstrations calling for legislative intervention in Trades Union affairs found little support amongst the new Members, or indeed in any section of the party. But an amendment to one of these Motions, which expressly rejected legislative interference, was strongly backed by the newcomers: 24 of the 27 signatories took their seats at the 1959 general election, or at post-1955 by-elections. A Motion sponsored by the Foreign Policy Right expressed concern at the expropriation of British assets in Cuba and urged the Government to replace imports from Cuba by goods from Commonwealth sources. The new Members were neither more nor less enthusiastic. In the division on homosexuality the newcomers were slightly more sympathetic than the rest of the party to the Wolfenden Committee's recommendations, but the difference was not significant.

In the second session however, there were signs of dissidence. There was considerable dissatisfaction with the liberal colonial policy of Mr. Macleod, the new Colonial Secretary, and Mr. Butler, the Home Secretary, incurred opposition as a result of his refusal to recommend the re-introduction of corporal punishment as a judicial penalty. In economic affairs, Mr. Selwyn Lloyd forestalled criticism by the large surtax concessions in his budget.

Opposition to Mr. Macleod crystallized during the negotiations to revise the Northern Rhodesian Constitution. The increasing coldness of the British Government towards South Africa met with virtually no criticism on the Conservative benches; nor was there any overt large scale resistance to Mr. Macleod's plans in Kenya and Nyasaland, though Lord Salisbury made clear his hostility to the whole tenor of the Government's policies in East and Central Africa. On the question of Rhodesia, the Government's apparent course alarmed many Conservatives. The early possibility of an African majority in the Northern Rhodesia Legislature aroused fears that the white community in Central Africa were being betrayed. The parallel with Ulster in 1914 was too close to be ignored. Mr. Macleod was rigorously questioned at a meeting of the Conservative Private Members' Commonwealth Affairs Committee; immediately after the meeting, Mr. Robin Turton, a former Minister, framed a Motion which implicitly criticized the Colonial Secretary. The sponsors of the Motion included well-known figures of the Right, such as Anthony Fell, John Biggs-Davison, and Lord Hinchingbrooke. The Motion laconically called upon the Government, when considering the future of Northern Rhodesia, to adhere to the principles of non-racial representation embodied in the Lennox-Boyd constitution of 1958. But the innocent form of the Motion concealed a dangerous import; for the Motion was an open warning to Mr. Macleod that he must not proceed with any plan which would ensure the Africans, *as such,* a majority in the territorial legislature. Moreover, the Motion was widely construed as a portent of Conservative dissatisfaction with the swift pace, if not with the ultimate goal of enfranchisement in Central Africa.

The Motion won wide support in the Conservative party. At one stage, more than a hundred Conservatives had signed. Fifteen M.P.s later withdrew their names—either in deference to the Government's appeal or because they had been genuinely mistaken about the purport of the Motion.

It would be wrong to regard the signatories of the Motion as nothing more than a White Settlers' Lobby at Westminster. The motives which prompted Members to support the protest appeared to vary widely. The hard core of the Right were said to be alarmed by the general course of the Government's African policy, and in particular they were disturbed by what seemed to them an impending betrayal of the British community in Central Africa, and the sacrifice of the Federation. Others were said to be unhappy at the pace of change in the Rhodesias, and at the apparent substitution of a policy of African majority rule for the goal of "non-racialism". There were others, doubtless including M.P.s of presumed liberal views on colonial matters, who were said to be guiltless of any wish to embarrass the Government; for them, the Motion seemed simply to re-iterate and emphasize established official policy. Such Members were able to assert that the complicated scheme of representation announced by Mr. Macleod embodied the principle of "non-racialism" proclaimed in the Motion.

Nevertheless, whatever subtle variation there may have been in the personal interpretation placed upon the Motion by its signatories, the protest was generally construed as a severe warning to the Government; those M.P.s who had intended no challenge had the opportunity to withdraw their names, as some of them did. Whatever the precise motives of the signatories, whatever the intensity of their feeling on the issue, most of the signatories whose names remained on the Order Paper intended the Motion to be a sign of disquiet about the speed of African political advancement.

An examination of the Members involved revealed that the group were broadly a cross-section of the whole party. But one clear and characteristic distinction did emerge; amongst graduates, the curious cleavage between Oxford and Cambridge members was evident again. Oxford M.P.s took the more liberal stand. Only 15 per cent of Oxford backbenchers signed the Motion; but Cambridge mustered more than a third of its Members, and the other universities nearly as many. The association between university and attitude reached the high level of 2·5 per cent. There were no significant differences between graduates as a class and non-graduates.

There were in addition some minor and not fully-established associations between opinions and backgrounds. Amongst businessmen, the directors of private companies were the most enthusiastic supporters of the Motion, whilst the combined business executive and business finance groups gave very little support. There were similar minor differences in the reactions of the major occupational groups. The Miscellaneous class were the most favourable to the Motion, the Farmers the least so. A provisional association, also at the ten per cent level, has been established between school and attitude—the Clarendon School M.P.s being the least, the Non-Public School M.P.s the most sympathetic, to the Motion.

There may have been some connection between age and attitude. The under-fifties were rather more liberal than the over-fifties. An association has been provisionally established—the level being 10 per cent. Likewise a provisional association has been established between year of entry and opinion. The Members who entered the House between 1955 and 1959 were less favourable to the Motion than those elected before 1955. The association is at the 10 per cent level and so is not fully established. The pre-1945 generation, a group which normally shows some reserve about signing Motions, came out in large numbers in support of Mr. Turton's protest. There is then, some limited evidence to show that the new generation of Conservative Members have a more liberal approach to colonial affairs than their seniors.

Amongst the survivors of the previous Parliament, there was a close overlap between the Foreign Policy Right and the signatories of the Motion. Two-thirds of the remaining Suez Diehards, and nearly half of the "Anti-Americans" were amongst the signers. However, not a solitary Suez Critic, and only a quarter of those who were uncommitted on Suez gave their support. Similarly, three-quarters of the anti-U.N. group signed, as against a handful of the United Nations sympathizers. But there was little co-incidence between Members' views on Rhodesia, and attitudes to the question of European and Commonwealth relationships. It is true that nearly half of the Empire Stalwarts signed the Motion—a disproportionately large fraction; but the European bloc supplied nearly as many signatories as the whole of the Commonwealth group—Empire Moderates and Empire Stalwarts combined. Sympathy for Europe rather than with the Commonwealth, does not necessarily connote enthusiasm for colonial emancipation; indeed, the fellow-feeling of colonial and ex-colonial nations is one of the

TABLE 14
Attitudes to Rhodesia 1960 and Foreign Policy 1955–59
Suez

	Diehards	*"Anti-Americans"*	*Critics*	*Uncom.*	*Exc.*	*Total*
Signers	17	27	—	17	2	63
Withdrawals	—	3	—	3	—	6
Non-Signers	10	33	12	46	7	108
TOTAL	27	63	12	66	9	177

$\chi^2_2 = 13 \cdot 66$. Significant at 0·5%
(Critics and Uncommitted grouped.) (Withdrawals omitted.)

United Nations

	Anti-U.N.	*Uncommitted*	*Pro-U.N.*	*Exc.*	*Total*
Signers	21	36	6	—	63
Withdrawals	—	2	4	—	6
Non-Signers	7	61	35	5	108
TOTAL	28	99	45	5	177

$\chi^2_2 = 25 \cdot 80$. Significant at 0·1%
(Withdrawals omitted.)

elements strengthening the drive towards European unity in the face of the Afro-Asian challenge.

Although there is a very close correlation between the composition of the Foreign Policy Right and the Rhodesia dissidents it is nonetheless noteworthy that six of the dissidents had expressed sympathy for the United Nations. The Right-wing is still very far from behaving as a rigid bloc, whose members display a common attitude to all the major questions of external policy.

There seems to have been no connection between views on social policy, and on Rhodesia. The signatories were fairly evenly distributed amongst the Left-, Centre- and Right-wings.

A month after the formidable challenge on Central Africa, another Conservative revolt took place. The demands for the re-introduction of corporal punishment as a judicial penalty, which had been a feature of the previous Parliament, were repeated in the new House of Commons. These demands were often backed by Conservative organizations outside Parliament. Mr. Butler, the Home Secretary, set up a committee under Sir Patrick Barry to consider whether there was a case for the restoration of judicial corporal punishment. The committee declared that there was not, but the backbench demands were nevertheless renewed, Sir Thomas Moore being the chief spokesman of the corporal punishment lobby. In April, 1961, Sir Thomas moved the addition of a new clause on the Report stage of the Criminal Justice Bill. The clause sought to empower the courts to award corporal punishment to young offenders convicted of a second or subsequent delinquency. The clause was strongly opposed by the Home Secretary. Nevertheless, in the division 69 Conservatives disobeyed the party Whip and voted for the inclusion of the clause. One hundred and two backbenchers followed Mr. Butler's advice.

Once again there was a significant cleavage on this issue between university men and non-graduates. Twenty-nine graduates voted for the clause, whilst 67 graduate backbenchers supported the Government; the non-graduates split in two—34 voting with Sir Thomas Moore and 33 with the Home Secretary.*

* Discrepancies between these figures and those cited in the preceding paragraph arise because those dissidents who entered the House at by-elections during the session have been disregarded; so have Members educated at Sandhurst.

Sir Thomas' support came to a disproportionate extent from the older and the more senior Members. Once more the 1959 entrants proved to be the most liberal group. Perhaps the greatest significance of the vote lay, however, in the overlap between the two dissident groups—the Rhodesia rebels and the supporters of corporal punishment. Mr. Turton himself followed the lead of the Home Secretary; but no less than 34 of his co-signatories flouted the government Whip and called for the re-introduction of corporal punishment. They constituted more than half the rebel total; in contrast, only 15 per cent of those who supported Mr. Butler's stand against corporal punishment had aligned themselves with the Rhodesia faction.

TABLE 15

Attitudes to Northern Rhodesia and Corporal Punishment

(EDM 64/1960 and Division on Criminal Justice Bill, 11th April, 1961)

	Humane (Pro-Govt.)	*Abstainers*	*Severe*	*Total*
Signers	16	34	34	84
Non-Signers & Withdrawals	86	90	32	208
TOTAL	102	124	66	292

$\bar{\chi}^2_3 = 25\cdot28$. Significant at $0\cdot1\%$

Some association had been found between views on penal reform and foreign policy in the previous Parliament. But the association in 1961 was much more pronounced. The extent of the overlap between the two dissident groups suggests that a new phenomenon may be occurring in the Conservative party—a consolidation of the Right. There is no sign yet of any coming together of the Social Right and the Foreign Policy Right. But in the fields of penal reform and foreign affairs, issues which often evoke a similar emotional attitude, we may be witnessing the emergence of a substantial and selfconsciously right-wing bloc. This fact, and the support enjoyed by the Rhodesia rebels amongst respected and senior backbench M.P.s may portend greater restiveness within the Parliamentary Party, and greater friction between Ministers and their nominal followers.

THE LABOUR PARTY

The conclusions of this study, as far as they concern the Labour party, find strong confirmation in the results of an investigation of the previous Parliament, 1951–55. The consequence of its peculiar structure, as outlined in the first pages of this chapter *viz,* the difficulty of keeping the Parliamentary party together, has also been most dramatically illustrated by the split over defence policy which has bedevilled it since the Scarborough Conference of 1960.

For the Parliament of 1951–55 we carried out more extensive tests than in the present study. Among other things, we inquired into whether there was any association between a Member's views and the region he represented, the size of his majority, his war service, and the like. Some associations have been firmly established, particularly between region and attitude; but neither war service nor size of majority have proved very important. On the other hand the associations which have proved persistent in the present study also prove to have been the most persistent for the 1951–55 period. In both cases *sponsorship* is the most important association, closely followed by *education* and *occupation.* To that extent therefore the present findings receive support from the experience of the previous Parliament.

Now it is precisely in these three respects that the 1959 backbench has changed least; and this suggests that the general attitude of the 1955–59 Labour Backbench is likely to be carried into the present Parliament. *Occupationally,* there has been a minute (3 per cent) rise in the proportion of Miscellaneous Occupations at the expense of the Workers. There is almost no change in the *sponsorship* proportions or in those of *educational* background.

The important changes have been confined to the factors of *age* and *political seniority,* as the following tables show:

TABLE 16

Age and political seniority in the Labour Party backbench, 1955–58 and 1959

AGE

	1955–58 % of backbench	1959 % of backbench
Under 41 years of age	6	12
41–50 years of age	23	28
51–60 years of age	37	37
Over 60 years of age	33	22

POLITICAL SENIORITY

	1955–58 % of backbench	1959 % of backbench
Post-1954	8	26
1950–1954	20	18
1945–1949	55	46
pre-1944	17	11

The question therefore is whether the infusion of younger and politically junior people in place of the older and senior will have any political effect?

It seems bound to have an effect, but a *limited* one, for the following reason: that the Members of the 1955-58 backbench who died before the end of that Parliament or who retired at the 1959 election, came predominantly from the *Right*-wing of the party. This is indeed what we would expect—for there is, as we have seen, some reason to believe that on some matters the older and more senior Members were more conservative than their juniors; and it is the older and more senior who tend to die or retire from politics. Of the 60 "most left-wing Members" of the 1955-59 Parliament, 8 failed to return to the new Parliament of 1959; of the 53 "most right-wing Members", however, 15 failed to return. The Left did worse at the polls than the Right: it lost 6 seats as against 2. But only 2 Left-wingers retired from politics, as against 13 Right-wingers who had either died before the election, or retired from the conflict. There has been therefore a marginal—but how very marginal! shift away from the extreme Right.

It is against this background that one must consider the present struggle between Left and Right in the Parliamentary Labour Party. "Unilateralism" is, it would seem, a coat of many colours. In the 1955–59 Parliament, it began with a demand for the unilateral renunciation of tests, and was shortly afterwards (when the bomb was built) accompanied by a demand for the unilateral renunciation of manufacture. At the same time agitation developed against the provision of fixed site missile bases. But by the middle of 1960 all these were either orthodox party policy or on the way to becoming so. Tests had been suspended while talks went on in Geneva between the U.S.S.R., the U.S.A. and the U.K.; and the Blue Streak missile had been abandoned, so that continued British H-bomb manufacture and the provision of fixed missile bases now became less and less defensible. Thus the objective of unilateralism in its 1955–59 guise were well within sight. But in 1960 "unilateralism" made explicit a further objective: the refusal to provide bases for any kind of nuclear weapon (thus denying the U.S.A. both airfields and submarine bases) and still more (in the words of Mr. Cousins' motion):

"A complete rejection of any defence policy based on the threat of the use of strategic or tactical nuclear weapons."

Interpreted by Mr. Gaitskell this was tantamount to saying that we should withdraw from NATO—that we should "go it alone", and it was certainly along these lines that the debate at Scarborough was conducted.*

The sequel is well known. The Scarborough Conference carried Mr. Cousins' unilateral motion with its anti-NATO implications. Thereupon Mr. Gaitskell reserved the right of the Parliamentary Party not to follow the Conference decision; and by re-electing him against the candidature of Mr. Wilson, by filling the Parliamentary Committee with his supporters and by giving a confidence vote to his defence policy the Parliamentary Party turned its back on the Conference line. And, moreover, it turned the parliamentary unilateralists into an oppositionist fraction.

---

* *Annual Conference of the Labour Party*, 1960, *Report*, p. 199.

Since that time this opposition has lost few opportunities by way of EDMs or floor-votes, to challenge the majority of the Parliamentary Party. Thus on February 16th, 1960, Mr. Swingler and others put down a Motion* calling for the unilateral renunciation of the testing and production of nuclear weapons and "the use of our soil for nuclear bases". It was signed by 46 Members. Later, on February 29th, 1960 when the House was to debate the White Paper on Defence, the unilateralists tabled their own unofficial amendment to the Government Motion. The Labour party's official amendment declared it had no confidence in the defence policy of the Government, but the unofficial Motion, sponsored by Messrs. Shinwell, Silverman, Wigg, Stephen Swingler, Zilliacus and Hale went further: it "deplored a defence policy based on a nuclear strategy . . .". When the division took place on the official Motion, 44 Labour Members ostentatiously abstained.

The climax came on December 13th, 1960. When the House divided on the Labour party's defence Motion no less than 72 Labour M.P.s abstained.

It is still too early to say precisely how many of these are convinced "unilateralists" in the anti-NATO sense; the *Daily Herald* has suggested that "The bulk" abstained because of the terms of the Motion which they thought an unnecessary "flouting of the Scarborough decision".† This seems unlikely in the light of the antecedents of the abstainers, as we shall now see.

From what quarters did the abstainers come? The question provokes a fascinating exercise in the shifts of party opinion: for the "72" derived mostly from inter-shifts of opinion among those who had sat in the previous Parliament, and only partly from newcomers.

First, we must look at the original unilateralists, i.e., "the 45", as defined on p. 25 above. Four had failed in the election; but more significantly no less than 14 appear to have moved away from their unilateralist opinion. Very few of the fourteen for instance, had either signed EDM 37/59, or abstained on the division of February 29th. Among these backsliders were Members like Messrs. Stross, King, Hunter and Robinson. It would appear that their views did not carry them into unilateralism's new phase, i.e., the possibility

* EDM 37/1959.
† December 15th, 1960.

of quitting NATO. Indeed, Messrs. King and Mason are today among the pro-Gaitskell "Campaign for Democratic Socialism" group, which supports the multilateral approach.

Thus the "original" unilateralists were reduced to a hard core of 27. But these have been joined by no less than 20 Members who had previously formed the "Centre Group", i.e., those who had not (1955–59) overtly gone beyond opposition to missile bases and H-patrols. There is no reason not to believe that their views had moved leftwards. Thus the unilateralist figures rose from twenty-seven "hard-core" plus twenty who had moved leftwards from the centre: a total of 47. Another 5 members including Mr. Wigg and Mr. Hale joined them from the previous category of "no opinion", and 3 former frontbenchers (e.g. Mr. Greenwood also). Thus the numbers rose to 55. Some of these, e.g., Messrs. Wigg and Shinwell were, of course, not pacifists or even neutralists: they were convinced of the need for an alternative defence *strategy*.

The remainder of the "72", 17 in all, were newcomers. Five of them had joined the 1955–59 Parliament too late for inclusion in our calculations—Messrs. Abse, Spriggs, Stonehouse and Mendelson, for instance. Eight more were elected in the 1959 election, and two—Mr. Foot and Mr. Milne—in 1960.

The outstanding feature of this group is its association with the *sponsorship* background of its members. Unlike the original "45", there was no pronounced association with occupation. The Miscellaneous Occupations were somewhat more prominent than the others, but to nothing like the degree they were in the previous parliament. The educational backgrounds were strikingly similar to the 1955–59 unilateralists. Age was not significant either. There was some difference between the post-1955 and the pre-1955 generations, the more junior being more unilateralist than their seniors. But the pattern was significantly determined by sponsorship. Once again, the Trades Unionists were the least responsive, and the Co-operatives most so.

This is interesting—and important—on three counts. First because it follows the previous and well attested pattern of behaviour of these sponsorship groupings. Secondly, it is connected with a deliberate political decision on the part of the Trades Union bloc in the party. In October, 1960, just before the election of the Leader of the Parliamentary Party, the Trades Union group received

TABLE 17

Composition of the 72 Abstainers by Sponsorship

	No. abstaining	*Total numbers*	*% abstaining*
Trade Union sponsored	17	81	21
Co-operative sponsored	9	17	53
Constituency Labour party	46	132	35
	72	230	

$\chi^2_2 = 8 \cdot 50$. Significant at 2.5%

a report from Mr. Pannell, (its secretary) which called on it to act as a body in the internal politics of the party. "Our position in the past," it said, "has been to assert that we are not a pressure group, so we have concentrated our energies on electoral matters. In the new and strange circumstances of today, while still wishing to maintain the principle that there shall not be parties within the party, nevertheless we, as trustees of those who founded this party and for whom it primarily exists, must now consider whether we should widen the scope of our discussions so that, with colleagues of like mind, we may ensure the effective electoral continuance of our movement".*

Thirdly, it throws light on the nature of sponsored candidates. That the Co-operators should be the most enthusiastic of the groupings is not surprising; for it was the Co-operative Party Congress, meeting in Easter 1960, which first came out with a resolution for unilateralism, and so started the ball rolling towards the fatal Scarborough Conference. But the nature of such Trades Unionist participation in this floor revolt as did occur is somewhat paradoxical. The T.G.W.U. was of course the architect of the unilateralist victory at Scarborough: yet of its 14 M.P.s, only *one* was among the 72 abstainers. The Shopworkers were also unilateralists at Scarborough: yet only three of their 9 M.P.s abstained. Likewise with the N.U.R., also unilateralists, of whose five M.P.s only one abstained. Of the unilateralist A.E.U.'s eight M.P.s, none abstained. Yet, on the other side, among the anti-unilateralist N.U.M.'s, 32 M.P.s, as many as 7 abstained; and four of these came from the Yorkshire and Durham areas, which, in the N.U.M. Conference had strenuously opposed and helped defeat the unilateralist cause. No more striking evidence can be advanced of the political independence of the Trades Union sponsored M.P. The

* *Daily Telegraph* October 28th, 1960.

Trades Union Group in the House of Commons does *not* reflect the views of the sponsoring unions: but it does appear—whether this view can be consciously manufactured or whether it merely reflects a common temperament—to have a view that opposes the ideological left of the party. This group, more than ever, is the sheet anchor of the Parliamentary Party; and Mr. Gaitskell's success in riding out the unilateralist storm clearly depends on its continuing and solid support.

TABLE 18

The "72"

Occupation	*Abstainers*	*Total*	%
Workers	20	68	29
Misc. Occupat'ns	27	71	38
Business	6	23	26
Professions	19	68	28
	72	230	

Sponsorship	*Abstainers*	*Total*	%
Trades Union	17	81	21
Co-operative	9	17	53
CLP	46	132	35
	72	230	

Education	*Abstainers*	*Total*	%
Not known	1	4	2
Elementary	21	73	29
Secondary	10	38	26
Ely/Sec. +	9	21	43
University	31	94	33
	72	230	

University	*Abstainers*	*Total*	%
U.1	6	25	24
U.2	4	13	31
U.3	4	11	36
U.4	17	42	40
	31	91	

Year of first entering Parliament	*Abstainers*	*Total*	%
1959	8	29	28
1955–8	13	30	43
1950–54	9	41	22
1945–9	35	105	33
pre-1945	7	25	28
	72	230	

Annex 1 · Some Problems of Method

In the compiling and the interpretation of our tables, a number of points must be made clear. Before proceeding to these tables, therefore, we offer some comments on these points.

1. First, there is no reason to suppose that Motions on serious subjects are not signed seriously. This is agreed by all informants without exception. It is consistent with the subsequent behaviour of the signatories of certain Motions, for instance, the Suez Motion of December 1953, out of whose 42 signatories 27 actually went into the division lobby to vote against the evacuation of the base, when this was debated eight months later. It is impossible to penetrate beyond the fact of signature to the mood inspiring it. For all practical purposes Members have made public attestation that they support a particular attitude.

2. It is not claimed that the Motions signed by any individual M.P. yield a complete picture of his political personality. An individual may not have signed because of some personal idiosyncrasy, or may have been absent when a particular Motion was tabled. It is for these reasons, that we have declined to publish lists of Members signing particular Motions. Our tables deal only in aggregates. In the absence of evidence to the contrary, we assume that Members who, for purely personal reasons, fail to sign a particular Motion are randomly distributed throughout the social and other categories into which we have classified each party. Furthermore, the probability that a Member has abstained from supporting a given attitude because of fortuitous or personal circumstances diminishes with the number of opportunities supplied him. Hence the larger the train of Motions supporting a particular attitude, not one of which a Member signs, the less the probability that this is due to fortuitous or personal factors and the higher the probability that it is deliberate.

3. Our earlier description of the way in which signatures are collected* may suggest that the lists of signatories are purely haphazard. However, the fundamental objective of all our analyses is, precisely, to find out whether the signatures do occur at random or not. To this end, every table has been subjected to the chi-square test of association. (See Statistical Appendix p. 146.)

4. The various categories into which we have divided each of the two parties do not always show equal propensities to sign Motions. For instance, in the Labour party, the pre-1945 Members tend to sign fewer Motions per head than those elected in and after 1945. This gives rise to the question, whether it is desirable to compensate for this general propensity not to sign, by inflating by some coefficient the figure of pre-1945 signers in our tables. This in turn depends on how we interpret the fact that some categories are "low-signers" compared with others.

If it could be shown, for instance, that the sickness and absenteeism rate of the pre-1945's was grossly higher than that of the remainder we might argue that their non-signature was due to a fortuitous outside circumstance, and we might well feel obliged to introduce some compensation factor into their out-turn as shown in the tables. The point is that the reason for doing so would be coming from *outside* our statistical data. In the absence of outside evidence, we can do no other than merely record the neutral fact, that pre-1945 M.P.s tend to sign less than others. It is true we can suggest hypotheses for such low signing. It may be that after years of signing Motions they have concluded that they are a waste of time. It may equally well be, however, that after years of service as M.P.s, they are no longer as interested as their juniors. In the former case we might feel justified in artificially inflating their signature rate: in the latter case we should certainly not. But in the absence of any outside proof, we have no alternative but to accept their low signature rate as a neutral fact—indeed, as one of the present characteristics of the pre-1945 generation.

5. An allied problem arises in the treatment of those who did not sign a particular Motion. If signing be taken as an index of interest, may non-signing be taken as indicating lack of interest?

For reasons dealt with in detail at page 143-5 below, there seem to be good reasons for inferring that this is broadly so. It is subject,

* Above pp. 9-10.

however, to an important qualification—whether the Member may be presumed to have had the physical opportunity of signing. In the Labour party the number of Motions put down on any given topic was usually large enough to permit such a presumption. Where a number of Motions, ranging from five to seven or eight or more, were tabled on a particular topic, it is not reasonable to assume that the Member was absent from the House on each and everyone of the occasions when Motions were signed.

In the Conservative party, however, the position is less clear. In general there were fewer Motions on any topic, and a much larger proportion of non-signatories. It seems very doubtful whether we can assume that the "uncommitted" deliberately withheld their signature, since they had fewer opportunities to sign than did Labour Members. For this reason the following method of analysis has been adopted.

(a) The first stage was to consider only those who did sign at least one Motion, and to test for associations between the strength of attitude revealed and the background factors.

(b) Secondly, the whole of the committed group was compared with the uncommitted.

If the committed and uncommitted groups do not differ in respect of any background factor, then we may conclude that they are alike in every *observed* respect. This is what would be expected if the uncommitted simply did not have an opportunity to sign. (However, before the conclusions reached for the committed can be extended to cover the uncommitted, we have necessarily assumed that the two groups do not differ in any *unobserved* respect.)

On the other hand, when we do find significant differences between the committed and uncommitted we have a prima facie case that non-signing was deliberate. In this case we are prevented from applying, and have not applied the conclusions reached for the committed, to all Conservative M.P.s.

6. Not all our tables have been constructed on the same basis. We have, in fact, used two different types of construction. These may be called qualitative and quantitative constructions. The difference calls for some explanation.

(a) *The Qualitative Tables*

All but one of the Conservative tables, and in the Labour party the Defence and Foreign Affairs tables, are of this type. In such cases it has proved possible to identify different viewpoints, and to list and classify the Members who hold these different viewpoints. Thus in the table cited at page 162 below, we have distinguished three broad viewpoints on Defence, which we have characterized as Left Pacificist, Centre Pacificist and Right Pacificist.

The only matter that calls for comment here is that the authors and the authors alone are responsible for "identifying" these viewpoints and arranging them in a scale. This is a subjective exercise. Others might have arranged the Motions differently, or drawn distinctions we have not made. The only answer to this is to say that what we have done we have done deliberately and overtly, giving our reasons.

(b) *The Quantitative Tables*

In some cases, however—the Labour party's views on anti-colonialism, social welfare, civil liberties and humanitarianism—we did not find shades or differences of opinion. All the Motions were in favour of social welfare, or civil liberties and so forth. In such cases, no one Motion is by itself more or less extreme than any other.

Here we have established the number of Motions a Member has signed, and have classified him as Left, Centre, Right, according to the numbers signed. All that is established here, at the very best, is a rank-order. We do not say that a Member who has signed six Motions is six times as keen as a Member who has signed only one, but simply that he is more keen. The numbers in each rank are an arbitrary matter. If one chose to specify 6–4 Motions, 3–2 Motions, and 1 Motion only as the criteria of each rank, the numbers in each such rank would be different from a classification based on 6–5; 4–2; 1; and no Motions.

These ranks are therefore *contingent*. We are in effect saying "Given present information, the Members may be ranked in the following order, with the following numbers in each rank. With further information it might be possible to introduce a finer scale i.e., more ranks; in which case it would be necessary to modify the numbers in each rank accordingly".

Furthermore in such a rank-order, the intervals between the ranks are not measureable and are not necessarily equal.
but do not in themselves raise questions of principle. There is,
These characteristics limit the utility of such quantitative tables,

however, an objection to the very principle on which these tables have been constructed, for they equate keenness or enthusiasm for a topic with the number of Motions a Member has signed. This is connected with the discussion at p. 140-1, above.

Against this assumption it may justly be urged that some Members are fond of signing Motions while others are reluctant to sign; and that this equation of keenness with the number of Motions signed, factitiously inflates the panjandrums in the Party, and by the same token, deflates the men of sober judgment. To the extent that these two classes of Member exist, the tables give a false picture, although this would affect these tables only if the Panjandra and/or the more reticent Members could be shown to fall predominantly within one or other of the social categories we have employed.

None the less, there are certain weighty considerations to be urged on the other side. Such evidence as we have (p. 41-2 above) does suggest that those who did not sign Motions were predominantly *not* enthusiastic about the topic of such motions. In one case it has proved possible to check the findings of one of these "quantitative" tables with the results of a free vote in the Commons. This was the Civil Liberties scale and it was checked against the way Labour Members voted in the division on the Street Offences Bill. The behaviour of Members in that division was highly consistent with the findings of the table. Secondly, the number of signatories of each class varies with the topic under discussion. Yet if the number of signatures depended primarily on whether Members were generally "high signers" or "low signers" (i.e., irrespective of topic) one would expect certain categories to be high signers in *every* case, regardless of the topic. This is not so. For instance: on anti-colonialism, civil liberties, and humanitarianism, the Worker category signed fewer Motions per head than any other occupational group. Yet in all social welfare matters it signed more Motions per head than any other group.

Thirdly, there is some evidence to support the view that "high signers" also tend to be more persistent at question time and more vocal in debate than the reluctant signers. This suggests that the latter tend to be men with few strongly marked opinions on the issues dividing the party, men who are content to follow the initiative of their leaders.

The evidence for this assertion has been found by counting up the number of questions asked by Members and the number of interventions in debate. This was done for the Conservative party for the 1957–58 session and figures were compared with the number of Motions signed on selected political matters* between 1955 and 1958. The results are shown in Tables 19 and 20 below.

The number of questions asked is the more accurate index of Parliamentary activity, for each Member has an equal chance of

TABLE 19

Questions and Number of Motions Signed†

No. of Motions Signed	*No. of Questions Asked* 0	%	1-10	%	11-20	%	21-50	%	Over 51	%	Total	%
1 and 2	8	23	18	53	5	15	3	9	—	—	34	100
3–5	11	15	44	62	8	11	5	7	3	4	71	100
6–10	7	8	47	57	16	19	9	11	4	5	83	100
Over 10	1	3	13	37	6	17	5	14	10	29	35	100
	27	12	122	55	35	16	22	10	17	8	223	100

$\tau c = 0 \cdot 24$. Significant at 1%

TABLE 20

Number of Interventions in Debate and Number of Motions Signed

No. of Motions Signed	**No. of Interventions** 0	%	1	%	2-5	%	6-10	%	10-20	%	Over 20	%	Total	%
1-2	10	29	1	3	12	35	8	23	2	6	1	3	34	100
3-5	8	11	7	10	28	39	19	27	7	10	2	3	71	100
6-10	4	5	4	5	21	25	30	36	19	23	5	6	83	100
Over 10	3	9	—	—	9	26	10	29	10	29	3	9	35	100
	25	11	12	5	70	31	67	30	38	17	11	5	223	100

$\tau c = 0 \cdot 26$. Significant at 0·5%

* Motions on Commonwealth and European relations, on the Suez crisis, the United Nations, social policy, penal reform and civil liberties.

† Two questions on exactly the same topic counted as one. Speeches on different stages of a Bill counted as separate speeches, but interventions on the same stage were counted as one. Only Members who were backbenchers for the whole of our period were counted.

asking questions, and there is no limit on the total number a Member may put.* There is a large fortuitous element in debate, though, for a Member can only speak in debate if called upon by the Speaker or Chairman. Presumably, however, a Member who attends frequently, and persistently tries to catch the Speaker's eye is more likely to be called than one who comes rarely, and does not bother to engage the Speaker's attention. To this extent, interventions in debate provide some yardstick of a Member's parliamentary keenness. But whichever criterion is used, a propensity to sign EDMs is associated with a high degree of parliamentary activity. A quarter of the lowest signers (1 and 2) asked no questions at all, and another half asked fewer than ten; in contrast, only one of the highest signers (over ten) asked no questions, and three-fifths asked more than ten. Similarly, a third of the low signers did not speak in debate and less than a tenth spoke more than ten times; but of the high signers nearly two-fifths intervened frequently, and fewer than a tenth of them spoke not at all. We cannot, of course, probe behind the index of *Hansard* and measure the activity that goes on in party committees, and party meetings; we can only compare the propensity to sign with certain overt and easily measurable forms of parliamentary work.†

Broadly speaking, therefore, it does not seem unreasonable to assume that those who sign a high number of Motions on a given topic are more interested in it than those who sign few, and these in turn are more "interested" than those who sign none at all.

STATISTICAL APPENDIX TO ANNEX 1

The purpose of this Appendix is to describe the statistical tests and measures which have been used in the book and to discuss some of the problems which have arisen in their application to our data.

---

* Though questions for *oral* reply were of course restricted to three a day.

† One further qualification which must be made is that the number of Motions signed is not a completely fair measure of a Member's *propensity* to sign. The number signed is not independent of the kind of Motions tabled. An ardent United Nations Conservative had the opportunity of signing no less than four Motions to express his sympathy. But a Member critical of the U.N. had only one to sign between 1955 and 1959. Low signing, therefore, may reflect not merely apathy but an absence of congenial motions.

1. *The χ^2 test for association.*

The typical method of analysis has been to divide the M.P.s into categories according to occupation, education, etc., and then to compare the distribution of these groups over a spectrum of attitudes. In statistical terminology we have tested for associations between background factors and viewpoints on various issues. The test which we have used in this situation is χ^2. The method of calculation and the tables of significance levels may be found in any elementary text so will not be discussed here. There are, however, some details of application which call for special comment.

The justification for using the tabled significance levels depends upon no "expected" frequency being "too small". It is customary to regard expected frequencies of 5 as being the smallest which can be permitted without serious error. However, it has been shown (e.g. Cochran) that in large tables little error results if some expectations are smaller than this. In the absence of clear theoretical guidance on this matter we have usually kept to a minimum of 5, but a few exceptions to this rule have been allowed.

Two methods of avoiding small expected frequencies have been used. In the majority of cases we have omitted the whole category which gives rise to them. Thus, for example, the "business" category for Labour and some of the school groupings for the Conservatives were very small. The conclusions do not therefore apply to categories too small for inclusion in the analysis. A second alternative is to combine adjacent "wings". For example, if the "Left" contains too few Members it can be conflated with the "Centre". This method is specially suitable where small groups, such as the Co-op sponsored members in the Labour party, are in marked contrast to other M.P.s. Rather than leave them out altogether it seemed preferable to use a coarser grouping of attitudes.

Having applied a χ^2 test to a table and obtained a non-significant (or just significant) result, we have sometimes been faced with the following dilemma. Inspection of the table has suggested that a higher level of significance might have been reached by grouping some categories to bring out a contrast more sharply. This point can be illustrated by the "Size of majority" analyses for the Conservative Members. Examination of the tables often showed that the real contrast was between "marginal" and "non-marginal". A test using this dichotomy was sometimes significant even when the original analysis based on the full classification failed to indicate an association. Unfortunately, when the grouping is chosen as being that most likely to yield significance it is no longer true that the significance level measures the chance of erroneously rejecting the null hypothesis. In fact it will, in general, under-estimate this probability. In spite of this drawback we have sometimes given the results of tests under alternative groupings as being a useful means of indicating the way for further investigation.

Any omissions or groupings which have been made are noted beneath the tables along with the value of χ^2, and the significance level reached. The suffix attached to χ^2, for example χ^2_5, denotes the number of degrees of freedom.

2. *The* $\bar{\chi}^2$ *test.*

Some of our tables were constructed to reveal a trend in proportions. For example, in chapter 2 we wished to test whether the proportion voting against the Street Offences Bill decreased as we moved from left to right across the civil liberties spectrum. Although the χ^2 test can be used in this situation, it is not particularly sensitive to the presence of a trend as opposed to other kinds of inequality. A more powerful alternative test is provided by $\bar{\chi}^2$, which is a modified form of χ^2 specially designed for detecting trends. This is a new test described by one of us (D.J.B.) in two recent papers (*Biometrika* **46** (1959) pp. 36-48 and 328-335) where special tables of significance levels are given. In some cases the problem specifies the direction of the trend (if it exists) and in others it does not. This information has been taken into account in determining the level of significance.

The suffix attached to $\bar{\chi}^2$ refers to the numbers of proportions involved in the test, and is used in entering the tables of percentage points. The remarks about the size of expected frequencies for χ^2 apply also to $\bar{\chi}^2$ where relevant.

3. *The coefficient* τc

This is a coefficient of rank correlation. It has been used to correlate the position of Members on one attitude scale with their position on another. The coefficient has been used both for a test of significance and as a *measure* of the association. It thus enables us to compare the strengths of association in different tables.

When we say that τc is significant we mean that it differs significantly from zero; in other words there is definite evidence for the existence of a correlation. The suffix c distinguishes τc from two other, closely related, coefficients which have not been used in this book. For a full discussion of this topic the reader is referred to *Rank Correlation Methods* by M. G. Kendall.

The average rank correlation coefficient has been used in chapter 2 as a measure of overall concordance in a set of rankings. This method was suggested by A. S. C. Ehrenberg (*Biometrika*, 1962, page 82) but no method of testing significance is known.

In deciding whether or not an association has been established we have adopted the following rule: —

(a) If the test attains significance at the 5 per cent level (or higher) we have concluded that the association cannot be ascribed to chance and is therefore real.

(b) If the test is significant at the 10 per cent level but not at the 5 per cent level we have described the association as tentatively, or "provisionally" established. This is because we do not wish these cases to pass unnoticed. But we do not feel that the evidence is strong enough to merit an unqualified acceptance.

(c) All other associations can reasonably be explained in terms of chance fluctuations.

Annex 2 · The Composition of the Parliamentary Parties

ONE major difference in treatment between the two parties arises because certain Members have to be excluded from the count, because they were Whips, or frontbenchers, or because they died or resigned their seats and the like. For the Labour party these Members have been excluded from all counts; as a result a fixed number or population* of 236 Labour Members only has been considered. For the Conservative party, however, Members have been excluded from certain counts and included for others. Thus a fluctuating number has been taken into consideration. The reason for this difference of method is that the movement of back-benchers in and out of the front-bench was greater amongst the Conservatives (as the Government party) than in the Labour party. Now the Conservative population in any case formed a smaller proportion of M.P.s in the party than the Labour population, because of the many Members who continuously occupied Government posts and were therefore precluded from signing Motions. Some Members, moreover, held office for part of the period only and others died during the Parliament or came in at a by-election. This sometimes meant that a Member had the opportunity to sign all the Motions on one topic but not on another. To exclude such Members altogether would unnecessarily reduce the size of an already depleted population. With the Conservatives, therefore, the device was adopted of a "working" population for each subject; some Members were excluded from the working population for one topic but included for another. Members were excluded from particular working population for one broad reason—that they were not on the backbenches long enough to have the opportunity to sign an adequate range of Motions on a topic. This general reason covers a number of specific grounds—government office; entry into the House after the 1955 General Election; retirement; death; or elevation to the House of Lords. It does not include such reasons as

* Population is a term used by statisticians to connote the aggregate of units which are being studied.

illness or prolonged travel, information about which is difficult to obtain.

There would have been little to be gained from applying this device to the Labour party: there were few Members who were backbenchers for only part of the time, and as the Labour party tabled twice as many Motions as the Conservatives there was much less likelihood of a Labour M.P. being eligible to sign a full train of Motions on one topic but an incomplete train on another.

A second difference arises because some categories are relevant to one party and not to the other. Categories common to both parties are: Education, Occupation, Age, and Year of first entering Parliament. But in the Labour party it was desirable to analyse Members according to their sponsoring body: the Trades Unions or the Co-operative party, or Constituency Party. Such a distinction is inapplicable to the Conservative party. On the other hand, two categories established for the Conservative party find no counterpart in the analysis of the Labour party. The Conservative party has been divided according to the urban, rural or semi-rural character of the constituency: but there is little point in doing this for the Labour party which is overwhelmingly representative of urban areas. Again, the Conservative Members have been classified according to the size of their majority. For the Labour party, however, a sample analysis showed little correlation between size of majority and political behaviour. Accordingly, this classification by size of majority has been omitted in respect of the Labour party.

The third difference lies in the sub-classifications of two of the tables which are common to both the parties, viz., Occupation and Education; and this is due to the very different social composition of the two parties. There is nothing in the Conservative party that corresponds to the "Worker" category in the Labour party. The Miscellaneous Occupations cover a much wider range for the Labour party than for the Conservatives. Business, which accounts for less than one-tenth of the Labour party, accounts for over one-half of the Conservatives and accordingly has to be sub-divided when dealing with this party. Farmers and the Services are so few among the Labour Members that there they have to be classified along with either the Business group or the Professions.

The same kind of consideration applies to the educational categories in the two parties. The elementary school category which forms about one-third of the Labour ranks hardly exists in the Conservative party. Hence in this party the category "Non-Public Schools" has to cover the few elementary school Members and the secondary schools. In the Labour party these two categories have been shown separately: and a category of those proceeding to higher education by way of teacher training or Ruskin College has been distinguished in the Labour party, but not for the Conservatives where this type hardly existed. Likewise, the Oxford and Cambridge group in the Conservative party was big enough to permit their being segregated into distinct categories: in the Labour party it was too small to allow of this. These and the other differences which will be noticed in the tables are unavoidable since they reflect the vastly different educational composition of the two parties. Had identical categories been established for both parties alike it would have led, in either case, to separating certain types such as "elementary education" in the Conservative party or "Clarendon School only" in the Labour party, which would have been much too small for the least ambitious statistical operations.

To put these matters in a general way: it was never our intention to compare and contrast the composition of the Labour and Conservative parties for its own sake. Such an exercise is perfectly fitting in such works as Ross's *Elections and Electors,* or Butler's election surveys.* Our categories are operational: they have to be both relevant to the analysis of political attitudes and large enough to permit conclusions to be drawn from their behaviour.

THE LABOUR PARTY

OCCUPATION

All occupational classifications present difficulties. We decided to follow the four main categories established by Mr. Butler in his election surveys, and accordingly distinguished Workers, Miscellaneous Occupations, Business men and Professional men. Unlike his, however, our criterion of occupation is not the Member's earliest occupation but the one in which he was currently engaged, or failing that, in which he was last engaged previous to his

* *D. J. Butler. The British General Election of* 1951 (and successors for 1955,1959).

election.* Some Members were pursuing two or three vocations simultaneously and here it became arbitrary as to which one was to select as the main occupation. Finally some of Mr. Butler's sub-classifications admit of different interpretations. Is a part-time lecturer for the National Council of Labour Colleges to be deemed an "Adult Education Teacher"? Thus, although our categories are based on Mr. Butler's, the detail diverges.

Workers: Self-explanatory.

Professions: This includes, lawyers, doctors, dentists, school, university and adult-education teachers.

Business: This includes employers, most of whom were small business men such as butchers, painters and owner-managers, and managers and consultants.

Miscellaneous Occupations: This includes housewives, professional politicians, welfare workers, local government officers, insurance agents and estate valuers. It also includes journalists, party publicists, professional party organizers, and lecturers for bodies such as the National Council of Labour Colleges.

SPONSORSHIP OF CANDIDATES

Members were classified according to their sponsoring bodies, viz.

Trades Unions
Co-operative Party
Constituency Labour Party (C.L.P.)

EDUCATION

Elementary: This includes Members who had further education at night-school.

Elementary/Secondary+: This consists of Members from elementary or secondary schools who had some form of technical training or teacher training. It also includes those who attended Ruskin College, Oxford.

---

* Exception is made in the case of the "Workers". Most of these are Trades Union sponsored and a high proportion had become full time union officials prior to election. However, they have been classified as *Workers*, not as Miscellaneous Occupations.

Secondary:	Members whose education stopped at the secondary level.
University:	All graduates including Members who attended Inns of Court.

UNIVERSITY EDUCATION

*U*1:	Public school and Oxford or Cambridge.
*U*2:	Public school and other universities.
*U*3:	Grammar school and Oxford or Cambridge.
*U*4:	Grammar school and other universities.

AGE:

Members were classified according to their age on 31st December, 1958.

THE CONSERVATIVE PARTY

The Conservative "Population"

Two hundred and seventy Conservative backbenchers are included in our study and we are referring to them as the Conservative "population". Members who were in the government throughout the period were naturally excluded as Ministers do not sign backbench Motions. There were also a few backbenchers who did not sign any of the selected political Motions. Usually, there were obvious reasons for this restraint; some, like Sir Donald Kaberry, held office in the Conservative party hierarchy and presumably did not wish to commit themselves publicly on contentious matters; others held politically sensitive posts, like that of Parliamentary Private Secretary to the Prime Minister. Others died or retired early in the life of the Parliament, or entered late at a by-election. Where there were reasons of this kind for particular Members not signing any of the selected Motions, the Members were excluded altogether from the "population". When all such Members were accounted for, only three persistent non-signers were left. The other 267 Members committed themselves on at least one of the political topics discussed later—foreign affairs, social policy, penal reform and civil liberties.

The effect of excluding some M.P.s from a particular topic but not from others is that the size and composition of the "working" population varies a little from subject to subject. Members excluded from the population were not a cross-section of the party. They included a disproportionately large number of M.P.s from the most exclusive public schools, of M.P.s in their forties, and of M.P.s from rural constituencies. The reason for this is that the Members who accepted or vacated office during the three years were drawn, to a disproportionate extent, from these groups. The three habitual non-signers were excluded, from each and every count. These exclusions, of course, do not affect our findings about the behaviour of different groups. In each case we confine ourselves to those M.P.s who were not precluded by office or any similar impediment, from signing a full range of Motions on a given topic.

The Conservative population has been analysed by seven different criteria: occupation; school; university; age; date of first election to Parliament; size of majority; and type of constituency.

OCCUPATIONS

Members have been classified according to the occupation they followed during the period under review. Members who were devoting their whole time to their political work were classified according to the occupation they followed immediately before election. Where a Member was following some business occupation simultaneously with another vocation such as law, or farming, he was regarded as a business man.

Business:

Director of Public Companies: Directors of companies whose shares are quoted on the London Stock Exchange.

Directors of Private Companies: Directors of companies whose shares are not quoted on the London Stock Exchange.

Business Executives: This includes all Members in a managerial role who were not also company directors.

Business (Finance): Stock brokers, bullion brokers, underwriters, etc.

Farmers: This category includes landowners, etc.

Professions:

Lawyers: Self-explanatory.

H.M. Forces: Officers in the Regular Forces.

Other Professions: All other recognized professions.

Miscellaneous: Occupations: Journalists, publicists, political organizers, miscellaneous administrators, housewives, and Members with no employment.

A considerable number of M.P.s holding some kind of business directorship also pursued at one time a profession such as the law or the armed services. It is possible that it was the former profession, rather than the current directorship, which most influenced a Member's outlook. A second classification, therefore, took all Members who followed law at any time, and all Members who were in the regular forces, irrespective of their occupation in the present or the immediate past. In the event, however, no significant differences in attitude were found between these categories based on former occupation.

TABLE 21
The Conservative Party: by Occupations

	No.	%
All Law	69	26
All H.M.F.	42	16
	111	42
Ex-Law	33	12
Ex-H.M.F.	25	9
	58	21

SCHOOL

Clarendon Public Schools: * Eton, Harrow, Winchester, Charterhouse, Shrewsbury, Rugby, Westminster, St. Paul's and Merchant Taylors.

Other Public Schools: All other schools represented at the Headmasters' Conference or on the Governing Bodies Association of Public Schools. The Royal Naval College is also included.

Non-Public Schools: All other British boys' schools.

* This category has been chosen because it includes the most expensive and exclusive public schools; other definitions might have been used based on school fees or a subjective assessment. It seemed, however, that the simplest method was to take the Clarendon Public Schools which were so named because they were the subject of a Royal Commission under Lord Clarendon in 1864.

The Rest: All women; male Members who went to school in the Commonwealth.

Where a Member attended more than one school and these schools were in different categories he has been classified under the school which enjoys the greater social esteem.

UNIVERSITIES

Oxford: Self-explanatory.

Cambridge: Self-explanatory.

Other Universities: All other recognized universities, whether in Great Britain, Ireland, or abroad, and the Inns of Court.

Sandhurst: Self-explanatory.

None: This includes Members who attended military, naval and air-force colleges other than Sandhurst.

Where a Member attended two or more universities he has been classified under the university enjoying the greater social prestige.

MAJORITY

The majority has been calculated as the Member's majority over his nearest opponent at the 1955 General Election, the figure being calculated as a percentage of the total votes cast. Where a Member was elected at a by-election after the 1955 General Election his predecessor's majority has been taken.

Marginal: 5% or less majority.
Semi-Marginal: 6%–11% majority.
Comfortable: 11%–16% majority.
Safe: 17%–31% majority.
Impregnable: Over 31% majority.

TYPE OF CONSTITUENCY

Constituencies are classified as urban, semi-rural and rural according to the proportion of the population living in urban or rural areas. Population figures are normally those obtaining at the 1951 census. In some cases however, there were alterations to the local government boundaries between 1951 and 1955 and in these constituencies the populations of the adjusted areas at the date of the change were taken.

All P.	Misc.	Cl.	O.P.	O.B.	Oth.	Ox.	C.	Oth.	S.	None	U. 41	41/50	51/60	Ov. 60	1955	1951	1950	1945	War	Pre-war	M.	M.C.	C.	S.	Imp.	U.	S./R.	R.
	8																											
	7																											
	5																											
	38																											
	9	67	24	8	1																							
	10	43	50	3	3																							
	9	3	52	39	6																							
	6	56	44	—	—																							
	7	12	36	43	9																							
	12	45	33	17	5	40	26	12	2	19																		
	6	42	38	18	2	25	27	7	6	36																		
	10	30	41	23	6	27	18	16	6	33																		
	7	26	37	30	7	23	19	16	9	33																		
	11	35	37	21	6	27	29	11	—	32	39	35	26	—														
	11	40	38	19	2	26	17	11	9	38	21	49	21	9														
	8	38	28	28	5	27	23	15	3	32	12	37	42	10														
	—	29	42	26	3	18	11	8	13	50	3	42	37	18														
	7	33	53	13	—	47	33	13	—	7	—	20	60	20														
	10	33	44	15	8	33	23	15	10	19	—	6	46	48														
	14	19	42	33	6	22	19	6	3	50	31	19	33	19	58	22	11	3	—	6								
	10	41	31	21	7	34	14	17	7	28	24	52	17	7	31	21	31	3	—	14								
	7	29	45	21	5	19	29	19	5	29	17	29	40	14	26	10	33	7	10	14								
	10	44	29	22	5	30	24	13	5	28	10	37	41	12	10	17	28	20	5	20								
	4	35	45	16	4	30	21	9	9	31	10	30	35	25	16	18	12	21	9	25								
	10	32	39	24	4	25	22	14	7	32	15	32	39	14	22	20	26	8	5	19	15	14	16	32	23			
	5	33	29	33	5	29	19	19	14	19	19	43	24	14	19	10	24	29	5	14	5	5	24	48	19			
	5	47	36	12	5	39	25	3	3	30	19	36	34	11	23	14	22	20	6	14	11	9	19	33	28			
	14	27	41	30	3	22	22	24	3	30	14	30	41	16	19	16	38	3	5	19	16	11	8	32	32	100	—	—
	7	33	40	21	6	37	21	3	9	30	15	39	31	15	19	16	28	12	9	15	9	9	18	37	27	58	9	33
	7	43	29	21	7	36	7	14	14	29	14	29	50	7	21	14	14	29	—	21	29	7	36	21	7	21	14	64
	4	46	31	19	4	23	38	12	—	27	23	31	31	15	23	23	15	15	4	19	19	8	12	27	35	65	4	31
	—	36	36	28	—	32	24	16	4	24	24	40	24	12	36	12	24	16	—	12	8	8	24	48	12	56	20	24
	6	29	46	23	3	17	23	11	11	37	9	29	51	11	17	23	17	17	—	26	11	17	14	29	29	83	6	11
	14	54	29	11	7	36	21	7	4	32	21	36	32	11	29	14	21	14	11	11	11	21	25	32	11	29	18	54
	12	35	38	19	8	23	15	12	4	46	4	23	35	38	15	15	—	27	12	31	15	8	4	23	50	—	—	—

This method of calculation has not been applied to Scotland because her local government structure and nomenclature differ from that of England and Wales. Scottish constituencies have been shown separately and divided into burghs and counties. Ulster has not been divided into rural and urban categories.

Urban: Constituencies in which less than a third of the population lived in rural districts.

Semi-rural: Constituencies in which between a third and a half lived in rural districts.

Rural: Constituencies where more than a half of the population lived in rural districts.

Scottish Burghs: Self-explanatory.

Scottish Counties: Self-explanatory.

Ulster: Self-explanatory.

Annex 3 · Pacificism in the Labour Party

WE have noted that a revulsion from the use of force in international affairs is a pronounced feature of the Labour party. In its extreme form this appears as pacifism. For the most part, however, it appears in qualified and conditional form. This generalized form of the sentiment we call "pacificism".

Many Motions expressed this sentiment, but in different degrees of intensity. It is therefore possible to range them in a crude scale of intensity.

There are really two alternative ways of doing this, according to the criterion we choose to adopt. One way would be to segregate the signatories of all Motions expressing a special degree of concern about the H-bomb, and to treat these as the more pacifist of the two halves of the party. The number of such signatories is 79. The number of Members expressing no opinion is 41. Thus we could divide the party into three groups:

Those expressing a special concern over the H-bomb	79
Those expressing other opinions on defence	116
Those expressing no views	41
Total	236

For certain purposes this classification has its advantages. It is useful to be able to see how far these 79 Members had social characteristics in common, and how far they were different from the rest of the party. It is also useful in analysing Members' views on foreign policy.

It is questionable, however, whether this is the best classification for detecting degrees of pacificism, and for this reason. Of the 79 Members described here as "expressing special concern", 45 committed themselves in one Motion or another, to the unilateral renunciation of H-bomb tests *while this was still contrary to party policy* and/or to the unilateral renunciation of H-Bomb manufacture—which is still contrary to party policy.* These 45 unilateralists expressed the most extreme pacificistic sentiments in the

* At the time of writing.

party, and may be grouped together as the Extreme wing.

The remaining 34 Members of the original 79 did indeed express concern about the testing of H-bombs, in one or both of two Motions—EDM 49/1955, tabled on February 13th, 1956, and EDM 48/1956 tabled on March 4th, 1957. But in neither case did these Motions go beyond urging the Government to take the initiative in securing international agreement on the banning of H-bomb tests; and "that Britain should propose the immediate cessation of H-bomb tests" had formed part of the Labour election manifesto of 1955. Thus signature of these Motions does not, by itself, imply a special degree of pacificism. On the other hand, it must fairly be admitted that some of these 34 Members subsequently expressed themselves in terms such as to suggest they were willing to contemplate unilateral nuclear disarmament of Britain. Furthermore, they may have signed these two Motions, rather than the unilateral Motions, in order not to embarrass their party.

Nevertheless, the fact remains that by official party line standards, these motions were innocuous. We have therefore decided not to consider them as expressing a degree of pacificism unless we find signature of them associated with the signature of other Motions. The effect of this on our subsequent analysis is that the Left-wing is cut down to its minimum proportions.

Thus our Left-wing consists of 45 unilateralists. Less extreme than these, but exhibiting a high degree of pacificism were the Members who, though not unilateralists, nevertheless signed one or other of the three Motions which opposed H-patrols and/or missile bases. It will be remembered from p. 24 above that these three Motions succeeded one another rapidly, between December 4th, 1957 and February 12th, 1958, when the party was labouring under the emotions raised by the Russian sputniks and the Russian pressure for a summit conference. Furthermore, these Motions were neither "orthodox" nor "unorthodox"; there was no official policy on these matters at the time the Motions were tabled, and indeed the last of the three Motions, appearing on February 12th, antedated the party's official statement in "Disarmament and Nuclear War" (March 6th, 1958).

UNILATERALISTS AND OTHERS

The group of EDM's signatories whose rank as *Left,* consists of four Motions. EDM 32/1955 was tabled on November 29th, 1955. It deplored the testing of H-bombs by the U.S.A. and the U.S.S.R. It believed that the deterrent effects of such weapons were disproportionate to the risks involved and that the tests might be dangerous in themselves. It therefore asked the Government not to undertake tests, and to ask the U.S.A. and the U.S.S.R. to follow suit. EDM 89/1955 was tabled on June 25th, 1956. It drew attention to the Medical Research Council's report on the hazards of nuclear radiations and baldly stated that the Government should announce the ending of its experimental explosions of atomic and thermo-nuclear weapons.

At June 25th, 1956 no British tests of thermo-nuclear weapons had, in fact, been carried out. Hence the effect of the Motions would have prevented a British H-bomb from ever being tested. As Mr. George Brown pointed out on March 29th, 1957, if we wished to show the aggressor that we had a bomb, i.e., if we wanted to use the possession of the bomb as a deterrent, we must first show that it had been successfully tested. And as Mr. Bevan was to point out in October, 1957, an end to testing meant *pro hac tempore* an end to manufacture. Thus the effect of the Motion would have prevented the bomb's being manufactured, or robbed it of deterrent value. Finally, it must be noticed this decision not to proceed to tests was to be unilateral and unconditional.

For these reasons we draw no distinction between the Motions calling for unilateral abandonment of testing and those calling for unilateral abandonment of manufacture. The first of the latter, since it was signed by Mr. Pargiter and nobody else, does not call for further mention. The second was technically an amendment to another Motion, EDM 54/1957. This amendment was tabled on March 12th, 1958 and can only be considered as a deliberate affront to the party leaders who, on March 6th, had published the policy statement on "*Disarmament and Nuclear War*". This went no further along the unilateralist road than to declare that, if returned to power, the Party would unilaterally *suspend* tests, and for a limited period. The amendment to EDM 54/1957, signed by 27 Members, demanded, however, the immediate and unilateral cessation of "tests or production of nuclear weapons".

The second group, the signatories of which we call Centre, consists of three Motions concerned with H-patrols and missile bases.

We have already described the circumstances in which they were conceived.* EDM 14/1957 believed that the H-patrols "created a state of emergency which is not warranted by the facts of the international situation", and went on to opine that "the safety and well-being of the British and the peace of the world would be far better assured by the ending of this panic measure." Eighty-five Members signed it. EDM 20/1957 deplored the Prime Minister's action "in committing this country to the establishment of four ballistic missile bases in Scotland at the cost of many millions of pounds" and "condemned his acquiescence in American custody and control of the nuclear warheads and the exposure of the areas concerned as enemy targets while means of defence are still lacking". Ninety Members signed this. EDM 32/1957 called on the Government "not to enter into, or ratify, or implement any agreement by which any foreign power became entitled to acquire further British bases or to use these for missile warfare until after a General Election". This was signed by only 26 Members. Despite the large number of Members signing these Motions, when the 45 "unilateralists" are withdrawn only 68 remain who had signed one or more of these three Motions.

The third group of Motions is one which may be described as the "Strengthen UNO" group. It contains three Motions. One was EDM 66/1956, tabled in May 1957. This asked for the reform of the U.N. Charter so as to give the UNO a permanent army, and bases on which to deploy it. Thirty-eight Labour Members signed this. Another was EDM 11/1957, calling for an UN police force of 20,000 men to patrol the area between hostile or belligerent states. One hundred and twenty-seven Members signed this, of whom 111 were Labour. The most important Motion, however, was EDM 55/1957, tabled on March 13th, 1958. This Motion was a deliberate retort to the amendment to EDM 54/1957, by which 27 Labour Members, in flat defiance of their party's official policy statement, had demanded the unilateral abandonment of H-tests and production. It was conceived as an all-party Motion, and indeed 2 Liberals and 34 Conservatives signed it: but the bulk of its support came from the Labour party who contributed 175 signatures. The Motion ran:

---

* Pp. 23-4 above.

"This House, appreciating the deep concern of the people of this nation over the hydrogen bomb, urges the necessity to concentrate on the fundamental issue which is the design and provision of an authority to be set up by the United Nations, responsible for the abolition under effective control of all nuclear and conventional weapons of mass destruction and for the effective reduction of conventional forces and armaments."

Despite the very large numbers signing the last two of the Motions, the total number of Members signing any of these, and not already signing Motions in the Centre and Left group, was only 82. Many Left-wingers and still more of the Centre sensed no incompatability between signing these rather unspecific Motions, and the more extreme Motions. Those Members who signed only Motions in this group we have styled Right-wingers.

Some Members signed none of the Motions listed here. These are brought together under the heading "Uncommitted".

The numbers and proportions of Members in each of these categories is shown in table 24.

TABLE 24

Distribution of Pacificist Attitudes in the Labour Party

Left: (Unilateral banners)	45	19%
Centre: (Anti-Missile bases and/or H-patrols)	68	29%
Right: (Strengthen U.N.)	82	35%
Uncommitted:	41	17%
Total	236	100%

How far do various strata in the Labour party display similar degrees of pacificism? We proceed to compare the attitudes of social categories within the Labour party to the degrees of pacificism which were displayed.

Miscellaneous Occupations were much the most pacificistic, and conversely fell off in support of the Right position. By contrast, the Workers were poorly represented among the Left, (only 1 in 8 of their number) and their proportion rose as the viewpoint became less extreme. The same tendency is noticeable among the Professions.

TABLE 25

The Pacificism of the Labour Party: by occupational groups

	Left Unilateral banners (tests &/or mnfr.)	%	*Centre* Anti-Missile bases &/or H-patrols	%	*Right* Strengthen U.N.	%	*Uncom-mitted*	%	*Totals*	%
Workers:	10	13	24	30	35	44	10	13	79	100
Miscellaneous Occupations:	18	30	19	30	15	25	9	15	61	100
Business:	6	26	5	22	9	39	3	13	23	100
Professions:	11	15	20	27	23	32	19	26	73	100
	45	19	68	29	82	35	41	17	236	100

Business omitted, $\chi^2_6 = 14 \cdot 57$. Significant at 2·5%

The main lines are clear: Workers, Professions and to a much less degree Business "polled" *more* heavily the more moderate the pacificism. By contrast the Miscellaneous Occupations came out in their greatest numbers on the Left and Centre positions.

TABLE 26

The Pacificism of the Labour Party: by sponsorship of M.P.s

	Left	%	*Centre*	%	*Right*	%	*Uncom-mitted*	%	*Total*	%
T.U.s	10	13	24	31	34	44	10	13	78	100
Co-ops	6	29	9	43	5	24	1	4	21	100
CLP	29	21	35	26	43	31	30	22	137	100
	45	19	68	29	82	35	41	17	236	100

T.U.'s + CLP vs. Co-ops.
Left + Centre, Right + Uncommitted.
$\chi^2_1 = 4 \cdot 13$. Significant at 5%

This is an interesting table. In the first place it appears that the Co-operators, Trades Unionists and CLP candidates did not act as "blocs"; for each category is to be found distributed over the whole range of attitudes. Secondly, the degree of commitment is noteworthy. It is often said that the CLP candidates tend to be more "aware" of foreign policy matters than the Trades Union candidates. The table shows that this is unjustified: only 13 per cent of the T.U. group failed to express an opinion as against 22 per cent of the CLP candidates.

Thirdly, there does not appear to be very much difference between the viewpoints of the T.U. group and the CLP group. Trades union candidates were less extreme than the CLP, but were more heavily represented in the Centre. If one added Left and Centre together, the T.U. and CLP groups behaved rather similarly. This is reflected in the results of the χ^2 test—if the Co-operators are left out of account, the table is significant only at a 10 per cent. level. In other words, only a provisional association can be asserted between pacificism and membership of either the T.U.-sponsored or the CLP group of candidates.

The situation is transformed when the Co-operators are taken into account. As the table shows, these were both "aware" and extreme. All but one of their members expressed a view, and nearly three out of four were in the Left and Centre categories. When they are included, the table becomes significant at the 5 per cent level which is high.

There *is* therefore an association between sponsorship and pacificism; but this is mostly if not entirely due to the markedly distinctive behaviour of the Co-operators as compared with the rest of the Labour party.

This result is consistent with the association, already established, between pacificism and occupation. There it was shown that the Miscellaneous Occupations were the most pacificistic, and that the Workers and Professions reacted similarly and were the least pacificistic. Now the T.U.-sponsored group is largely co-incident with Workers who make up 81 per cent of its numbers: while 54 per cent of the CLP group is made up of Professions or Workers. By contrast, the small Co-op group consists, to the extent of 52 per cent, of Miscellaneous Occupations. This is not to say that the behaviour of the sponsorship-groups is to be interpreted as *due* to their occupational make-up; it might equally well be true that the behaviour of the occupational groups is due to their sponsoring bodies. We are merely drawing attention to the fact that there is a connexion between the sponsorship-groups and occupational background, and that a degree of consistency between the results of the two tables is, therefore, only to be expected.

There was no association between the degree of pacificism and the kind of education received: those educated at elementary schools, secondary schools or universities all reacted similarly. There were important differences, however, *inside* the category of the university-educated. This is not homogenous: on the contrary we have established four categories here.

U.1: Public Schools + Oxford or Cambridge	25
U.2: Public Schools + All other universities	15
U.3: Secondary Schools + Oxford or Cambridge	10
U.4: Secondary Schools + All other universities	40
Not known	3
	93

TABLE 27

The Pacificism of the University-educated: in the Labour Party

	Left	%	*Centre*	%	*Right*	%	*Uncommitted*	%	*Total*	%
U.1:	1	4	4	16	14	56	6	24	25	100
U.2:	4	27	2	13	3	20	6	40	15	100
U.3:	1	10	3	30	5	50	1	10	10	100
U.4:	10	25	18	45	8	20	4	10	40	100
	16		30		27		17		90	

U.1 + U.2 vs. U.3 + U.4: $\chi^2_4 = 12 \cdot 71$
U.1 + U.3 vs. U.2 + U.4: $\chi^2_4 = 11 \cdot 92$
(Significant at 1 per cent)

From this table we can find out if there was any association between pacificism and the type of school attended (irrespective of the type of university); and between pacificism and the type of university attended (irrespective of the kind of school).

Those who attended grammar schools were more pacificistic than those coming from public schools. Those who went to universities other than Oxford and Cambridge were more pacifistic than those who went to Oxford and Cambridge. In both cases the association is established at the highly significant level of 1 per cent. As the table shows, this double association is strikingly evident when the behaviour of the U.1's is contrasted with the U.4's: the first, from public school to Oxford and Cambridge were overwhelmingly less pacifistic than those proceeding from grammar schools to other universities.

These results throw an important light on the relative importance of education and occupation. The Professions were almost wholly (86 per cent) university-educated, but the U.4's outnumbered the U.1's by two to one. Again, the grammar schools outnumbered those from public schools by four to three; and the other universities outnumbered those from Oxford and Cambridge by nearly two to one. On any count, therefore, one might have expected the Professions to be distinctively pacifistic; but they were preponderantly Right-wing or uncommitted. The only conclusion possible is, therefore, that those university men who were Professionals tended to be predominantly Right-wing and uncommitted, whereas those of them who were Miscellaneous Occupations or Business men were correspondingly very pacifistic. Thus, it is the profession, not the educational background, which is the relevant factor in the shaping of attitudes.

No association can be established between pacificism and age; the reactions of all age-groups were rather similar.

There remains one more question—were the more recently elected less or more pacificistic than the long established? The findings for this problem are set out in Table 28.

TABLE 28

Pacificism in the Labour Party: By first year entering Parliament

	Left	%	*Centre*	%	*Right*	%	*Uncommitted*	%	*Total*	%
1955– :	5	26	8	43	5	26	1	5	19	100
1950–54:	6	13	13	27	13	27	15	33	47	100
1945–49:	30	23	31	24	52	40	18	13	131	100
1940–44:	—	—	4	44	3	33	2	23	9	100
Pre-War:	4	13	12	40	9	30	5	17	30	100
	45		68		82		41		236	

$\chi^2_6 = 11\cdot18$. Significant at 10%
'55 + 50, '45 + 40–44.

This hints at the possibility that the post-1954 generation were somewhat more pacificistic than their seniors; but the association is only provisional.

Annex 4 · The Parliamentary Labour Party and Foreign Affairs

THE GERMAN PROBLEM

Members have been divided into Left-, Centre-, and Right-wing factions on the issue of European disengagement and the future of Germany. The basis of this classification consists of a group of three Motions and Amendments tabled in February, 1959. On these we have superimposed three Motions tabled between June 1955 and December 1958.

The scale is as follows:

		Total
The Left		
Signatories of EDM 26/1958	37	
Signatories (other than the above)	7	
	——	44
The Centre		
Signatories of EDM 38/1958 only +		
Signatories of EDM 38/1958 other than the above ...	44	44
The Right		
Signatories of Amendment to EDM 26/1958 only ...	70	
Signatories of EDM 60/1957 only	16	
	——	86
Remainder		62
		——
		236

The basic EDM's were 26/1958, the so-called Silverman Motion, accounting for 37 of the 44 members of the Left; the Amendment to this Motion (the Bellenger-Morrison Amendment), accounting for 70 of the 86 Members of the Right; and the signatories of EDM 38/1958, the so-called "United" Motion accounting for the 44 Members of the Centre.

To explain the classification, it is first of all necessary to explain these three basic EDMs.

In April 1958, the National Executive of the Labour party had formulated its views on Germany and disengagement, in its policy pronouncement called *"Disengagement in Europe"*, and this was adopted by the Conference in October 1958. For once the party seemed united on its European policy. The plan was:

"(1) Gradual withdrawal under effective international control of foreign forces of all kinds from East and West Germany, Poland, Czechoslovakia and Hungary.

(2) Establishment of effective international control over the level and type of national armaments and armed forces agreed for these countries.

(3) German reunification within a framework to be agreed and guaranteed by the four Powers (Britain, France, U.S.A. and U.S.S.R.) including free elections, leaving the ways and means to be settled by the Germans themselves.

(4) Negotiation of a European security treaty, backed by the four powers, to guarantee the territorial integrity of countries in the area.

(5) Withdrawal of the countries in the area from NATO and the Warsaw Pact—"

Now some of this is very ambiguous indeed, and notably item (3). It was from this ambiguity that the controversy of February 1959 sprang, and it appeared, not for the first time, that what seemed clear and specific had been acceptable to factions with differing standpoints.

For in November 1958 Mr. Khrushchev suddenly resurrected the problem of Germany. Questioning the status of West Berlin, he gave the West till May 17th 1959, in which either to accept his solution or else come to some kind of understanding with him. Hence, in January 1959, Mr. Macmillan and Mr. Selwyn Lloyd decided to visit Khrushchev on a "voyage of exploration". The trouble in the Labour party sprang up on February 2nd, just before the Prime Minister and Foreign Secretary were due to set off. Mr. Sydney Silverman tabled his EDM 26/1958, which ran thus:

"This House, realising that the present international tension cannot be relieved without a solution of the problem of Germany and without a peace treaty which safeguards Germany's neighbours against a resurgence of German military aggression, would welcome the *de facto* recognition of the German Democratic Republic by Her Majesty's Government and the formation by agreement between that Republic and the German Federal Republic, of an all-German Federal Council with which a treaty of peace could be negotiated, providing for the admission of a United Germany to the United Nations and her exclusion from military alliances, in pursuance of a policy of disengagement—"

This Motion quite certainly went beyond official policy by demanding the *de facto* recognition of the East German Government. (Mr. Bevan himself made this point.)* To this Mr. Zilliacus retorted that the Motion merely "made explicit some of the things implicit in (party) policy". And indeed, even if this view be unacceptable, it is hard to say that the *de facto* recognition of East Germany, and the formation of an all-German Federal Council is logically or verbally inconsistent with item 3 of the 5-point policy statement cited above.

Forty-eight Members had signed Mr. Silverman's Motion, when the Labour Right reacted. On Thursday, February 5th, there appeared on the Order Paper what was technically an amendment to Mr. Silverman's Motion but was in practice, a quite different one. This Motion was sponsored by Messrs. J. B. Hynd, Bellenger, Morrison, Arthur Henderson, Creech Jones and Kenneth Younger. All six were former Ministers. They were rapidly joined by 108 others, including twelve former Ministers, and six Members who now withdraw their names from Silverman's Motion.

The "Amendment" ran:

> "This House realising that the present international tension cannot be relieved without a solution of the problem of Germany, therefore urges Her Majesty's Government to take the initiative in convening a Four Power Conference for the purpose of seeking agreement on terms for the re-unification of Germany under a freely elected government, and the drafting of a peace treaty which would enable Germany, in membership of the United Nations, to play her full part in the maintenance of world peace and economic advancement."

This was as vague as the Silverman Motion was specific, and the sponsors of the Silverman Motion were not slow to point this out. "The question is what Britain should propose at such a conference," they said, "To keep on insisting that not only must Germany be united by free elections but also that a German Government so elected must be free to join NATO is to ensure that such a conference would fail. Any Labour Member who insisted on that would be in direct conflict with Labour policy—"† In fact, the Bellenger-Morrison Amendment not only did not " '*Insist*' on that". but did not even suggest it. Nevertheless Zilliacus, for the Leftist group, maintained that this was what Morrison and Bellenger secretly meant when they talked of Germany being "enabled to play her full part in the maintenance of world peace". "Mr.

* *Manchester Guardian,* February 13th, 1959.
† *Manchester Guardian,* February 10th, 1959.

Morrison and Mr. Bellenger approved of that wording," he said, "because they believe that the North Atlantic Treaty Organization is essential to 'the maintenance of world peace' and consequently that to play her full part in that laudable endeavour united Germany must be allowed to enter NATO—".*

The tabling of the "Amendment" to Silverman's Motion and the explanations and charges put out by both sides first brought discredit on the Party, and then ridicule. (Nineteen Members who signed the Amendment found that their names had been printed as supporting Silverman's Motion, and one of these names turned out to be Dr. Donald Johnson, the Conservative Member for Carlisle, instead of Douglas Johnston the Labour Member for Paisley.) In the House of Commons a Conservative Member drew the Prime Minister's attention to the Motion and the Amendment standing on the Order Paper, and asked whether the coming foreign affairs debate would provide an opportunity "to find out what their foreign policy on Germany is"; to which the Prime Minister returned: "I find a certain delicacy in pressing this question too far. I am reminded of the answer to a question in a theology paper about the major and minor prophets to which the examinee replied: "Far be it from me to distinguish between these holy men—"†

Furthermore, the Opposition wished to debate foreign affairs, and the problem of Germany in particular, before the Prime Minister set off on his voyage to Moscow. In these circumstances, the Foreign Affairs group of the Labour Party composed a new Motion, designed to attract signatories from both camps and present a united front in Parliament. This Motion, EDM 38/1958, tabled on February 12th, 1959, simply reprinted the official five-point policy of the Party as set out in "*Disengagement in Europe*" and adopted by the Scarborough Conference. Here at any rate was something the whole party could subscribe to, since it was the Scarborough official policy with neither additions or omissions. With this in view, it seems to have been agreed that Mr. Silverman should withdraw his Motion No. 26, and with two of his coadjutors become the sponsor of the new Motion, while Mr. Hynd, Mr. Morrison and Mr. Bellenger should act as the other three sponsors.‡

* *Manchester Guardian,* February 24th, 1959.
† *H.C. Debates,* February 12th, 1959, col. 1362.
‡ *Manchester Guardian,* February 18th, 1959.

But this neither Mr. Morrison nor Mr. Bellenger would consent to do! And their refusal set off another round of recrimination, and resulted in this farcical—and humiliating—consequence, that whereas 150 Members had signed either the Silverman Motion or the "amendment", less that half put their names to the "unified" Motion EDM 38! "The omission of the names of Mr. Bellenger and Mr. Morrison is not accidental," said the *Manchester Guardian*. "Mr. Bellenger said yesterday that he had been disinclined to sign a Motion which had been designed to patch over the distinct differences of approach to the German problem which were evident in the contrast between the wording of Mr. Silverman's original Motion and that of (the) amendment."*

To this Mr. Zilliacus replied that the real reason for their not signing was that "it reproduced the terms of the party's policy as framed by the N.E.C. and adopted by the Scarborough Conference —and that policy is explicit on the point that united Germany must be excluded from membership of NATO and of the Warsaw alliance. In short, Mr. Morrison and Mr. Bellenger agree with the Government and disagree with the Labour party about admitting united Germany to NATO—"† To this charge, neither Bellenger nor Morrison made any specific reply. It became clear from the foreign affairs debate on February 19th that to Mr. Zilliacus the five-point programme of the Labour party meant that "West Germany should be compelled to leave NATO": a view from which even his co-signatory Mr. Hynd, vigorously dissented.‡

Thus Labour Members fell into three main groups. First, there were the original signatories of the Silverman Motion excluding six backsliders who removed their names and supported Morrison and Bellenger. They numbered 37 of the 236 Members with whom we are concerned. These Members also signed the "unified" Motion, it is true. "The Left," explained Mr. Zilliacus "had no difficulty in signing the 'reunified' Motion, because it reproduced the five points of the party's disengagement policy on Germany and we agree with that policy—our Motion merely made explicit some of the things implicit in it." Thus the "*Left*" is defined as the signa-

---

* *Manchester Guardian*, February 18th, 1959.

† *Manchester Guardian*, February 24th, 1959.

‡ *H.C. Debates*, February 19th, 1959. Col. 637.

tories of the Silverman Motion, irrespective of whether they signed the re-unified Motion (38/1958) or not.

The second group, the Centre, consists of all Members, not being members of the Left, who signed the re-unified Motion, re-asserting the party line without any kind of gloss. Some had signed the Morrison-Bellenger amendment and some had not. Irrespective of this, all signatories of this Motion (38/1955) not already Members of the Left, were classified as Centre.

The Right, consisting of 70 Members, comprises those who opposed the Silverman Motion by supporting the Bellenger-Morrison amendment and *declined* to re-interpret this by signing the "re-unified Motion". Some must have failed to do so because they felt it unnecessary, or because they were absent or because they were tired of the business. Others, like Morrison and Bellenger declined to sign out of conviction. Thus this group of 70 is a *maximal* list.

The result of this analysis is to produce a classification thus:

Left
Signatories of EDM 26/1958 37
Centre
Signatories of EDM 38/1958. Other than above 44
Right
Signatories of Amendment to EDM 26/1958 other than above ... 70

Now to the numbers as here defined it is possible to add *seven* Members to the Left and 16 to the Right.

(a) *Additions to the Left*

These consist of seven Members who did *not* sign the Silverman Motion but had signed one or both of two earlier Motions: EDM 9/1955, and EDM 15/1957.

EDM 9/1955, signed by only 9 Members on July 21st, 1955, represents a "disengagement" policy long before disengagement became official Labour party policy. A European settlement was to be based on the U.N. Charter and to this end Germany was to be united within the Oder-Neisse frontiers by free elections under international supervision; and to be admitted with all European ex-enemy states to the U.N. Her armaments were to be limited under the Peace Treaty. All "occupation forces" were to be withdrawn from "ex-enemy states". There was to be an "all European" regional security and economic pact. Finally, the manufacture or testing of nuclear weapons was to cease immediately, pending the conclusion of a general disarmament convention. Thus the Motion implicitly rejected NATO as the basis of a European settlement.

The second Motion, EDM 15/1957 was tabled on December 5th, 1957, shortly before the NATO Council was due to meet. At first sight it appears remote from the question of Germany, for it called on the House not to respect any agreement which, in theory and practice would divest the House of its control of foreign and defence policies and its right to decide the "ultimate issues" of war and peace. At first blush, it appears to be a recrudescence of the demand, made by Macdonald, Morel, and Trevelyan, when they founded the Union of Democratic Control in 1914, for democratic control of foreign policy.

In fact, the circumstances of the time suggest a different interpretation. It was widely rumoured that the NATO Council would adopt a policy for siting American IRBM's throughout Western Europe to counter Russian missile superiority and it was this that worried the sponsors of the Motion. Accordingly, it attracted support from different quarters. It was supported by the pacifists and near pacifists because they did not want American missile bases in Britain. It was also supported by the extreme Right who objected to Britain becoming a client state of the U.S.A. But its chief appeal was to those who opposed the cold war and the policy of negotiation from strength, and hence to NATO as an instrument of these policies. It is no surprise that *every one* of the nine signatories of the earlier EDM 9/199, signed this one also.

The *Left* thus consists of 44 Members: (a) 37 signatories of the Silverman Motion and (b) 7 the signatories of either EDM 9/1955 or 15/1957.

(b) *Additions to the Right*

These comprise 16 Members whose sole expression of opinion on German affairs was to have signed EDM 60/1957. Tabled on March 18th, 1958, it opposed the rumoured arming of West Germany with nuclear weapons, on the grounds that this would "make it more difficult to secure the disengagement of forces and the nuclear free zone in central Europe on which the relaxation of tension between East and West will depend". Ninety-eight Members had signed this Motion. All but 16 however, signed one or other of the left-wing, right-wing or centre Motions. These 16 were therefore a residual category committed in very vague terms to the disengagement of forces in central Europe. They have consequently been grouped with the Right, bringing the total to 86.

This brings us to the classification adopted at p. 168 above. This classification is reproduced below, in Table 29, where it is now related to Members' pacificism. There is a strong association between "Leftism" on Germany, and pacificism in relation to the H-bomb. The table is significant at the level of 0·5 per cent, i.e., the probability of the association's occurring fortuitously is 199 to 1 against.

TABLE 29

Labour Attitudes to Germany and Disengagement as at February 19th, 1958: in their Relationship to Varying Degrees of Pacificism

	Left Pacificists		%	*Centre*		%	*Right Pacificists*		%	*No opinion*		%	*Total*	
The Left:														
Signatories of EDM 26/1958	26	30	66	11	14	21	0	0	—	0	0	—	37	44
Signatories of EDM 9/1955 &/or 13/1957, other than the above	4			3			0			0			7	
The Centre:														
Signatories of EDM 60/1957+38/1958	3			2			4			0			9	
Signatories of Amendment to EDM 26/1958+EDM38/1958	3	6	13	8	14	21	15	22	27	0	2	5	26	44
Signatories of EDM 38/1958 only	0			4			3			2			9	
The Right:														
Signatories of EDM 60/1957, only	3	5	11	9	24	35	2	38	46	2	19	46	16	86
Signatories of Amendment to EDM 26/1958, only	2			15			36			17			70	

TABLE 29 (continued)

		%		%		%		%	
*Other Views**	3		16		11		9		39
	4	9	16	24	22	27	20	49	62
No Views	1		0		11		11		23
	45	100	68	100	82	100	41	100	236

$\tau c = 0 \cdot 39$. Significant at $0 \cdot 5\%$

In this, the relationship between views on Germany and disengagement and pacificism reached as far as information permitted.

Since the Foreign Policy "Centre" was considerably further to the left than in 1955–57 when the Left pacificists' Motions were being tabled, it is easy to understand why 13 per cent of the unilateralists took the straight party line as their guide: and of the five Members who belong to the Right, three had gone on record for a "nuclear-free zone in Eastern Europe". In interpreting the results, it must be remembered that, even for Zilliacus, "the party had come about two-thirds of the way towards a Socialist foreign policy—"†

Of the Centre pacificists, the proportions subscribing to the Left and the Centre were 21 per cent in each case, rising to 35 per cent in the Right and as many as 24 per cent expressing no opinion. Among the Right pacificists this trend was more pronounced still; none of them belonged to the Left, as many as 27 per cent to the Centre, 46 per cent to the Right. Among the "No opinions on Pacificism" not only were there no Members on the Left but only 5 per cent in the Centre. Forty-six per cent belonged to the Right and 49 per cent to the "Other" or "No opinion" group.

In short, the more extreme the pacificism of a group, the more Left-wingers it contained, and the fewer Right-wingers: defining Left-wing and Right-wing here in respect to Members' views on the German problem.

These views can be expressed, once again, in terms of the signatories' views on the H-bomb, using the simpler category of "special concern at the H-bomb" (pp. 27-28, pp. 158-9).

These figures, where one quarter of the anti-H-bomb faction are on the Right-wing of the party's German policy suggest, as before, that "anti-H-bomb" is a less well-defined category than "extreme pacificists", as used in Table 24.

* i.e., views on other foreign policy matters, *not* on Germany.
† *Manchester Guardian*, March 2nd, 1959.

TABLE 30

Labour Attitudes to Germany and Disengagement as at February 19th, 1958: in their Relationship to Views on the H-bomb

	Anti-H-bomb		*Other Views*		*No Views*		*Total*
	(Unilateral banners of tests and/or manufacture + signatories of Motions calling for immediate initiative in securing international agreement on banning tests)	%		%		%	
Left	37	47	7	6	0	0	44
Centre	14	18	28	24	2	5	44
Right	19	24	48	41	19	46	86
Other Views	7		23		9		39
	}9	11	}33	29	}20	49	}62
No Views	2		10		11		23
	79	100	116	100	41	100	236

$\tau c = 0\cdot45$. Significant at $0\cdot5\%$

Nevertheless, here too, there is a strong association between "anti-H-bomb" and views on Germany. The correlation is significant at the level of 0.5 per cent.

It remains to ask whether attitudes to Germany and disengagement were associated with Members' characteristics. Perhaps sur-

TABLE 31

Labour Party Attitudes on Germany and Disengagement, by Sponsorship

	Left	%	*Centre*	%	*Right*	%	*Other Views*	%	*No Views*	%	*Total*	
Trades Union sponsored:	9	12	22	28	29	37	12	15	6	8	78	100
Co-op sponsored:	6	29	4	19	8	38	3	14	0	0	21	100
CLP	29	21	18	13	49	36	24	18	17	12	137	100
Total	44		44		86		39		23		236	

Other Views+No Views. $\chi^2_6 = 11\cdot94$. Significant at 10%

prisingly, there was no association with either occupation, education, age or year of entering Parliament. But, as Table 31 shows, there is a possibility that the attitude was associated with sponsorship. The table is significant at a figure of 10 per cent, so that the possibility cannot be entirely dismissed.

The table suggests that the Co-operators were the most Left, and the Trades Union sponsored the most Right, with the CLP candidates somewhere between these two.

Annex 5 · Social Welfare in the Labour Party

HERE again we gauged the intensity of Members' attitudes on social welfare by the number of Motions they signed. There are nine Motions available, but we have disregarded EDM 54/1955, which dealt with widows' pensions, since it was signed by only ten Labour Members; and also EDM 65/1956 which certainly attracted 35 signatures, but was concerned with the somewhat narrow point of the value of "disregards" in the NAB scales. (It asked the Government to raise these so as to restore their real value in terms of purchasing power.)

The seven Motions selected for consideration cover three aspects of "social welfare" viz. the high cost of living and industrial relations; social security payments; and the social services. The first of the high cost of living Motions is EDM 10/1957.* It condemned the Government for its "destructive interference with established processes of collective bargaining in nationalized industries and attempting to condition the minds of these who serve on Arbitration Tribunals to refuse applications for increases in wages, irrespective of the merits of such claims". It went on to claim that a continuation of these practices would result in the breakdown of the negotiating machinery in those industries. It attracted 75 names. The second and third Motions are here treated as alternatives: we

---

* *Tabled November 26th,* 1957. Bank rate was raised to 7 per cent on September 19th, 1957. In a two-day debate on the economic situation, 29th–30th October, the Chancellor of the Exchequer (Mr. Thorneycroft) stated that those who adjudicated about wages ought to bear "in the forefront of their minds" the interest of the nation as a whole. This was characterized by the TUC as "goodbye to impartial arbitration". On November 1st, the Minister of Health refused to confirm a Whitley Council award of 3 per cent increased pay to clerical and administrative staffs in the N.H.S. This was characterized as "the negation of collective bargaining". The Minister defended his decision in the House on November 6th. On November 12th, the Opposition amendment to the address regretted the omission of policies designed to increase production and establish better relations in industry. In the last week of November the engineering unions' claim for a 40-hour week was rejected by the employers, and likewise the T.G.W.U. claim for a 25/- per week rise for busmen.

have conflated together all those Members, who signed either or both. This is because both dealt with the cost of living and only a brief interval of time elapsed between them.

EDM 11/1955* attracting 35 signatures, "viewed with alarm" the recent steep rise in the cost of living. Blaming the Government for this, it accused it of "depressing the standard of life of many millions of lower paid workers and pensioners to a bare subsistence level". It called on the Government to reduce the cost of living, ending with an exhortation to "alleviate the plight of those who are suffering poverty in the midst of plenty". EDM 45/1955,† signed by no less than 104 Members, was "gravely concerned" at the rise in living costs at a time when world prices were falling; held the Government responsible; declared opposition to its policies; and condemned it also for "the irresponsible manner in which it continues to jeopardize industrial peace in pursuit of partisan ends—".

Of the social security motions, the first is EDM 23/1955,‡ calling on the Government to increase NAB scales substantially and as early as possible. One hundred and thirty-five Members signed. The second motion is EDM 72/1956§ which 147 signed. It urged the Government to raise the basic old-age pension to £3 a week before the House rose in August.

There are two welfare-service motions. EDM 69/1956|| urged the Government to give a high priority to the building of new hospitals or to their modernization; stated that the Government's policy was imperilling the N.H.S.; and ended by urging increased grants to the Regional Hospital Boards. Ninety-one Members signed

---

* *Tabled October 25th,* 1955. One of its sponsors, Mr. Sparks, was successful in the ballot for Private Members' Motions, and gave notice that he would introduce a Motion on the cost of living on December 2nd; but he does not appear to have done so.

† *Tabled January 25th,* 1956. The topic was dealt with in a general debate on economic affairs (see *H.C. Debates,* January 26th, 1956, col. 374; February 2nd, 1956, cols. 1085–6).

‡ *Tabled November 22nd,* 1955. The Annual Conference of the Labour Party had just carried a resolution demanding that NAB benefits should be raised immediately, to keep step with increases in National Insurance benefits. (Annual Conference of Labour Party, 1955, *Report* p. 193). Cf. also *H.C. Debates,* December 7th, col. 404).

§ *Tabled July 11th,* 1957.

|| *Tabled July 2nd,* 1957.

it. EDM 24/1957 was concerned with education. It maintained that the economies envisaged in the Ministry of Education Circular 334 of 1958 would cause "irreparable harm" to the education service, and especially (so it said) to the expansion of technical education. It ended by demanding the withdrawal of the Circular.

In the subsequent analysis we divide our 236 backbenchers according to the number of Motions they signed; six or five ranking as Very Keen, four or three as Keen, two or one as Moderate, and none as No Opinion. This indicates Members' feelings on the general issue of social welfare legislation.

ATTITUDES TOWARDS SOCIAL WELFARE

TABLE 32

Attitudes towards Social Welfare in the Labour Party: by Occupation

	Very Keen (6 or 5 Motions)	%	*Keen (4 or 3 Motions)*	%	*Moderate (2 or 1 Motion)*	%	*No opinion*	%	*Totals*	%
Workers:	21	27	31	39	20	25	7	9	79	100
Miscellaneous Professions:	10	16	17	28	29	48	5	8	61	100
Business:	3	13	11	48	8	35	1	4	23	100
Professions:	11	15	21	29	29	40	12	16	73	100
	45		80		86		25		236	

Omitting business, $\chi^2_6 = 12 \cdot 47$. Significant at 10%. "Workers" vs. remainder $\bar{\chi}^2_4 = 8 \cdot 66$. Significant at 2·5%

The Workers differed from the remainder. While there is little to choose between the reactions of the Professions and the Miscellaneous Occupations, the Workers were by far the most Keen. If contrasted with all "non-workers" including the business-men, the table is significant at the level of 2·5 per cent.

TABLE 33

Attitudes towards Social Welfare in the Labour Party: by Sponsorship of Candidates

	Very Keen	%	*Keen*	%	*Moderate*	%	*No opinion*	%	*Totals*	%
T.U. sponsored	22	28	33	42	18	23	5	6	78	100
Co-op sponsored	5	24	6	29	10	48	0	0	21	100
CLP	18	13	41	30	58	42	20	15	137	100
Totals	45		80		86		25		236	

(Omitting Co-ops, $\chi^2_4 = 16 \cdot 48$. Significant at 0·5%)

As the table shows, the Trades Union sponsored candidates were the keenest, and the C.L.P. candidates the least keen; the Co-op sponsored candidates were midway between the two. If the Co-op candidates be omitted (as they are too few for direct statistical comparison), the difference between the Trades Union sponsored candidates and that of the C.L.P. is so great that the table becomes significant at the very high level of 0·5 per cent.

Now, as we have had occasion to remark earlier, the inter-relationship between the Workers and the Trades Union sponsored group is so close that wherever the Workers behave significantly differently from the rest of the occupational groups, we should also expect to find a significant difference between the behaviour of the Trades Union sponsored members and the "rest" of the party. This is indeed what we find here. Furthermore, the reason for there being a closer association between attitude and sponsorship (0·5 per cent) than between attitude and occupation (2·5 per cent) lies in the omission of the Co-operators from the calculation for the sponsorship table. This group is only slightly less keen on social welfare than the Trades Unionists; if they are left out of account, this but serves to heighten the contrast between the Trades Unions (which largely overlaps the Workers' category), and what remains of the party once the Co-operators are excluded—viz, the C.L.P.

candidates. In both cases we are contrasting with the rest of the party a group of members that is nearly identical—the Workers or Trades Union sponsored members; but in the first instance (Table 32) these are contrasted with "rest of the party" and in the second (Table 33, with the rest of the party *minus* a fairly keen group, viz. the Co-operators.

Just as there is an inter-relationship between occupational groups and sponsorship, so there is between occupational groups and educational categories. Of the Workers, 84 per cent are in the Elementary or Elementary/Secondary+ categories; in the rest of the party the proportion is only 20 per cent. There was a significant difference between the attitude of the Workers as contrasted with the rest of the party: it would therefore be surprising if that did not reflect itself in a difference between the Elementary and Elementary/Secondary+ groups, as against the older educational groups. This is what the following table shows.

TABLE 34

Attitudes towards Social Welfare in the Labour Party: by Education

	Very Keen & Keen	%	*Moderate*	%	*No opinion*	%	*Totals*	%
Elementary	49	64	22	29	6	8	77	100
Ely/Secy+	18	86	2	10	1	5	21	100
Secondary	20	54	13	35	4	11	37	100
University	36	39	44	47	13	14	93	100
Not known	2		5		1		8	100
	125		86		25		236	

Omitting Not Known, $\chi^2_6 = 18 \cdot 05$. Significant at 1%

There is a *possible* association (significant at the 10 per cent level only) between the type of school background, and also between the type of university background, and attitudes to social welfare. Those from public schools (U.1 and U.2) are *less* Keen than those from grammar schools (U.3 and U.4), irrespective of the

TABLE 35

Attitudes towards Social Welfare in the Labour Party: by University

	Very Keen	%	*Keen*	%	*Moderate*	%	*No opinion*	%	*Totals*	%
U.1:	1	4	3	12	14	56	7	28	25	100
U.2:	2	13	6	40	5	33	2	13	15	100
U.3:	1	10	3	30	6	60	0	0	10	100
U.4:	8	20	9	23	19	48	4	10	40	100
	12		21		44		13		90	

U.1 + U.2 vs. U.3 + U.4 $\bar{\chi}^2_4 = 5{\cdot}11$. Significant at 10%

universities attended. Likewise, those who went to Oxford and Cambridge are less Keen than those who went to other universities. (U.1's and U.3's against U.2's U.4's). These tendencies meet in the U.1's (public school to Oxford and Cambridge) and U.4's (grammar schools to other universities), and explain the marked difference between their attitudes as shown in the table: the former being predominantly Moderate or Uncommitted, the latter being markedly more Keen and Very Keen.

No association can be established between attitudes and either Members' age, or their year of entry into Parliament.

Annex 6 · Foreign Affairs and Commonwealth Policy in the Conservative Party

DIFFERENCES over European and Commonwealth relations were manifested in backbench Motions put down by Conservative Members.

On the European side were two Motions tabled by Geoffrey Rippon, an enthusiastic partisan of European unity who had entered Parliament in 1955. The first was tabled in July 1956, and urged the Government to enter into negotiations with the Six Powers* with a view to ensuring that if the Common Market treaty were signed, the way would be open for British participation on an acceptable basis and in accordance with the interests of the Commonwealth.†

The second Motion, put down in December 1956, just after the failure of the Suez operation, dealt with the more general question of European unity. It called for a closer association between Britain and Western Europe, in conditions which safeguarded existing Commonwealth relationships and urged the Government to call a conference between Britain and Western Europe to consider further practical steps towards European unity.‡

Neither Motion was uncompromisingly European; each made some concession to the empire wing of the party by making provisos about the interests of the Commonwealth.

The Commonwealth Motions fell into three groups. The most moderate called for greater investment in the Commonwealth or for greater encouragement for intra-Commonwealth trade. Stronger Motions demanded a positive priority for plans to stimulate imperial trade and two extremist amendments declared open hostility to Britain's association with a more integrated Europe.

Of the moderate Motions, the first demanded that the Government economise in public expenditure and set aside a sum equal to 5 per cent of the national revenue for the express purpose of pro-

---

* i.e. Benelux, France, Germany and Italy.
† EDM 101/1955 tabled July 10th, 1956.
‡ EDM 28/1956 tabled December 12th, 1956.

viding the basic facilities of water, communications and power in the Empire.* Another, tabled in July 1958, urged the Government to take steps to increase Commonwealth trade, to use Commonwealth agricultural surpluses in order to raise living standards in Commonwealth countries, and to improve the machinery for Commonwealth investment and consultation. It concluded by exhorting the Government to give an inspiring lead at the Commonwealth Economic Conference at Montreal.†

Another was less specific than either of these; it simply welcomed Mr. Diefenbaker's proposals to hold a Commonwealth Economic Conference and to increase Anglo-Canadian trade, and urged the Government to give all possible support to these and other plans to encourage intra-Commonwealth trade.‡ Although these Motions were instigated by leading pro-Commonwealth backbenchers, they made no specific proposals which might have conflicted with Britain's obligations to Europe.

More extreme were two Motions which made it clear that the interests of the Commonwealth came first; one which called for a revision of G.A.T.T., re-emphasized the party's traditional support for Empire preference.§ The second Motion welcomed the holding of the Montreal Conference and sought a positive assurance from the Government that the terms on which Britain entered the European Free Trade Area should not in any way hamper efforts to secure an expansion of Commonwealth trade.||

There were, as well, two Amendments to the pro-European Motions, which were sponsored by the extreme Commonwealth fringe of the party. Both Motions, which were tabled by Major Legge-Bourke, rejected Britain's participation in any supra-national economic organization. Nine M.P.s signed at least one of these two Amendments, and eight of them can be regarded as constituting the ultra-imperialist wing of the Conservative party in the House of Commons.**

These Motions and Amendments enable us to construct a scale marking extreme concern for Europe at one end, and extreme

* EDM 72/1955, tabled April 26th, 1956.
† EDM 97/1957, tabled July 15th, 1958.
‡ EDM 81/1956, tabled July 17th, 1957.
§ EDM 110/1955, tabled July 30th, 1956.
|| EDM 4/1957, tabled November 11th, 1957.
** See footnote on p. 187.

support for the Commonwealth at the other. By examining a Member's record, it is possible to assign him a place on the scale according to the type of Motion he signed. Members have been divided into two main blocs, "Europe" and "Commonwealth", and each of these blocs has been subdivided into two groups: "Europe" has been split into "European Stalwart" and "Europe and Empire", and the "Commonwealth" bloc into "Empire Moderates" and "Empire Stalwarts". The table below shows how Members have been allocated to the appropriate bloc.

EUROPE (104 M.P.s)

(a) *European Stalwart.* (28 M.P.s)

This small group of 28 M.P.s consisted of Members who signed either or both of the European Motions but did not support any of the Commonwealth EDMs. They appear to have had little interest in the claims of the Commonwealth, for although the two European Motions acknowledged our existing Commonwealth commitments, not one of these Members signed the five Commonwealth EDMs,

** EDM 4/1957 was actually debated and carried. Its sponsor, Mr. Russell, won a place in the ballot for Private Members' Motions. No significance need be attached either to its being carried, or to the cordial reception given it by the Government. Only half an hour was available for discussion, the debate beginning at 3.31 p.m. and finishing at 4 o'clock. Mr. Vaughan-Morgan, Minister of State for the Board of Trade began by warmly welcoming the Motion and concluded by divesting his welcome of any import. "I think that if my Hon. Friend studies the communiqué issued on that occasion (at the Montreal Economic Conference) he will see that the nations gathered at Mont Tremblant were well aware of the need to discuss most of the subjects he has mentioned today. I therefore warmly welcome his Motion in that spirit." The Motion was then put and carried without dissent. One of the nine Members has been regarded as "Uncommitted" because he signed another Motion which seems incompatible with the Common Market amendment. This other Motion looked forward to Government proposals to create a North Atlantic Treaty Organization based on economic and political as well as military factors and stipulated that "narrow considerations of national sovereignty alone" should not be allowed to stand in the way (EDM 22/1957, tabled January 21st, 1958). This Motion and the Common Market Amendment could perhaps be reconciled with some logical ingenuity, but the spirit of the Common Market Amendment seems to be in conflict with the NATO Motion. The Member in question should probably be counted as belonging to the Commonwealth wing because he also signed the Motion calling for a revision of G.A.T.T. But in view of the apparent inconsistency, it was thought better to treat him as "Uncommitted".

which afforded M.P.s an opportunity to express a more positive interest in the Empire. It is assumed that these Members were more concerned about Britain's relationship with Europe than about her Commonwealth links.

(b) *Europe and Empire.* (76 M.P.s)

This group of 76 Members comprises those who signed either the Common Market or the European Unity Motion (or both) *plus* at least one of the "Empire Moderate" Motions.* This group sought the best of both worlds. It was anxious that Britain should be linked with a more united Europe but was also in favour of greater Commonwealth economic co-operation and development. Its members, however, did not sign any Motion which specifically put the Commonwealth before Europe.

COMMONWEALTH (127 M.P.s)

M.P.s signing any of the three moderate Empire Motions† without signing either the more extreme Commonwealth Motions and Amendments‡ or the European motions (§) have been called "Empire Moderates".

These Members displayed no enthusiasm at all about our relations with Europe. On the other hand, they offered no support to the advocates of imperial preference or to the opponents of a closer British involvement with Western Europe. This group consisted of 63 Members.

Empire Stalwarts. (64 M.P.s)

There were 64 Members who signed one or more of the following Motions:

EDM 101A/1955—Anti-Common Market Amendment.
EDM 28A/1956—Anti-European unity Amendment.
EDM 110/1955—Increased Empire preference.
EDM 5/1957—Empire trade before Free Trade Area.

---

* That is, those Motions calling either for increased Commonwealth development or which called for the encouragement of Commonwealth trade without clearly putting the Commonwealth before Europe (EDMs 72/1955, 81/1956 and 97/1957).

† EDMs 72/1955, 97/1957 and 81/1956.

‡ EDMs 110/1955, 4/1957, 101A/1955, and 28A/1956.

§ EDMs 28/1956 and 101/1955.

Any Member signing one or more of these Motions has been labelled as "Empire Stalwart" whether or not he signed either of the European Motions. Nearly half of this group signed at least one of the European Motions; but by signing the more extreme Empire Motions they made it plain that their first allegiance was to the Commonwealth.

UNCOMMITTED (27 M.P.s)

There were 26 backbenchers who signed no Motions at all on this subject, though signing on other political topics, and one Member who signed with apparent inconsistency (see p. 187). They have been regarded as "Uncommitted".

EXCLUSIONS (12 M.P.s)

Some M.P.s have been excluded from the inquiry on this topic because either through death, retirement, office or late entry into the House, they were not in a position to sign when the relevant Motions were put down.

Attitudes to Europe and the Commonwealth and M.P.s Backgrounds

Let us now try to relate these attitudes to the backgrounds of Members—to their education, their occupations and other characteristics.

TABLE 36

The Conservative Party and Relations with Europe and the Commonwealth: By Occupation

	European Stalwarts		Europe and Empire		All Europe		Empire Moderates		Empire Stalwarts		All Commonwealth		Uncommitted		Total
		%		%		%		%		%		%		%	
Law	4	12	14	42	18	55	5	15	5	15	10	30	5	15	33
H.M. Forces	—	—	2	12	2	12	8	47	5	29	13	76	2	12	17

Europe vs. Commonwealth, $\chi^2_1=8\cdot26$. Significant at 0·5%

There were no significant differences of attitude amongst the major occupational classes, but there was a sharp contrast in the behaviour of lawyers and regular officers. Lawyers inclined to Europe, whilst the few servicemen were overwhelmingly pro-Commonwealth.

There were no significant differences, however, when ex-lawyers were compared with former regular servicemen.

Nor were there any significant variations in the attitudes of those coming from different kinds of schools. But there were differences in the degree of commitment, the Members from Other Public schools being the least, and those from Non-Public schools being the most interested.

TABLE 37

The Conservative Party and Relations with Europe and the Commonwealth: by Universities attended

	European Stalwarts		Europe and Empire		All Europe		Empire Moderates		Empire Stalwarts		All Commonwealth		Uncommitted		Total
		%		%		%		%		%		%		%	
Oxford	11	16	23	33	34	49	15	22	11	16	26	38	9	13	69
Cambridge	5	9	8	15	13	24	15	27	18	33	33	60	9	16	55
Other	2	6	12	36	14	42	8	24	8	24	16	48	3	9	33
Sandhurst	—	—	4	25	4	25	7	44	4	25	11	69	1	6	16
None	10	12	29	34	39	46	18	21	23	27	41	48	5	6	85
Total	28	11	76	29	104	40	63	24	64	25	127	49	27	10	258

Europe vs. Commonwealth, Omitting None,
$\chi^2_3=10\cdot49$. Significant at 2·5%
Oxford vs. Cambridge: $\chi^2_1=7\cdot41$. Significant at 1%

The differences between graduates as a class, and non-graduates were small and not statistically significant. But there were considerable variations amongst graduates of different universities. Cambridge graduates, and men from Sandhurst, were strongly pro-Commonwealth whilst Members with an Oxford background leant towards Europe. Other University M.P.s were slightly pro-Empire but much less so than the Cambridge and Sandhurst blocs.

TABLE 38

The Conservative Party and Relations with Europe and the Commonwealth: by Age

	European Stalwarts		Europe and Empire		All Europe		Empire Moderates		Empire Stalwarts		All Commonwealth		Uncommitted		Total
		%		%		%		%		%		%		%	
Under 41	5	12	17	41	22	54	8	20	8	20	16	39	3	7	41
41–50	11	14	22	28	33	42	18	23	21	27	39	50	6	8	78
51–60	9	9	32	33	41	43	25	26	22	23	47	49	8	8	96
Over 60	3	7	5	12	8	19	12	28	13	30	25	58	10	23	43
Total	28	11	76	29	104	40	63	24	64	25	127	49	27	10	258

Europe vs. Commonwealth, $\chi^2_3 = 8\cdot41$. Significant at 5%

The youngest Members showed a small majority in favour of Europe: the middle age range behaved rather like the party as a whole. The oldest Members, who were also the least committed, showed a three to one majority for the Empire.

There seems to have been a marked connexion between the year of entry into Parliament and a Member's opinions. Members first elected before the war inclined to the Empire, but the 1945 and 1950 intakes were even more strongly pro-Commonwealth. A sharp break occurred, however, in 1951; the "Europeans" almost obtained parity with the Commonwealth lobby, mustering 20 against 23. This change was confirmed by the 1955 intake, the "Europeans" having a strong lead of nearly two to one. Out of the 55 new M.P.s committing themselves on this question, 36 leaned towards Europe and nearly a fifth of them displayed no overt interest in the Commonwealth.

The election of 1951 was a watershed; up to 1950 Conservative candidates selected for winnable seats were predominantly Empire-minded; from 1951, however, sympathy for the European idea increased rapidly. Indeed, in one sense the change had taken place

TABLE 39

The Conservative Party and Relations with Europe and the Commonwealth: by Year of Entry into Parliament

	European Stalwarts		Europe and Empire		All Europe		Empire Moderates		Empire Stalwarts		All Commonwealth		Uncommitted		Total
		%		%		%		%		%		%		%	
1955	10	17	26	43	36	60	9	15	10	17	19	32	5	8	60
1951	4	9	16	35	20	43	11	24	12	26	23	50	3	7	46
1950	1	2	16	29	17	31	13	24	19	35	32	58	6	11	55
1945	7	19	4	11	11	31	15	42	10	28	25	69	—	—	36
War	1	8	3	23	4	31	4	31	1	8	5	38	4	31	13
Pre-War	5	10	11	23	16	33	11	23	12	25	23	48	9	19	48
Total	28	11	76	29	104	40	63	24	64	25	127	49	27	10	258

Europe vs. Commonwealth, War and Pre-War grouped:
$\chi^2_4 = 14{\cdot}69$. Significant at 0·5%

Committed vs. Uncommitted: War and Pre-War grouped:
$\chi^2_4 = 12{\cdot}93$. Significant at 1%

as early as 1950. If we compare the figures for M.P.s signing any European Motion with those signing Commonwealth Motions only we find the following result:

	All signing any European Motion	Commonwealth Signatories Only
1955	42	13
1951	24	19
1950	26	23
1945	12	24
War	5	4
Pre-War	19	20
	128	103

$\chi^2_5 = 17{\cdot}69$. Significant at 0·5%

On the other hand, this intake of 1950 contained a high proportion of the most militant Commonwealth men—19 of the 32 were classed as "Empire Stalwarts". While sensitive to Europe's problems, many of them left no doubt that their first loyalty was to the Empire, and indeed nearly all of the 1950 intake who committed themselves signed at least one Empire Motion.

TABLE 40

The Conservative Party and Relations with Europe and the Commonwealth: by Size of Majority

	European Stalwarts		Europe and Empire		All Europe		Empire Moderates		Empire Stalwarts		All Commonwealth		Uncommitted		Total
		%		%		%		%		%		%		%	
Marginal	5	14	13	36	18	50	3	8	11	31	14	39	4	11	36
Semi-Marginal	3	11	11	41	14	52	2	7	8	30	10	37	3	11	27
Comfortable	6	14	13	32	19	46	10	24	6	15	16	39	6	15	41
Safe	8	10	22	28	30	38	25	32	19	24	44	56	4	5	78
Impregnable	6	8	17	22	23	30	23	30	20	26	43	57	10	13	76
Total	28	11	76	29	104	40	63	24	64	25	127	49	27	10	258

Europe vs. Commonwealth: Marginal + Semi-Marginal + Comfortable (grouped) vs. Safe + Impregnable (grouped):

$\bar{\chi}^2_4 = 5 \cdot 57$. Significant at 5%

Views on European and Commonwealth relationships seem also to have been associated with the size of majority. This is to be expected since the size of majority and date of first election are closely connected. The marginal, semi-marginal and comfortable seats all showed majorities for Europe. When these were aggregated and compared with the combined safe and impregnable classes, whose Members leant predominantly to the Empire, an association was established at the significant level of 5 per cent.

The other notable feature was the extreme position of those

supporters of the Commonwealth bloc who had small majorities. Commonwealth men from the marginal and semi-marginal seats came overwhelmingly from the Empire Stalwart wing, whilst the Empire Moderates were strongly entrenched in the safe constituencies. This association within the Commonwealth bloc between intensity of feeling and size of majority is significant at the 5 per cent level.

TABLE 41

The Conservative Party and Relations with Europe and the Commonwealth: by Town and Country

	European Stalwarts		Europe and Empire		All Europe		Empire Moderates		Empire Stalwarts		All Commonwealth		Uncommitted		Total
		%		%		%		%		%		%		%	
Urban	15	11	47	33	62	44	25	18	40	28	65	46	15	11	142
Semi-rural	3	14	3	14	6	29	9	43	3	14	12	57	3	14	21
Rural	9	16	14	24	23	40	22	38	9	16	31	53	4	7	58
Total United Kingdom*	28	11	76	29	104	40	63	24	64	25	127	49	27	10	258

Empire Moderates vs. Empire Stalwarts: $\chi^2_2 = 11 \cdot 24$. Significant at 0·5%

The chief interest of this table lies in the distribution of the two wings of the Commonwealth bloc. Nearly two-thirds of the urban Commonwealthers were Empire Stalwarts. The rural Commonwealth Members, however, were overwhelmingly moderate. These differences are significant at a very high level—0·5 per cent.

There was little variation in the distribution of Commonwealth M.P.s and Europeans between rural and urban constituencies.

* Includes Scotland and Ulster.

Annex 7 · Penal Reform in the Conservative Party

Two Motions were connected with the death penalty abolition controversy in 1955 and 1956. One, tabled in November 1955, declared that the death penalty should be suspended for an experimental period of five years. This was put down by the Labour Member, Geoffrey de Freitas.* The next day, Sydney Silverman tabled a second Motion, asking that time might be provided for a Second Reading debate for his own Death Penalty (Abolition) Bill.† Each Motion attracted some Conservative support: altogether, 25 Conservatives identified themselves with either or both of these abolitionist Motions.

In contrast, there were three Motions which declared that the courts should be given back the power to award corporal punishment, and one, tabled after the passing of the Homicide Act, called for both the return of corporal punishment and the extension of the death penalty. The mildest of these "severe" Motions called for the restoration of birching "in appropriate cases" for crimes of violence.‡

The most extreme Motion was tabled by Sir Thomas Moore. This asked the Government to amend the Criminal Justice and Homicide Acts so as to allow the courts to inflict corporal punishment for crimes of violence, and capital punishment for *all* crimes of murder.§ Twenty-five other Conservatives supported Sir Thomas' appeal. In all 54 Conservatives signed at least one "severe" Motion.

The death penalty and corporal punishment Motions have been consolidated to give a scale of "humanitarianism". At one pole are the "humane" M.P.s, at the other, the "severe".

---

* EDM 18/1955, tabled November 15th, 1955.

† EDM 20/1955, tabled November 16th, 1955.

‡ EDM 53/1955, tabled February 28th, 1956. The other motions were EDM 27/1957, tabled February 4th, 1958 and EDM 67/1957, tabled April 4th, 1958 and EDM 26/1957, tabled February 3rd, 1958.

§ EDM 26/1957, tabled February 3rd, 1958.

Members were allocated to the appropriate group in the following way:

Humane (23 Members)*

Those who signed either the Motion calling for the suspension of the death penalty, (EDM 18/1955) or the Motion calling for facilities for Mr. Silverman's Bill (EDM 20/1955) without signing any of the corporal punishment Motions.

Severe (49 Members)†

Those who signed any of the Motions calling for birching or other forms of corporal punishment, or the extension of the death penalty (EDMs 53/1955, 27/1957, 67/1957, 26/1957) but did not sign either of the abolitionist Motions.

Uncommitted (175 Members)

Members signing none of these Motions, or signing Motions of both kinds.

---

* There is a slight difference between the total number of signatures given earlier and these figures. The first disparity is due to two M.P.s who signed Motions in favour both of the Silverman Bill and the restoration of birching. They have been omitted from this scale. There is an inconsistency of attitude here (though not an intellectual inconsistency) which makes it difficult to assign them to a definite group. This dual approach—support for abolition of the death penalty and for the re-introduction of corporal punishment—is not uncommon in the Conservative party. Five Members who entered the House after the General Election signed one of the Motions calling for the restoration of corporal punishment. They were not in the House when the abolitionist Motions were tabled. It is possible, though unlikely, that they might have signed one of these Motions had they been in the House. They have therefore been excluded.

† We have had some difficulty in deciding whether to take the signatories of the abolitionist Motions as our "humane" category, or whether to enlarge it by taking all those M.P.s who voted for the abolitionist amendment tabled by Mr. Ede, and carried on February 16th, 1956. We finally decided to restrict it to the signers of the EDMs. However, the distribution of the Conservative supporters of the Ede amendment is shown by university, age and year of entry later in this chapter. Those readers who wish to can substitute the figures of abolitionist voters for the signers of the abolitionist EDMs. Whichever source is used makes no differences to our conclusions. Two of the "humane" M.P.s actually voted against the Ede amendment, and for the government's Motion in favour of retaining the death penalty but limiting its application. Another abstained. The question arises whether signature of the Motions or the vote in the division lobbies was the more expressive of these Members' attitudes. We have chosen the EDMs.

Exclusions

These number 23 M.P.s.

The only significant difference between the occupational groups was in the degree of commitment. The Miscellaneous Occupations M.P.s were the most committed, and the Professions the least.

TABLE 42

The Conservative Party and Penal Reform: by Schools Attended

	Humane	%	*Severe*	%	*Uncommitted*	%	*Total*	%
Clarendon	8	10	11	14	60	76	79	100
Other Pub.	10	10	18	18	72	72	100	100
Non-Public	2	4	18	33	35	64	55	100
The Rest	3	23	2	15	8	62	13	100
Total	23	9	49	20	175	71	247	100

Humane vs. Severe, $\chi^2_3 = 7{\cdot}33$. Significant at 10%

Amongst the committed Members there was some cleavage between the Public School and Non-Public School M.P.s. The Clarendon School M.P.s were the most humane, M.P.s from the newer public schools were rather less so, and Members from private and council schools were overwhelmingly severe. This association, however, has not been fully established, the significance level being only 10 per cent. As the next table shows, sharper differences were found between graduates and non-graduates.

The division here lay between graduates and non-graduates. Amongst the committed graduates there was a majority of abolitionists, but the non-graduates revealed a very big majority for severe penal policies. The association is significant at the high level of 0.5 per cent.

There were also significant differences in the degree of commitment: non-graduates were more committed than graduates.

Amongst graduates, there were no significant variations, but Oxford had the highest proportion of Humane Members. The

TABLE 43
The Conservative Party and Penal Reform: by Universities Attended

	Humane	%	*Severe*	%	*Uncommitted*	%	*Total*	%
Oxford	9	14	5	8	49	78	63	100
Cambridge	5	10	7	13	40	77	52	100
Others	4	12	5	15	24	73	33	100
Sandhurst	—	—	5	31	11	69	16	100
None	5	6	27	53	51	41	83	100
Total	23	9	49	20	175	71	247	100

Graduates vs. Non-graduates (omitting Sandhurst):
$\chi^2_3=13\cdot92$. Significant at 0·5%
Graduates vs. Non-graduates, Committed vs. Uncommitted (Sandhurst omitted):
$\chi^2_1=5\cdot04$. Significant at 2·5%

number of Sandhurst men expressing a view was very small, but it is noteworthy that all five of them were in favour of more Severe penalties: and of the twenty-five Members who had been educated at some military or naval college, eight were Severe and none Humane.

There is an association between attitudes and both school and university attendance. In each case, Members with a higher educational background were more Humane than their colleagues. In fact, the association between school and attitude reflects the association between university and attitude. Nearly all of the Clarendon Members, and two-thirds of the newer Public School M.P.s went on to university: but only a third of the "Non-Public School" class had had a university training. Given the association between university and attitude, we should expect to find a similar relationship between school and attitude. That the university rather than the school is the crucial factor can be shown by comparing

Public School M.P.s who went on to university with those who did not. The former were predominantly Humane, the latter heavily Severe.

TABLE 44

The Conservative Party and Penal Reform: by Age

	Humane	%	*Severe*	%	*Uncommitted*	%	*Total*	%
Below 41	10	28	4	11	22	61	36	100
41–50	6	8	17	22	54	70	77	100
51–60	6	7	23	25	62	68	91	100
Over 60	1	2	5	12	37	86	43	100
Total	23	9	49	20	175	71	247	100

51–60 + Over 60: $\chi^2_2 = 12 \cdot 71$ Significant at 0·5%
Humane vs. Severe, Committed vs. Uncommitted:
$\chi^2_3 = 6 \cdot 79$. Significant at 10%

There is also an association between age and attitude. The committed younger Members were the most Humane, and the older Members the most Severe. When the two oldest age-groups are combined, the significance level reaches 0·5 per cent. There is also some evidence that the interest shown varied with age—the youngest Members being the most committed, and the oldest the least. The association however, is only provisional, the significance level falling between 5 and 10 per cent.

The association between age and attitude is somewhat complex. To some extent it reflects the association between attitude and university attendance. The youngest age-group contained a disproportionately large number of graduates, and especially of Oxonians. About two-fifths of the under forty-ones had been to Oxford, compared with a quarter of each of the other three age groups. Moreover, four-fifths were graduates as against two-thirds of the older groups. We should expect younger Members therefore to have been more Humane than older Members. But in turn, the younger graduates were markedly more Humane than the older graduates. In the case of university Members, therefore, it is true today that the younger the Member, the more likely he was to have taken the Humane side; but this was not so of non-graduates.

TABLE 45

The Conservative Party and Penal Reform: by Year of First Entering Parliament

	Humane	%	*Severe*	%	*Uncommitted*	%	*Total*	%
1955	12	23	13	25	28	53	53	100
1951	3	7	10	22	33	72	46	100
1950	4	7	14	25	38	68	56	100
1945	1	3	6	17	28	80	35	100
War	1	9	—	—	10	91	11	100
Pre-war	2	4	6	13	38	83	46	100
Total	23	9	49	20	175	71	247	100

1955 vs. All other groups combined: $\chi^2_1 = 3 \cdot 47$. Significant at 5%
All groups (War and Pre-war combined), Committed vs. Uncommitted: $\chi^2_4 = 14 \cdot 91$. Significant at 0·5%

There were significant differences both in attitude and the degree of commitment. If the 1955 intake is compared with all other intakes combined, the association reaches the significance level of 5 per cent. Committed Members entering the House in 1955 were more Humane than those elected earlier.

Differences in commitment were much more pronounced. The 1955 intake was by far the most committed, and the war and pre-war intakes the least so. The association here reaches the high level of 0·5 per cent, the war and pre-war intakes being treated as one.

The number of M.P.s expressing an opinion on crime and punishment was small, and this makes it difficult for us to draw firm conclusions about the whole Party. However, we are able to compare the figures given by this study of backbench Motions with the results of some free votes on the floor of the House. Three divisions have been selected for examination. One took place on a Private Members' Bill which was debated in February 1953. This Bill, the Criminal Justice Act, 1948 (Amendment) Bill, which was brought in by W/Cdr. Bullus, proposed to re-introduce corporal punishment for crimes of violence. The Government opposed the Bill, and with the aid of the Labour party were able to defeat it.

The second division took place on Mr. Ede's Amendment, calling on the Government to bring in legislation suspending the death penalty, which was debated in February 1956. This Motion was carried, to the embarrassment of the Government, who escaped from their dilemma by granting time for Mr. Silverman's Abolition Bill.

The third division occurred during the passage of the Silverman Bill. A Conservative, Mr. Arbuthnot, tabled an Amendment which would have allowed the courts to impose a double sentence upon convicted murderers: as well as suffering life imprisonment, they could now also be sentenced to be flogged. This Amendment was easily defeated though it actually won the support of one or two Conservative abolitionists; conversely, several Conservative opponents of abolition voted against it.

It should be noted that these three divisions did not pose the issue in quite the same way as the penal reform scale. In the penal reform scale, the question lay between the penal "progressives" and the penal "reactionaries", with the uncommitted presumably wanting no change in either direction. But on the Bullus Bill and the Arbuthnot Amendment the dispute was between the Severe, and the supporters of the *status quo*: and over the Ede Amendment, the situation was reversed, the initiative being taken by the supporters of a milder penal system, with both the Severe and the defenders of the *status quo* opposing them.

The Motion to suspend the death penalty aroused the greatest interest: 240 backbench Conservatives voted in this division, and its size makes it statistically the most important of the three. The other two divisions seemed to cause much less feeling. Just over a hundred voted on the Bullus Bill, and less than 90 on the Arbuthnot Amendment.

These divisions have been analysed in the same way as the Early Day Motions. The analysis has been confined to the background characteristics which appear important—school, university, age and year of entering Parliament. Members of the Government have been excluded; to count them would falsify the result for even though the divisions were free votes, by convention they were obliged, if they voted at all, to vote with the Government. Ministers and other office holders with views opposed to the collective policy of the Government are required to abstain, even on free votes. For the sake of simplicity, the same terminology—"Humane" and "Severe" —that was used to describe the attitudes embodied in the Early Day Motions has been used here.

TABLE 46
The Conservative Party and Penal Reform: by Schools
Arbuthnot Amendment

	Humane	%	*Severe*	%	*Total*	%
Clarendon	16	52	15	48	31	100
Other Public	9	29	22	71	31	100
Non-Public	3	15	17	85	20	100
The Rest	1	20	4	80	5	100
Total	29	33	58	67	87	100*

Clarendon vs. Other Public vs. Non-Public:
$\chi^2_2 = 8 \cdot 11$. Significant at 2·5%

The breakdown of the Arbuthnot Amendment endorses the results derived from the Early Day Motions. The Clarendon School M.P.s were the most Humane, the Non-Public School Members the most Severe. These differences are significant at the 2·5 per cent level. Over the Bullus Bill, and the Abolition Amendment, the differences are not significant but are consistent with the findings of the EDMs. In each case, the Clarendon School Members were the most Humane, and the Non-Public School Members the most Severe, though on the abolition amendment the differences were small.

* The percentages here are calculated on the number voting.

TABLE 47

The Conservative Party and Penal Reform: by Universities.
Bullus Bill, 1953

	Humane	%	*Severe*	%	*Total*	%
Oxford	19	56	15	44	34	100
Cambridge	10	48	11	52	21	100
Others	4	36	7	64	11	100
Sandhurst	2	40	3	60	5	100
None	3	10	28	90	31	100
Total	38	37	64	63	102*	100

Graduates vs. Non-graduates: $\chi^2_1 = 12 \cdot 84$. Significant at 0·1%

Arbuthnot Amendment

	Humane	%	*Severe*	%	*Total*	%
Oxford	18	67	9	33	27	100
Cambridge	7	39	11	61	18	100
Others	2	18	9	82	11	100
Sandhurst	—	—	2	100	2	100
None	2	7	27	93	29	100
Total	29	33	58	67	87	100

Oxford vs. Cambridge vs. Others: $\chi^2_2 = 8 \cdot 26$. Significant at 2·5%
Graduates vs. Non-graduates: $\chi^2_1 = 11 \cdot 97$. Significant at 0·1%

* It was not possible to trace the age or education of one Member who voted for the Bill.

Abolition Amendment

	Humane	%	Severe	%	Total	%
Oxford	24	38	39	62	63	100
Cambridge	7	13	45	87	52	100
Others	7	22	25	78	32	100
Sandhurst	1	6	16	94	17	100
None	9	12	67	88	76	100
Total	48	20	192	80	240	100

Oxford vs. Cambridge vs. Others: $\chi^2_2=9 \cdot 36$. Significant at 1%
Graduates vs. Non-Graduates: $\chi^2_1=3 \cdot 91$. Significant at 5%

Each of the university tests revealed a significant association. In each, graduates were markedly more Humane than non-graduates. Where the issue lay between the *status quo* and harsher penalties, the association reached the very high significance level of 0·1 per cent. Two of the divisions also disclosed significant variations in the attitudes of graduates from different universities. Oxford graduates showed themselves to be more Humane than graduates from Cambridge and Other Universities over both the Arbuthnot Amendment and the Abolition Amendment. Over the latter, the difference was strongly marked, reaching a significance level of 1 per cent.

TABLE 48

The Conservative Party and Penal Reform: by Age.
Arbuthnot Amendment

	Humane	%	Severe	%	Total	%
Under 41	11	85	2	15	13	100
41–50	10	36	18	64	28	100
51–60	6	18	28	82	34	100
Over 60	2	17	10	83	12	100
Total	29	33	58	67	87	100

Under 51 vs. 51 and over: $\chi^2_1=9 \cdot 68$. Significant at 0·5%

Only the Arbuthnot Amendment yields a significant association between age and attitude, the level of significance reaching 0·5 per cent. But although the differences over the Bullus Bill (debated in the preceding Parliament) and the Ede Amendment were not marked enough to give a statistical association, such variations as there were, were consistent with the hypothesis that the younger the Member, the more likely he would be to have Humane views. More than half of those under forty-one voted for the abolition of the death penalty: by contrast 95 per cent of those over sixty wanted to retain it. In every case the older Members were less in sympathy with modern approaches to punishment than were the younger Members.

TABLE 49

The Conservative Party and Penal Reform: by Date of First Entering Parliament

Abolition Amendment

	Humane	%	*Severe*	%	*Total*	%
1955	18	34	35	66	53	100
1951	7	16	36	84	43	100
1950	12	22	43	78	55	100
1945	4	13	27	87	31	100
War	3	27	8	73	11	100
Pre-war	4	9	43	91	47	100
Total	48	20	192	80	240	100

War and pre-war combined: $\chi^2_4 = 10 \cdot 20$. Significant at 5%

On the Abolition Amendment, the 1955 intake again showed that they differed markedly from their seniors, over a third of them voting for abolition. The association between intake and attitude is here significant at the 5 per cent level: the 1945 and pre-1945 groups were the most severe.

This analysis of division lists shows remarkable agreement with the main conclusions derived from the study of EDMs. Support for penal reform was strongest amongst the young, amongst Oxonians, and amongst Members with a university education.

The older M.P.s and those who did not go to university were consistently and markedly Severe. The abolitionists found hardly any support amongst them but the advocates of birching and flogging could always count on their signatures and their votes.

Annex 8 · The Conservatives and Social Policy

THERE were several Motions which are useful indicators of Conservative attitudes to social policy. These do not give a perfect cross-section of opinion in the Conservative party, but there are enough of them to permit some tentative and cautious generalizations.

The Motions have been divided into two classes. Those favourable to wage-earners' claims and supporting a wider distribution of property have been called left-wing whilst those sympathetic to existing property owners have been described as right-wing.

The two most emphatic of the left-wing Motions arose out of the dismissal of workers from the British Motor Corporation factories in Birmingham, Oxford and South Wales. One Motion deplored the management's failure to consult representatives of the workpeople.* A second Motion deplored the short notice which had been given and called on the corporation to do all in its power to mitigate individual hardship during the period of transitional unemployment.†

Another strongly-worded Motion concerned individual ownership of property. The Motion called on the Government to take all necessary steps to promote individual ownership of property on the widest possible scale, and urged that such steps should be given the highest priority.‡

A further Motion which attracted only one Conservative signature, that of Sir Robert Boothby, deplored the decision of the Minister of Pensions and National Insurance not to raise the pension of the "ten shilling widow" and asked the Minister to reconsider the matter favourably.§

---

* EDM 93/1955, tabled June 26th, 1956.
† EDM 94/1955, tabled June 26th, 1956.
‡ EDM 82/1957, tabled May 21st, 1958.
§ There were about 175,000 "ten shilling widows" in 1956. They were widows whose title to a pension derived from their husband's insurance under the pre-1948 scheme. As their title indicates, their pension was ten shillings a week.

Finally, another Motion pleaded the cause of formerly unestablished civil servants. Established civil servants, who had previously served on a temporary basis, had their unestablished service before 1949 reckoned to the extent of one half, instead of in full, when their pensions were calculated.* A Motion tabled in 1957 declared that all such service should be counted in full for superannuation purposes.†

Although this Motion was of a sectional nature, it is appropriate to class it as "Left-wing", for it espoused the claims of a large number of wage-earners, or pensioners.

On the right, there was only one Motion and one Amendment. The Motion expressed concern at the scale of compensation awarded for land which was compulsory acquired by public authorities and asked the Government to accept that the principle of fair market value should be the basis of future compensation.‡ An amendment embodying a similar principle was tabled to a Motion calling for the acquisition of a site which would permit an extension of the National Gallery.§

The two kinds of Motions represent competing, possibly conflicting, claims and contrasting tendencies. One group of Motions was concerned with the well-being of wage-earners, and with the broader diffusion of property. The other championed the rights of existing property owners. On this assumption, a scale of "social attitudes" has been constructed. The scale is both quantitative and qualitative: it takes into account both the number and kinds of Motions signed. Members have been divided into three blocs—Left, Centre, and Right. Although this nomenclature may not be altogether appropriate to the Conservative party, it has the advantage of being both simple and intelligible.

Social Policy Scale

Left (50)	All signatories of the B.M.C. protest Motion, irrespective of whether they signed the Compensation Motion.

(*see over*)

* Nearly half a million civil servants were affected; most of them were in the lower grades. The annual cost of reckoning their unestablished service in full would rise from about £5,500,000 in 1958/59 to about £10,000,000 in 1973/74. See *H.C. Debates,* October 31st, 1957, col. 97.

† EDM 2/1957, tabled November 5th, 1957.

‡ EDM 75/1957, tabled May 6th, 1958.

§ EDM 83A/1957, tabled June 12th, 1958.

	All Members who signed two or more other left-wing Motions, irrespective of whether they signed the Compensation Motion. All Members who signed one left-wing Motion but did not sign the Compensation Motion.
Centre (40)	All Members signing one left-wing Motion (other than the B.M.C. protest), and the Compensation motion or National Gallery Amendment.
Right (73)	All Members signing either the Compensation Motions and National Gallery Amendment, and none of the left-wing Motions.
Uncommitted (71)	Members signing none of the Motions in the scale.
Excluded (36)	Members whose position is doubtful because they were unable to sign the whole range of Motions, because of death, retirement, office or late entry into Parliament.

At this point, a few possible objections must be considered. Superficially it may seem inconsistent to treat the Motion calling for a greater dispersion of property ownership as Left-wing and the compensation Motion as Right-wing. The difference is that the compensation Motion was concerned with the rights of existing property-owners; the other Motion wanted the Government to take steps to widen the ownership of property, to enable those without property to acquire it.

It will also be noticed that the *Left* comprises all signatories of either of the B.M.C. protest Motions *or*, amongst signers of the compensation Motions, all signatories of at least *two* other left-wing motions. This is tantamount to saying that we regard the signature of a B.M.C. Motion as worth the signature of any other two Left-wing Motions; in this sense it may be described as weighted.

This is because these two Motions were by far the most advanced. Both explicitly condemned the B.M.C.'s decision; one insisted that prior consultation was "an essential and a right" and the other charged the Corporation with the duty of mitigating any individual hardship caused by the sackings.

Wherever possible, the findings of this study have been checked against independent sources of evidence such as free votes in the House, or floor revolts. Unfortunately, there was only one limited piece of external evidence against which the "Social Policy" scales could be measured. This was the vote on the Office Charter Bill, a Private Member's Bill brought in by a Labour M.P., Mr. Marsh at the beginning of the 1959 Parliament. Only a few backbench

Conservatives voted: excluding Members not covered by this study (those who entered the House at by-elections or at the 1959 General Election) only five voted for the Bill and 38 against.

The Bill, which was opposed by the Government, aimed at implementing the recommendations of the Gowers Committee about working conditions in offices. Those Conservatives who voted for the Bill can be regarded as being more enthusiastic for social welfare than their colleagues, while those who voted *against* the Bill were presumably more indifferent. We would expect the Right, therefore, to mobilize more of its members against the Bill than the Left.* Table 50 shows how the various blocs—Left, Centre and Right—voted on this question. M.P.s who were uncommitted under our scale, or excluded, have been omitted.

TABLE 50

Distribution of Voting on Office Charter Bill (Second Reading, December 11th, 1959) Social Policy Scale

	Left		*Centre*		*Right*		*Total*
For the Bill	2		2		—		4
Against the Bill	5	13%	6	20%	16	26%	27
Not Against	34	87%	24	80%	46	74%	104
Total	39		30		62		131

Against vs. Not Against. All groups $\chi^2_3=2\cdot48$. Significant at 10%

The trend was quite regular. The Left was less hostile to the Bill than the Centre and the Centre less hostile than the Right. An association has been provisionally established, the significance level being 10 per cent. An analysis of this division does therefore

* The votes of a few Members who wanted to vote against the Bill were not counted. When the House divided, some opponents of the Bill passed through the Noes lobby before the doors were locked and their votes were not recorded. A second division was called, but some of these Members had apparently already left the House.

† The totals differ from those in pp. 208–9 because some Members retired, etc., at the General Election.

confirm the validity of the scale which has been built up from the EDMs.

TABLE 51

Social Policy and the Conservatives: By Occupation

	Left	%	*Centre*	%	*Right*	%	*Uncom-mitted*	%	*Total*
Pub. Coys.	11	14	8	10	28	35	32	40	79
Pte. Coys.	14	26	13	25	13	25	13	25	53

All committed: Pub. Coy. vs. Pte. Coy. $\chi^2_2=6\cdot52$. Significant at 5%
Committed vs. Uncommitted: Pub. Coy. vs. Pte. Coy.
$\chi^2_1=2\cdot94$. Significant at 10%
(To simplify the table, only figures for the occupational groups which yield significant differences have been included.)

Committed private company directors were more left-wing than public company directors. There is also a provisional association between the degree of commitment and occupation, the private company directors being more committed.

TABLE 52

Social Policy and the Conservatives: by Schools Attended

	Left	%	*Centre*	%	*Right*	%	*Uncom-mitted*	%	*Total*
Clarendon	11	15	7	9	27	36	29	39	74
Other Public	24	26	15	16	31	33	24	26	94
Non-Public	12	23	15	28	11	21	15	28	53
The Rest	3	23	3	23	4	31	3	23	13
Total	50	21	40	17	73	31	71	30	234

Omitting The Rest: $\chi^2_4=10\cdot58$. Significant at 5%

Clarendon School M.P.s were the most right-wing and Non-Public School M.P.s the most left-wing. There is no association under this scale between schools attended and the degree of commitment, the variations in commitment being small, which suggests that the association between school and attitude obtained throughout the party.

TABLE 53

Social Policy and the Conservatives: by Universities Attended

	Left	%	*Centre*	%	*Right*	%	*Uncom-mitted*	%	*Total*
Oxford	6	10	10	17	28	47	16	27	60
Cambridge	12	26	3	7	17	37	14	30	46
Others	7	23	7	23	5	17	11	37	30
Sandhurst	6	38	2	13	2	13	6	38	16
None	19	23	18	22	21	26	24	29	82
Total	50	21	40	17	73	31	71	30	234

Between Universities for Committed (omitting Sandhurst): $\chi^2_4=12\cdot91$. Significant at 2·5%
Oxford vs. Cambridge for Committed: $\chi^2_2=6\cdot74$. Significant at 5%

There were significant variations between graduates of different universities, Oxford being the most right-wing, but there was no difference between graduates and non-graduates. There were no significant differences in the degree of commitment.

TABLE 54

Social Policy and the Conservatives: by Size of Majority

	Left	%	*Centre*	%	*Right*	%	*Uncom-mitted*	%	*Total*
Marginal	11	33	5	15	5	15	12	36	33
Semi-Marginal	3	13	8	33	7	29	6	25	24
Comfortable	13	32	4	10	17	41	7	17	41
Safe	8	12	11	17	22	34	24	37	65
Impregnable	15	21	12	17	22	31	22	31	71
Total	50	21	40	17	73	31	71	30	234

Committed only. All groups: $\chi^2_8=15\cdot06$. Significant at 10%
Marginal vs. Non-Marginal: $\chi^2_2=6\cdot08$. Significant at 5%

There were no significant associations between attitudes and age, or between attitudes and date of entry into Parliament. But there was an association between the degree of commitment and date of entry into Parliament. The 1950 and 1955 intakes were more committed than the other groups.

Differences of attitude may have been related to the size of majority, for there is an association at the low significance level of 10 per cent: M.P.s from marginal seats were the most left-wing group, and M.P.s from safe seats the most right-wing. But there was no regular trend, for M.P.s with impregnable majorities behaved like the party as a whole.

Marginal Members considered as a class were again more left-wing than their colleagues. When their behaviour is compared with that of all of their colleagues there is an association of 5 per cent.

There were no significant differences between the attitudes of rural and urban Members.

INDEX